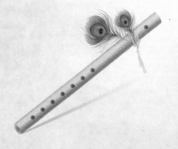

.

TALKS ON
The Gita

Published under licence by
Spiritual Hierarchy Publication Trust
Kolkata – 700 027

First edition: 2019

ISBN: 978-81-933109-3-9

Printed & Bound by
Srinivas Fine Arts, Pvt. Ltd,
340/3, Keelathiruthangal,
Sivakasi - 626130, India.

Introduction

The *Bhagavad Gita* is no stranger to the West. Nor is Vinoba Bhave, the author of these talks on the 'Song Celestial'. Since the death of Gandhi, one name that has sent, if not a wave, a ripple of hope throughout this frightened world is that of Vinoba.

During Gandhi's life Vinoba's name was not much known even in India. Today, however, the remotest villages resound with the words 'Vinoba' and Bhoodan. Even outside India, well-informed circles have sat up to take notice of the 'walking saint' and his land-gift mission. Many thinkers in the West have seen in Vinoba's message a solvent for that war of ideologies that has become the despair of the human race.

Vinoba was born in a Brahmin family of Maharashtra (India) in September 1895. From his childhood he showed a remarkable lack of interest in worldly affairs. A brilliant undergraduate, he gave up college because that sort of education was not what his soul craved for. The idea of utilizing his education in order to make money never entered his head. So, he went to Benaras (Varanasi—India's holiest city and acknowledged as the premier seat of Sanskrit scholarship) to study Sanskrit and Philosophy and to live a life of contemplation and brahmacharya (self-discipline in the most comprehensive sense).

Though he gave up college, Vinoba has remained a student all his life. Unlike Gandhi, he is an erudite pundit of Sanskrit, Philosophy and the religious literature of the world. He has studied the Koran in Arabic, which language he learnt only to be able to read that holy book in the original. He knows the Bible and Christian religious literature as well perhaps as a Doctor of Divinity.

I shall not forget the occasion when the Rev. Dr. Martin Luther King, the leader of the Montgomery, Alabama movement of non-violent resistance to racial segregation, met Vinoba with his wife. Jim Bristol of the Quaker Centre, Delhi, it was, I think, who in introducing Mrs. King spoke of her proficiency in music and suggested that she might sing some hymns and Negro spirituals for Vinoba. Everyone was delighted at the suggestion. I looked at Vinoba and wondered loudly if he knew what the Negro spirituals were. We were all startled, most of all the Americans, when Vinoba, as if in answer, raised his ever-downcast eyes towards Mrs. King and intoned softly, 'Were you there, Were you there, When they crucified my Lord?' When Mrs. King sang that spiritual, it had an added poignancy for us.

Vinoba is a linguist. Besides Sanskrit, Pali and Arabic, he knows English well; reads French; was recently learning German; knows all the major Indian languages. He loves Mathematics. His quest for knowledge is insatiable. But it is not knowledge as ordinarily understood. Most knowledge he regards as superficial and is interested in seeking after the fundamental truths of life. He has an uncanny capacity for separating the chaff from the grain and going to the root of a question. I have not met another person with as keen, razor-like a mind as Vinoba's.

'Vinoba literature', i.e. the collection of his writings and speeches, is already a voluminous affair and is ever-growing. It deals mostly with Philosophy and the theory and practice of non-violence.

To go back to his early days again. There were from the beginning two urges, or rather two tributaries of a single stream of urge, that impelled Vinoba onward. The one came from his identification with his fellow-creatures and impelled him, naturally, to work for the freedom of his country. Due to this urge he felt strongly attracted by the courage, dedication, sincerity and spirit of self-immolation of the revolutionaries of Bengal (whom the British unjustly called 'terrorists').

The other urge pulled him towards the Himalayas—the traditional home of spiritual seekers—for a life of meditation and spiritual fulfilment. While torn between these urges (whose essential unity was not yet clear to him), Vinoba came in touch with Gandhi, who seemed to synthesize beautifully the two urges in his own life. Therefore, he threw in his lot with that newcomer from South Africa who was saying strange and doing what was even stranger. That was way back in 1916. Vinoba was among the first to join Gandhi's Sabarmati Ashram, near

the textile city of Ahmedabad. It was from there
that Gandhi directed the freedom movement till the
beginning of the famous salt satyagraha of 1930.

From that first day of contact Vinoba remained
steadfast in his loyalty and devotion to his chosen
master, though it would be doing an injustice to him
to regard him as a disciple in any narrow sense of
the term. It was clear to those who came to know
him even during Gandhi's lifetime that he possessed
a mind and character, an originality, and above all,
a spiritual quality, that were destined to take him
beyond the limits of a mere follower—no matter
how brilliant—and make him a master in his own
right. Those who have followed closely Vinoba's
work and thought know how great have been his
own 'experiments with truth' and how significant
his contribution to human thought. Particularly
significant has been his development of the theory
and practice of satyagraha beyond the stage where
Gandhi left them.

When Gandhi was assassinated at the beginning of
1948, he was about to launch upon an even greater
undertaking than the winning of India's freedom.
Gandhi had his own vision of the future India and,
as he used to say jokingly, he wanted to live till
the age of 125 years in order to make that vision
a reality.

That vision was of a new social order—different
from the capitalist, socialist, communist orders of

society; a non-violent society, a society based on love and human values, a decentralized, self-governing, non-exploitative, co-operative society. Gandhi gave that society the name of Sarvodaya—literally, the rise of all, i.e. a society in which the good of all is achieved.

To bring about this grand social revolution, Gandhi had conceived of different means from those followed in history—the means of love. He had used the same means in his struggle against the British. But Gandhi did not live to put his concept into practice. Nothing was more natural than that the task should have devolved upon Vinoba.

This is not the place to write about the Bhoodan movement. But this much must be said, that it is the first attempt in history to bring about a social revolution and reconstruction by the means of love. Vinoba is doing a path-finding job in this field. The results of his experiment may have a far-reaching impact on a world that is so torn with hatred and charged with violence.

One final word about Vinoba is essential so that he may be truly understood. Vinoba is not a politician, not a social reformer, nor a revolutionary. He is first and last a man of God. Service of man is to him nothing but an effort to unite with God. He endeavours every second to blot himself out, to make himself empty so that God may fill him up and make him His instrument.

The talks of such a man of Self-realization on one of the profoundest spiritual works of all times should be of inestimable value to all—irrespective of race, creed or nationality.

—Jayaprakash Narayan

Specially written for the foreign edition of the 'Talks on the Gita' published by George Allen and Unwin Ltd., London.

Note from the Publisher

Vinoba's 'Gita Pravachan' or the 'Talks on the Gita' is a work unique and wonderful in many respects. It not only interprets the Gita in a novel and refreshingly different way and brings out the quintessential message of that great spiritual classic in a language that is simple, lucid and intelligible even to ordinary readers, but also lays bare the essence of true spirituality that includes whatever is the best and the most enduring in the religious traditions of the world and still transcends all of them. Needless to say, its power to purify the hearts and the lives of the readers has few parallels. That it has been translated in 24 languages and around 2.5 million copies have been sold is a testimony to its popularity and potency.

The work has been translated in English as well and 22 editions of the English translation have so far been published. An edition has also been published by George Allen and Unwin Ltd., London.

The work had earlier been translated by Shri K. Swaminathan. It has now been almost re-translated by Dr. Parag Cholkar, although he has liberally drawn on the earlier translation as well as the relevant portion in 'The Intimate and The Ultimate' edited by Satish Kumar. Several persons have gone through the new version and made suggestions which have been taken care of. Labours taken by Shri Sarvanarayandas and Shri Vasant Palshikar deserve special mention. It has also received the blessings of Ms. Vimla Thakar, one of the tallest spiritual guides, who is unfortunately no more. This revised edition also has the benefit of the suggestions of Shri B.J.K. Tampi (Director General of Police retd). We are obliged to all of them. Several footnotes on important philosophical terms as well as individuals and incidents from the Indian mythology and epics have also been added.

These talks were delivered in 1932 in the Dhule jail where Vinoba had been incarcerated by the British for his participation in the freedom movement. There were hundreds of political prisoners lodged in that jail. How Vinoba transformed the jail life and how the jailor who was a strict disciplinarian became his admirer is a fascinating story, but one must avoid the temptation to recount that story for paucity of space. Prison inmates expressed a desire that Vinoba should speak on the Gita. Vinoba agreed to give a talk every Sunday and delivered 18 talks on the 18 Chapters. P.S. Sane alias Sane Guruji, a great writer and freedom-fighter, wrote them down in long hand. There was no question of their being taped and their publication was also not thought of. In fact, Vinoba had given talks on the Gita many times in the past, but none of them had been published. However, Sane Guruji preserved the notebooks and the talks were published first in the weekly edited by him, and then in the form of a book in 1945 when Vinoba was in jail even before he could find time to go through them for necessary editing. It was only thereafter that Vinoba edited the talks. He also divided them into 108 sub-divisions and 432 paragraphs and wrote aphorisms (totalling 540) on each of them in Sanskrit so that the contents could be reflected upon and understood with ease. The collection of those aphorisms, named 'Samyasutra-vritti' has been appended to most of the editions in Indian languages.

As has already been mentioned, these talks were written down from the notes taken by Sane Guruji, whose literary style is evident to any discerning reader. The spirit, of course, has been kept intact, and that is perhaps why Vinoba put his seal of approval on their publication. That these talks were taken down by a man of rare purity like Sane Guruji had a special significance for Vinoba.

Few liberties have been taken with the text while translating and the stress is on the communication of the content even at the cost of the flow and lucidity of the language, if necessary. Only a few words or a sentence or two have been deleted or added. It may be added that the talks are replete with analogies and examples and sometimes they may appear a bit out of place to the modern rational mind, which may also fail to grasp some of them because of their milieu. This is inevitable in the translation of any work in a foreign language. In fact, Vinoba had doubts whether English readers could appreciate these talks. That the English translation has also been well received is clear from the fact that it had already run into twenty one editions totalling 101,000 copies. What is, after all, important is the spirit and the essence.

It is not an academic treatise on the Gita. These are the talks given before ordinary individuals from different walks of life. It was Vinoba's firm conviction that the Gita is meant to spiritualize human life; to tranform and make it divine. That is exactly what these talks too are meant to bring about. Their success in doing so in good measure has been amply testified. That is why Vinoba considered this work as a vehicle for the propagation of the Bhoodan (Land-gift) movement; in fact, for the revolutionary transformation of the individual and social life.

Glossary has also been added.

The readers are requested to convey their comments and suggestions so that necessary changes could be made in the next edition, and the translation made as authentic as possible.

Vinoba on the 'Talks on the Gita'

It was a period of intense agitation of 1932. Many patriots and saintly men were gathered together in the Dhule jail. The jail life is marked with excitement and uncertainty. Nobody would have thought then that these talks delivered in the jail would reach the whole nation through all of its languages. But, ultimately, what happens is what the Lord wills. I or Sane Guruji, who wrote down these talks could have been shifted to another jail, as some of the inmates were. But this did not happen, and the talks could be through.

'Talks on the Gita' should be carefully read and assimilated. Its style is not that of the scriptures; it is for the general public. There are instances of repetition also. Like a singer I have harped again and again on the tune that I like most. In fact, I had no idea that these talks could ever be published. Had a man of pure heart like Sane Guruji who could do 'short-hand' writing in long hand not been there, these talks could have remained confined to the speaker and the listeners. And for me, that was enough. It was for my own sake that I delivered these talks; for me, it was like reciting the sacred Name of the Lord. What actually happened was beyond imagination. That is why one feels that it was His will.

Bhagavad-Gita was told in the battlefield; and that is why it is something different and no other treatise can match her. The Lord Himself told the Gita again, which is known as the Anugita. But it is a pale shadow of the original. My writings and talks on the Gita elsewhere would not have the magic touch that these 'Talks' have, as these were delivered in jail which, for us, was a battlefield, before the soldiers in the freedom struggle. Those who heard these talks can never forget those moments. The atmosphere of the jail at that time was charged with a spiritual elan.

It is a matter of satisfaction for me that, by the grace of God, these talks on the Gita are proving to be of great use to social workers and spiritual seekers in purifying their minds. There are individuals who have read them hundreds of times. When selfless workers derive inspiration from these talks, that enhances their potency. Thousands have thus derived strength from these talks and have, in turn, contributed to the enhancement of their potency.

As this book became a vehicle for the Bhoodan (land-gift) movement, it was translated into all the Indian languages and thousands of its copies reached the people. This book has brought about revolutionary changes. Wherever it has reached, it has been instumental in removing the veil of ignorance and delusions.

I cannot describe in words the state of my being while delivering these talks. If it could be assumed that God does speak at times through human beings, then these are such words. While delivering these talks, I had no awareness that 'I am talking' and the listeners too did not feel that it was Vinoba who was talking. The individual delivering the talks was merely instrumental.

Both the speaker and the listeners felt that some different power was speaking.

It was God's grace that I could have an opportunity to offer this humble service to the Gita. The place of Gita in my life is unique. She is always there to help me in need. I have strived in these talks to explain the meaning of the Gita as I have understood it.

Here, I have not concerned myself with the literal meaning of the verses; rather, there is reflection on the essence of every Chapter. The use of scientific terminology has been kept to the minimum even while retaining the scientific approach. You will not find herein any academic discourse unrelated to life. I am confident that even ordinary labourers could find solace and peace herein.

Wherever these talks have reached, they have motivated people to purify their minds and transform their lives. I would like to see them being read, heard and reflected upon in every home.

The 'Talks on the Gita' is the story of my life, and it is also my message.

Foreword

Acharya Vinoba Bhave was a towering personality of the Indian freedom struggle. As a great social reformer and *ahimsavadi* he embodied the essence of the *Bhagavad Gita* – of skill in action, struggle for self-mastery and selfless service.

Acharya Vinoba was an advocate of non-violent change. He championed the rights of fellow Indians not only during the Independence struggle when he was repeatedly jailed for political resistance, but also as the founder of *Bhoodan* – a land-gift movement built on an appeal to landowners, big and small, to voluntarily part with some of their farm land to the landless and the land poor so they may earn a dignified living.

In the cause of *Bhoodan*, beginning in 1951 and for the next thirteen years, Acharya Vinoba walked tens of thousands of kilometres across his beloved country. His call, "Go with complete confidence in the heart of everyone you approach[1]," evoked his originality as an activist for social justice, and in his faith in the goodness of the human heart to respond in the face of dire humanitarian appeal.

The *Bhagavad Gita* was a significant influence in Acharya Vinoba's life and moral vision. In his reading of the *Gita's* high-minded aphorisms, he penetrated to its universal message of do unto others as you would

---

[1] *Principles and Philosophy of the Bhoodan Yagna*, by Acharya Vinoba Bhave, 1955, pp. 1-5, 15-16.

have them do unto you. He coined the slogan, "Jai Jagat", symbolising the well-being of all.

In 1916, at twenty-one years of age, Vinobaji met Mahatma Gandhi who became his political and spiritual mentor. Vinobaji actively participated in ashram life by the Sabarmati in Gujarat. Later, at the Wardha ashram, Vinobaji published his insights on the Upanishads and the devotional poetry of Bhakta Tukaram.

Between January and June of 1932, Acharya Vinoba was jailed for six months in Dhule in Maharashtra. Prison became his abode of reading, writing, and, the *Bhagavad Gita,* a source of wisdom and strength to continue the freedom struggle inside prison walls. Over the course of six months, Acharya Vinoba gave eighteen discourses on the *Bhagavad Gita* that were transcribed by Pandurang Sane known to all as Sane Guruji, a fellow inmate and freedom fighter.

Published in Marathi as *Gita Pravachan* or *Talks on the Gita,* they are laced with storybook telling of profound life truths and understood by even those with no knowledge of holy literature. The Acharya said, "My writings and talks on the *Gita* elsewhere would not have the magic touch that these talks have, as these were delivered in jail, which, for us, was a battlefield, before the soldiers in the freedom struggle."[2]

---

[2] Preface, *Talks on the Gita,* by Acharya Vinoba Bhave.

Shri Ram Chandra Mission is delighted to republish the *Talks on the Gita,* which Acharya Vinoba Bhave said was the story of his life and also his message[3].

Kamlesh Patel
President, Shri Ram Chandra Mission

---

[3] Preface, *Talks on the Gita,* by Acharya Vinoba Bhave.

Contents

TALKS ON
The Gita

CHAPTER 1

Introduction:
Arjuna's despondency

1. At the heart of the Mahabharata

1. Dear brothers, from today I shall be talking to you about *Shrimad Bhagavad Gita*. The bond between the Gita and me transcends reason. My heart and mind have received more nourishment from the Gita than my body has from my mother's milk. There is little place for logic in a relationship of loving tenderness. Moving beyond the intellect, I therefore soar high in the vast expanse of the Gita on the twin wings of faith and experimentation. All the time I live in the ambience of the Gita. The Gita is my life-breath. I am as it were afloat on the surface of this ocean of nectar when I am talking about the Gita and when alone, I dive deep into this ocean and rest there. Henceforth, every Sunday, I shall be giving a talk on the teaching of the Gita, who is verily our mother.

2. The Gita has been set in the Mahabharata. Standing in the middle of the great epic like a lighthouse, it illuminates the whole of the epic. Placed between six *parvas* (sections of the text) of the epic on one side and twelve on the other, its message is being unfolded in the middle of the battlefield with seven divisions of the Pandava army on one side and eleven divisions of the Kaurava army on the other.

3. The Mahabharata and the Ramayana are our national epics. The characters depicted therein have become an inseparable part of our lives. Since time immemorial, life in India has remained under the spell of the characters like Rama, Sita, Dharmaraj, Draupadi,

Bhishma and Hanuman. The characters in other epics of the world have not become one with the lives of the people in this way. The Mahabharata and the Ramayana are thus undoubtedly unique and wonderful works. The Ramayana is an enchanting ethical poem, while the Mahabharata is a comprehensive treatise on the working of society. In the Mahabharata, Vyasa has, in one hundred thousand verses, sketched the lives, personalities and characters of innumerable individuals with consummate skill. The Mahabharata vividly brings out the fact that none but God is completely faultless and good, and also that none can be said to be evil personifed. For instance, it points out faults even of moral giants like Bhishma and Dharmaraj, and virtues in the characters like Karna and Duryodhana, who had strayed from the path of righteousness. The Mahabharata tells us that human life is like a fabric woven with black and white threads – threads of good and evil. With perfect detachment Vyasa, the great sage, graphically depicts for us the complex reality of the vast web of worldly life. Because of Vyasa's great literary skill, noble as well detached, in depicting life the Mahabharata has become a veritable gold-mine. Everybody is free to explore it and take freely as much as he wants.

4. Vyasa wrote such a great epic, but did he have something of his own to tell? Has he told his special message somewhere? Where do we find him in a state of *samadhi*[1]? In the Mahabharata one comes

---

[1] *Samadhi* here means a state in which the mind is intensely concentrated and is in tune with the divine consciousness. This is the sense in which the term has been used in Chap. 2.15 as well. The word is used in a different sense in Chap. 9.2.

across a number of dense thickets of philosophies and preachings, but has Vyasa given anywhere the essence of all those and presented the central message of the whole epic? Yes, he has. He has presented it in the form of the Gita. The Gita is his principal message and the repository of his wisdom. It is because of the Gita that the Lord has extolled him as the sage among the sages, as His own manifestation among the sages.[2] The Gita has been accorded the status of an Upanishad[3] since ancient times. It is, in fact, the Supreme Upanishad. It is as if Lord Krishna has distilled the essence of all the Upanishads and offered it in the form of the Gita to the whole world. Arjuna's despondency provided only an occasion. Almost every idea and thought necessary for the blossoming of life can be found in the Gita. That is why the wise have rightly called it the encyclopaedia of *dharma*[4]. The Gita, although small in size, is the principal text of Hinduism.

5. It is well-known that the Gita was told by Lord Krishna. Arjuna, the devotee who listened to this great teaching, became one with it, so much so that he too came to be called 'Krishna'. Vyasa's empathy while narrating it earned him too the epithet 'Krishna'. Total identity was thus established between Krishna the teacher, Krishna the listener and Krishna the narrator.

---

[2] 'Of the sages, I am Vyasa.' – Gita, 10.37.

[3] Upanishads are the basic texts of Hindu philosophy and spiritual knowledge.

[4] *Dharma* is normally translated as 'religion', but is a much wider concept. *Dharma* is that which holds and supports everything in the world. Its meaning includes right conduct and duties that become obligatory to a man because of his nature and station.

One who wants to go deep into the Gita should also have concentration of this kind and degree.

2. Arjuna's standpoint and genesis of the Gita

6. There are many who feel that the Gita should be taken to begin with the Second Chapter. The actual teaching starts from the eleventh verse of the Second Chapter; so why not take it as the real beginning? A gentleman once argued that the Lord had called 'अ' (first letter of the Nagari alphabet)[5] as His *vibhuti* (manifestation) among the letters of the alphabet and the eleventh verse begins with it; therefore, it should be taken as the beginning. That apart, it would be right in more than one sense to take this as the real beginning of the Gita. Nonetheless, the preceding introductory portion has a value of its own. Without it we would not have properly understood Arjuna's standpoint and the genesis of the Gita.

7. Many contend that Arjuna was going weak at the knees and the Gita was preached to restore his manliness and induce him to fight. In their view the Gita preaches not only *karmayoga* (the philosophy of action) but also *yuddhayoga* (the philosophy of war). But a little thinking will show the error in this view. Eighteen divisions of army were ready for the battle. Can we say that the Lord, through exposition of the Gita, made Arjuna worthy to face that army in battle? It was Arjuna who quailed; not the army. Was then the army braver than Arjuna? It is just inconceivable. It was not out of fear that Arjuna was shying away from the battle. The great warrior had

---

[5] Gita, 10.33.

8

fought hundreds of battles. He had single-handedly routed Bhishma, Drona and Karna when they had invaded Virat's kingdom. He was, in fact, known as one who knew no defeat; a man among men. Valour was in every drop of his blood. Krishna, in fact, did try to needle him by attributing impotence to him; but it proved to be off the mark. He had then to go deep into different aspects of the spiritual knowledge. It is clearly too simplistic to think that the aim of the Gita is to remove unmanliness.

8. It is also said that the Gita is meant to make Arjuna willing to fight by removing his inclination towards non-violence. In my opinion this view also is not right. To understand this point, we have to examine Arjuna's standpoint. The First Chapter and its extension in the Second are useful in this context.

Arjuna had come to the battlefield with a firm resolve and a sense of duty. Being a *kshatriya*[6], fighting was in his blood. Every attempt to avoid war had failed. The Pandavas had pitched their claims at the minimum and Krishna Himself had tried to mediate, but all in vain, making the war inevitable. In these circumstances, Arjuna had brought together many kings, made Krishna his charioteer, and is now on the battle-field. He asks Krishna with heroic ardour, "Place my chariot between the two armies, so that I can have a look at the people who have assembled

---

[6] According to the Hindu scriptures, society is divided into four divisions or *varnas* : *Brahmin* (teachers, priests, intellectuals), *Kshatriya* (warriors, administrators, kings), *Vaishya* (those engaged in trading, farming, animal husbandry) and *Shudra* (artisans and those doing menial work).

here to fight with me." Krishna complies. Arjuna looks around. And what does he see? He finds his kith and kin, his near and dear ones arrayed on both the sides. He finds four generations of his own people intent on fighting to the finish. It is not that Arjuna had no idea of what he was going to see. But the actual sight, as is always the case, had a devastating impact. Seeing his kinsmen on the battlefield, Arjuna lost his nerve and deep anguish assailed his heart. In the past, he had slain innumerable warriors in many a battle, but he had never before felt so dejected, never had his bow Gandiva slipped from his hands, never had he trembled so, never had tears welled up in his eyes! Then, why was all this happening now? Was he coming to abhor violence like King Ashoka[7]? Certainly not. It was nothing but attachment to his kith and kin. Had those in front of him not been his kinsmen, he would even now have felt no qualms in severing their heads and merrily tossing them around. But attachment to the kith and kin clouded his sense of duty, and then he started philosophising. When a man with a sense of duty is caught in delusion, he cannot face his naked lapse from duty. He tries to justify it by citing lofty principles. The same thing happened with Arjuna. He now started putting before Krishna, to convince him, the specious argument that war in itself was sinful, that it would destroy the clan, eclipse *dharma* and lead to moral anarchy, scarcity

---

[7] King Ashoka turned away from violence, disgusted by the ghastly sights in the successful war against the kingdom of Kalinga. He then embraced Buddhism, the religion of non-violence, and thenceforth worked for its propagation.

and devastation, and bring many other disasters upon the society.

9. I am reminded here of the story of a judge. He had sentenced to death hundreds of criminals. But one day, his own son, accused of murder, was produced before him. The guilt was proved and the time came for the judge to pronounce the sentence. But then he hesitated, and started arguing, "The death sentence is inhuman. It does not behove a man to inflict such a punishment. It destroys all hopes of reforming the guilty. One commits murder in a fit of passion. The moment of bloodthirsty madness then passes off. Still we coolly take him to the gallows and hang him to death. It is disgraceful to humanity." Such were the judge's arguments. But, had his son not been there, he would have gone on sentencing people to death. His arguments lacked inner conviction; they were born out of attachment to his son.

10. Arjuna's condition was like that of the judge in this story. His arguments were not unsound. The world has witnessed precisely the same consequences of the First World War. But the point is that Arjuna was not voicing his own authentic conviction. His words were seemingly wise, but not really so. Krishna realised this. He, therefore, paid no attention to Arjuna's arguments and straightway proceeded to dispel his delusion. Had Arjuna really become a votary of non-violence, he would not have been satisfied until his arguments had been convincingly answered. But the Gita nowhere deals with them, and yet Arjuna was

ultimately satisfied. This means that Arjuna had not really become a votary of non-violence. The intrinsic propensity to fight was still very much a part of his nature. War was for him his natural and inescapable duty. But he was trying to evade it under the spell of delusion. And it is this delusion that the Gita attacks most pointedly.

3. Purpose of the Gita : Dispelling anti-swadharma[8] delusion

11. Arjuna had not only started talking of non-violence, he was also talking of *sannyasa*[9]. He was saying that *sannyasa* was preferable to the blood-stained *kshatra-dharma* (duty of the *Kshatriya*). But was this his *swadharma*? Was this in keeping with his nature? He could easily have donned the garb of a recluse, but how could he have acquired the mentality of a recluse? Had he gone to the forest to live the life of a recluse he would have started killing the deer there. The Lord tells him plainly, "O Arjuna! You are saying that you would not fight. This is an illusion. Your nature, which has been formed through all these years, will compel you to fight."

Arjuna is finding his *swadharma* devoid of merit. But even if it is so perceived, one has to find fulfilment

---

[8] 'Swadharma' can be translated as one's natural duty dictated by one's natural state of being, one's true self and one's station in life.

[9] *Sannyasa* means renunciation of the worldly possessions and attachments. Spiritual seekers take *sannyasa* and retire from the world to devote fully to the spiritual pursuit. According to the Hindu scriptures, it is the fourth *ashram*, which should be the last stage in every man's life.

through its practice only. There can be no pride attached to any particular *swadharma*. This is the law of growth. *Swadharma* is not something to be adopted because it is perceived to be great or noble; nor it is to be cast off because it appears lowly. *Swadharma* is neither great nor small; it is equal to our measure. It is that which fits us the best. श्रेयान्स्वधर्मो विगुण:[10] ('One's own *dharma*, even if it is devoid of merit is the best for oneself.'), the Gita says. The word *dharma* here does not mean a religion like Hinduism, Islam or Christianity. Every individual, in fact, has his own distinct *dharma*. Two hundred individuals sitting in front of me here have two hundred different *dharmas*. Even my own *dharma* today is not what it was ten years ago, and it will not be the same in ten years' time. As one's mind grows and develops through reflection and experience, the old *dharma* gets shed and one acquires new *dharma*. Nothing in this matter should be done obstinately.

12. It is not good for me to adopt another's *dharma*, however superior it may appear. I like sunlight. It helps my growth. I worship the sun. But if, for that reason, I try to get close to the sun, I would be burnt to ashes. Compared to the sun, the earth may appear worthless; it may not be self-luminous, still I should strive for self-development by staying on the earth, which is my rightful place, so long as I lack the capacity to stand the sun's powerful blaze. If someone were to say to a fish, "Milk is better than water.

---

[10] Gita, 3.35.

Come and swim in the milk", will it accept? It can survive in water only; in milk it will die.

13. Another's *dharma* is not to be adopted even if it appears easier to follow. Quite often, the apparent easiness is deceptive. If someone is unable to look after his family properly and gets fed up, renounces the world and becomes a recluse, it would be sheer hypocrisy and such renunciation would also be burdensome. His passions will reassert themselves at the slightest opportunity. Even if he goes to the forest, he would build a hut for himself, then he would put up a fence to protect it; and in the course of time, his involvement in worldly affairs will increase with a vengeance. On the other hand, there is nothing difficult in *sannyasa* if one's mind is truly detached. Indeed, there are many sayings in the Smritis[11] to this effect. It is the disposition of one's mind which matters, which decides one's *dharma*. The question is not whether it is high or low, easy or difficult; what matters is that there should be real inner growth and genuine fulfilment.

14. But the devout ask, "If *sannyasa* is always unquestionably superior to the way of fighting, then why did the Lord not make Arjuna a true *sannyasi*? Was this impossible for Him?" Certainly not. But, would it have done any credit to Arjuna? It would have offered no scope for Arjuna to exert himself and

---

[11] Smritis are compendiums of rules about individual and social behaviour and social relationships.

excel in his efforts. The Lord gives us freedom. Let everybody make efforts in his own way. Therein lies the charm. A child enjoys sketching figures with his own hands; he does not like anybody else holding his hands for this purpose. If a teacher just goes on rapidly solving all the mathematical problems himself for the students, how would their intellect develop? The teachers and the parents should only guide the children. God guides us from within. He does nothing more than that. There is no charm in God shaping us like a potter. We are not earthenware; we are beings full of consciousness.

15. From all this discussion, it is clear that the purpose of the Gita is to remove the delusion that stands between us and our *swadharma*. Arjuna was confused about his *dharma*. He was gripped by a delusion about his *swadharma*. When Krishna castigates him, he himself admits it. The Gita's main task is to remove that delusion, that attachment. The Lord asked Arjuna at the end of the Gita, "O Arjuna! Has your delusion gone now?" And Arjuna replied, "Yes, Lord. The delusion has fled away. I have realised what my *swadharma* is."[12] Thus, taking into consideration both the beginning and the end of the Gita, it is clear that the removal of delusion is its central message. This is the purpose of the Gita, as well as of the whole of the Mahabharata. Vyasa had said, right at the beginning of the Mahabharata, that he was lighting this lamp of history to dispel delusions in the minds of the people.

[12] Gita, 18.73

15

4. Honesty and straightforwardness make one worthy of the Gita's message

16. This introduction to Arjuna's condition helps us greatly in understanding the rest of the Gita. We should be grateful for this. It also helps us in another way. It reveals Arjuna's straightforwardness and honesty. The word 'Arjuna', in fact, means one who is honest and straightforward in nature. He candidly told Krishna all that he felt and thought, hid nothing from Him and ultimately surrendered to Him totally. In fact, he was already His devotee. When he made Krishna his charioteer and entrusted to Him the reins of his horses, he had got ready to give into His hands the reins of his mind also. Let us do likewise. Let us not think that, unlike Arjuna, we do not have Krishna to guide us. Let us not get caught in the fallacy that Krishna was a historical person. Everybody has Krishna residing in his heart as the indwelling Self. He is nearer to us than the nearest. Let us bare our heart, with all its impurities and weaknesses, before Him and say, "O Lord! I take refuge in you. You are my sole guide, my master. Show me the right path and I shall follow it." If we do so, Arjuna's charioteer will be our charioteer too. We shall hear the Gita from His own lips and He will lead us to victory.

(21.2.32)

CHAPTER 2

The Teaching in brief:
Self-knowledge and equanimity

5. The Gita's terminology

1. Brothers, last week we discussed Arjuna's state of despondency (*vishad*). Whenever there is Arjuna-like honesty, straightforwardness and total surrender to God, even a state of despondency attains the character of *yoga*[1]. It is the churning of heart which brings this about. The First Chapter of the Gita has been called *Arjuna-vishad-yoga*. I prefer to call it simply *Vishad-yoga*, as Arjuna provided only an occasion for the discourse. It is not for the sake of Pundalik[2] alone that the Lord took the form of Pandurang. Pundalik provided only a pretext for His descent on earth. We see that the Lord is standing for thousands of years at Pandharpur to redeem us all, ignorant creatures as we are, held captive by the bonds of this-worldliness. Similarly, although Arjuna provided an immediate cause for the overflowing of the Lord's compassion in the form of the Gita, it is really intended for all of us. That is why the general term *vishad-yoga* is more appropriate for this Chapter. Beginning from this *vishad-yoga* the Gita's teaching keeps on growing like a magnificent tree, finally bearing the fruit of *prasad-yoga* (God's grace) in the concluding Chapter. God

---

[1] *Yoga* means union or integration. It entails detachment from suffering and perverse propensities – in fact, from all outside interests – and integration with the Divine. Different types of *yoga* are different means or processes to achieve such integration or, in other words, spiritual liberation. *Yoga* can also be defined as the art of practising the fundamental truths of life for this purpose.

[2] The story of Pundalik has been described in detail in 9.17 of this Chapter.

willing, we too would reach that destination during the term of our imprisonment.

2. The Gita's teaching begins from the Second Chapter. At the very outset, the Lord enunciates the cardinal principles of life. The idea is that once the fundamental principles, which should be the foundation of life, are well-grasped, the way ahead would be clear. In my view, the term *sankhya-buddhi*[3] in the Second Chapter stands for the basic principles of life. We have now to take a look at these principles. But before that, it is better to have a clear understanding of the Gita's terminology.

The Gita has a penchant for using old philosophical terms in new senses. Grafting new meanings on to old terms is a non-violent process of bringing about revolution in thinking. Vyasa is adept in this process. This is the secret of the great potency and strength of the language of the Gita and its ever-freshness and vitality. Different thinkers could therefore read different meanings in the terms used by it in the light of their experiences and according to their needs. In my view, all those interpretations could be taken as valid from their respective standpoints and yet we can have a different interpretation of our own without ruling out any of them.

---

[3] It means the wisdom in accordance with the *Sankhya*. *Sankhya* is one of the six systems of the Indian philosophy. (Please also see Chap. 2.13 and the footnote in Chap. 7.2.) However, the Gita uses the term here in a different sense.

3. There is a beautiful story in an Upanishad which is worth recounting here. Once gods, demons and human beings went to Prajapati (the Creator) for advice. Prajapati gave all of them only one word of advice : the single syllable द (da). The gods said, "We are given to passions and sensual pleasures. So, Prajapati has advised us 'daman' (दमन) (subduing and conquering them)." The demons said, "We are given to anger and cruelty. So, Prajapati has advised us to cultivate 'daya' (दया) (compassion)." The human beings said, "We are greedy and are always hankering after possessions. So, Prajapati has advised us to practise 'dana' (दान) (charity and sharing)."[4] Prajapati approved all these interpretations, as all of them had arrived at their interpretations through their own experiences. We should bear in mind this story while interpreting the Gita's terminology.

6. Using the body for swadharma

4. Three cardinal principles have been enunciated in the Second Chapter —
   (i) The atman (the Self) is deathless and indivisible.
   (ii) The body is insignificant and transient.
   (iii) Swadharma must be followed.
Out of these, Swadharma is in the nature of duty to be performed while the other two are principles to be understood.

---

[4] The words daman (दमन), daya (दया) and dana (दान), all begin with the Nagari syllable द.

I have already said something about *swadharma*. For each of us, *swadharma* is 'given'. It comes to us naturally; we do not have to go out looking for it. We did not, as it were, drop from the sky; we are part of a stream of existence. Society, parents, neighbours – all existed before our birth. To serve the parents who gave me life, to serve the society in which I was born is my natural *dharma*. Our *swadharma* thus takes birth along with us; it can even be said that it is already there for us before our birth. In fact, fulfilment of *swadharma* is the very purpose behind our birth. Some people say that *swadharma* is like one's wife and say that the bond of *swadharma* is as inviolable and indissoluble as the bond of marriage.[5] But I do not think that this simile is quite apposite. I would rather say that *swadharma*, like one's mother, is not chosen but pre-determined. No matter what sort of person my mother is, she will ever remain my mother. This is precisely the case with *swadharma*. In this world, we have nothing else to rely on. To disown one's *swadharma* is to disown oneself, to commit suicide. Only in harmony with it can we move forward. That is why we should never lose sight of it.

5. *Swadharma* should, in fact, come easily and naturally. But because of several temptations and delusions this does not happen or becomes extremely difficult. Even if it is practised, the practice gets vitiated. The temptations and delusions that strew with thorns the

---

[5] In the Hindu tradition, marriage is not a mere civil contract that could be annulled at will. It is a life-long sacred bond.

path of *swadharma* have various forms. However, on analysis, we find only one thing at the bottom of it all : a restricted and shallow identification of oneself with one's body. I, and those related to me through the body, set the limits of my expansion. Those outside the circle are aliens or enemies. Besides, the attachment is restricted to only the physical bodies of the 'I and mine'. Caught in this double trap, we start putting up all sorts of little walls. Almost everyone does this. The size of the enclosure may vary, but they are enclosures all the same. And they are not thicker than one's skin. One man's enclosure is the family, another's the nation. One wall divides the so-called upper and lower castes, another divides the people on the basis of religions. Wherever you turn, you see nothing but such walls. Even in this jail, we differentiate between ordinary convicts and political prisoners. It is as if we cannot live without such walls. We revel in living in puddles. But what does this result into? Only in the multiplication of the germs of mean and vicious thoughts and destruction of the healthy state of *swadharma*.

7. Awareness of the Self that transcends the body

6. In this situation, commitment to *swadharma* is not enough. Constant awareness of two other principles is necessary. One of them is : 'I am not this feeble and mortal physical body; the body is only the outer shell.' The other is : 'I am the Self that is imperishable, indivisible and all-pervading.' These two together constitute a whole philosophy of life.

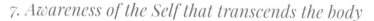

The Gita values this philosophy so much that it enunciates it at the very outset and only thereafter brings in the concept of *swadharma*. Some people wonder why such abstruse philosophical theorems are there at the very beginning. But to me it seems that if there are any verses in the Gita whose place cannot at all be changed, then these are such verses.

If this philosophy is imprinted on the mind, it will be easy to follow our *swadharma*. In fact, it will be difficult to follow something else. That the Self is eternal and indivisible and the body is worthless and transient is not difficult to comprehend, as it is the truth. But it needs to be reflected upon continuously in the mind. We should train ourselves to belittle the body and exalt the Self.

7. Look! This body is forever changing, caught in the cycle of childhood, youth and old age. Modern scientists say that every seven years it is renewed and not a drop of old blood remains. Our ancestors believed that this takes twelve years. That is why they prescribed a period of twelve years for study, penance, atonement of sins or wrongdoings etc. We often hear that mothers failed to recognise their own sons after years of separation. Is the body that changes every moment, dies every moment, your true form? Its sewers are flowing continuously, and despite your indefatigable scavenging it remains unclean; is this body you? No, the body is dirty; it is you who wash it. It gets ill; it is you who give it medicine. It fills three and a half cubits of space; you are free to

roam in the whole of the cosmos. It changes endlessly; you observe those changes. It is open to death; you make necessary arrangements in that regard. When the distinction between your body and yourself is so clear, why do you shrink into smallness? Why do you relate only with your kin? And why do you grieve over the death of the body? The Lord asks : "Is the destruction of the body a cause for grief?"

8. The body is, in fact, like a garment. We can put on a new garment as the old one gets worn out. Had the same body stuck to the Self for ever, the plight of the Self would have been really sad. That would have stopped all growth, extinguished all joy and dimmed the illuminating power of knowledge and wisdom. Hence, perishing of the body is not a thing to grieve. Had the Self been perishable, that would indeed have been a cause for grief. But the Self is imperishable. The eternal Self clothes itself in a succession of bodies. That is why it is utterly wrong to get attached to a particular body and its relations and grieve over their loss; and it is also wrong to consider some as kin and others as aliens. The universe is a beautifully woven whole. Were we to cut up the undivided Self, immanent in the whole universe, into bits of separate selves using the body as a pair of scissors like a child who wilfully cuts a whole piece of cloth with a pair of scissors, would it not be the height of childish folly, and moreover, an act of extreme violence?

It is really a pity that India, the land where *Brahmavidya* (the science of realising the *Brahman*[6]) was born, is now teeming with innumerable groups and castes. Our fear of death is perhaps unparalleled. No doubt, it is a consequence of a long period of subjection; but then one must not forget that it is also one of the causes of that subjection.

9. We dread the word 'death'. It is considered inauspicious. Jnanadeva had to write regretfully : 'अगा मर हा बोल न साहती । आणि मेलिया तरी रडती ॥' ('They cannot bear the word death and cry over death.') If someone dies, what tears! What wailing! We seem to think it a duty! People go to the extent of hiring professional mourners![7] Even when death is imminent, we do not tell the patient of it. He is kept in the dark even when a doctor has told us that the patient cannot live. Even doctors do not speak plainly to the patients and go on pouring medicines down their throats until the last moment. If, instead, the doctor were to tell the patient the truth, give him courage and direct his thoughts towards God, what a help that would be! But it is

---

[6] *Brahman* is the Absolute – the Supreme Truth, the Ultimate Reality. The concept is, in fact, too grand for conceptualisation and description. The Upanishad had, therefore, to speak of the *Brahman* in negative terms: 'The Real is not this, the Real is not that.' *Brahman* is the Supreme Principle that is the root cause of the generation, evolution and extinction of the world. It pervades everything and transcends everything. It is the Supreme Self. The individual self is a part of the *Brahman* and the consummation of its development and evolution lies in merging with the *Brahman*, that is, attaining spiritual liberation.

[7] This is a custom prevalent in some communities in India, particularly in Rajasthan and Gujarat.

feared that this little pot (of the body) might crack of shock before its time. But can death ever come before the right moment? Besides, even if it comes a little earlier, what does it matter? We should certainly not be loveless and hard-hearted; but attachment to the body is not love. On the contrary, true love emerges only when attachment to the body is overcome.

When we are freed of that attachment, we would realise that the body is an instrument for service; and then the body would gain its true dignity. But today we regard pampering of the body as the sole purpose of our lives. We have totally forgotten that life is to be lived for the fulfilment of *swadharma* and one has to look after the body for this purpose only. It should be given proper nourishment; but there is no need to indulge the palate. It is all the same to a ladle whether you use it to serve a sweet dessert or plain curry; it feels neither happy nor unhappy. The same should be the case with our tongue. It should, of course, be able to distinguish between different tastes, but should not feel any pleasure or repulsion. The body is to be paid its due hire, and nothing more. A spinning wheel has to be oiled regularly to keep it in working condition; in the same way we should provide fuel to the body as we have to take work from it. If that is our approach, the body, although having little intrinsic worth, would become worthy and valuable and gain true dignity.

10. But, instead of using the body as an instrument, we lose ourselves in it and stunt our spirit whereby

the body, which has little intrinsic worth, has its worth still reduced. That is why the saints vehemently say, 'देह आणि देहसंबंधें निंदावीं । इतरें वंदावीं श्वानसूकरें ।' ('One should censure the narrow confinement to the body and the blood-relations; one may rather venerate even the pigs and the dogs!') Do not, therefore, worship the body and its ties all the time. Learn to relate to others as well. The saints are thus exhorting us to widen our horizon. Do we ever open our hearts to those outside our narrow circle of friends and relatives? Do we ever try to identify ourselves with others? Do we let our swan-Self – the bird of the spirit – escape from the cage of the body and breathe freedom? Does it ever occur to us that we should widen the circle of our friends continually so as to ultimately encompass the whole world and feel that the whole world is ours and that we belong to the whole world? We write letters to our relatives from the jail. That is natural. But would you write to a thief convict – not a political prisoner – who has become your friend here, after his release?

11. The Self is ever restless to reach out to others. It longs to embrace the whole world. But we shut it up in a cell. We have imprisoned it and are not even conscious of it. From morning till evening, we are busy minding the body. Day and night we worry about how fat or thin we have become. Perhaps there is no other joy in the world. But even beasts experience the pleasures of the senses. Will you not like to experience the joy of sacrifice, the joy of controlling the palate? Experience the joy of giving away your plate of food

even though you yourself are hungry. A mother tastes this joy a little when she toils for her child. In fact, even when one limits oneself in the small circle of 'I and mine' one is striving unconsciously to experience the joy in the enlargement of the self. Thereby the self, otherwise encased in the body, is released to a limited extent and for a little while. But what sort of a release is this? It is like a prisoner coming out of his cell into the prison courtyard. This hardly satisfies the self's aspirations. It wants the joy of unbounded freedom.

12. In short, (i) A seeker after truth should avoid the by-lanes of *adharma* (unrighteousness) and *paradharma* (the *dharma* which is not his own) and take to the natural and straight path of *swadharma*; and never waver from it. (ii) Bearing in mind that the body is transient, it should be used for the sake of the performance of *swadharma* and should be given up for the sake of *swadharma* when the need arises. (iii) Remaining ever aware of the eternal and all-pervading nature of the Self, the distinction between 'I' and 'others' should be removed from the mind. The Lord has expounded these three principles of life. One who follows them would undoubtedly have, some day or the other, the experience of नरदेहाचेनि साधनें, सच्चिदानंद पदवी घेणें (Using the human body as an instrument, one can reach the exalted state of *sat-chit-ananda*.[8])

---

[8] The Supreme Truth, or the *Brahman*, is said to have three aspects – *sat*, *chit* and *ananda*. *Sat* means being, that which really exits. It also means abiding, actual, right, self-existent essence. *Chit* means perception, knowledge or consciousness, while *ananda* means bliss.

8. The way to harmonise the two principles : Renunciation of the fruit of actions

13. The Lord has no doubt enunciated the principles of life. But this, in itself, does not serve the purpose. These principles were already there in the Upanishads and the Smritis. To restate them is not the Gita's unique contribution; that lies in its explaining how these principles are to be translated into practice. It is in solving this great problem that the ingenuity and uniqueness of the Gita lie.

Yoga means nothing but the art of translating the principles of life into practice. The word *'sankhya'* means principles or science while *'yoga'* means the art of translating it into practice. Jnanadeva's saying, 'योगियां साधली जीवनकळा' ('The *yogis* have mastered the art of living'), proclaims this as an experiential fact. The Gita includes both *sankhya* and *yoga*, the science and art respectively; and this has made her complete and perfect. When science and art unite, the beauty of life blossoms into its fullness. Science, by itself, remains on an abstract level. One may know the theory of music quite well, but the many-splendoured beauty of *naad-brahma* (the Supreme Truth revealed in the sound of music) will be realised only when one has mastered the art of singing. That is why the Lord has taught not only the principles, but also the art of applying them to life. What then is this art – the art of practising *swadharma* while realising that the body is of little worth and that the Self is imperishable and indivisible?

Behind a man's action there are generally two types of attitude. One of them is : 'If I do something, I shall definitely enjoy the fruit of my actions; I am entitled to it.' The second attitude is : 'I shall not act at all if I am not going to enjoy the fruit of my actions.' The Gita prescribes an altogether different attitude. It says : 'You must, of course, act; but do not have any claim over the fruit of your actions'. One who acts is certainly entitled to enjoy the fruit of one's actions, but one should voluntarily give up that right. *Rajas*[9] says, "I shall act only if I am going to enjoy the fruit of my actions." *Tamas* says, "If I am not going to enjoy the fruit, I shall not act at all." These attitudes are like two sides of the same coin; there is nothing to choose between the two. One should go beyond both of them and adopt pure *sattva*; one should act and then relinquish the fruits of actions; and act without any claim over them. The desire for the fruit should never be there, either before or after the action.

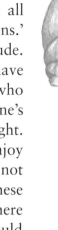

14. The Gita, while asking us not to have any desire for the fruit of actions, insists that the work must, however, be perfect. The work of a desireless doer can rightfully be expected to be better than that of one driven by desire for the fruit. The reason is

---

[9] *Gunas*, according to the *Sankhya* philosophy, mean basic elements. *Prakriti*, or the Nature, is constituted of three *gunas*, which can be called essential qualities or modes : *Sattva* is the principle of equilibrium and harmony; *rajas* is the principle of passion, restlessness, endeavour and initiation; and *tamas* is the principle of ignorance and inertia. Human nature and action is determined by the proportion of these *gunas* therein and their interaction.

that, because of attachment to the fruit, the latter is bound to waste at least some time and energy in daydreaming about it. On the other hand, every moment of the desireless doer's life and every bit of his energy would be spent in the work in hand. A river knows no respite; the wind takes no rest; the sun shines for ever. Likewise, a desireless doer is ever engaged in unremitting service. Who else can then achieve perfection in work, if not he? Secondly, mental poise, the equanimity of mind is a great quality; and the desireless doer has this quality in his own right. When equanimity of mind is combined with the skill of the hands, even the ordinary work of an artisan is bound to be better and more beautiful. Moreover, the difference between the outlook of a desireless doer and of one with attachment to desires is also conducive in making the former's work better. A man having an eye on securing the fruit looks at the work from a selfish point of view. In his view, the action as well as its fruit are exclusively his own. Therefore, he does not look upon any negligence in the work as a moral lapse. For him, it may, at the most, cause the output to be defective. But a desireless doer has a moral sense of duty towards his work. He is, therefore, extremely alert to avoid any shortcomings therein. Hence his work is bound to be more flawless. Thus, from whatever angle one may see, *falatyaga* (renunciation of the fruit of actions) proves to be a sound and effective principle. That is why it could be called a sort of *yoga* or the art of living.

15. Leaving aside the matter of desireless action, there is in the action itself a joy which you cannot find in the fruit. Total absorption in one's own work is an everlasting spring of joy. Were you to offer any amount of money to an artist for refraining from painting, would he agree? Certainly not. If you tell a farmer not to go and work in the field and offer him as much grains as he wants, he would certainly not agree to it if he were a true farmer. A farmer goes to the field in the early morning. There the Sun-god welcomes him. Birds sing for him. Cattle gather around him. He caresses them with affection, casts a loving glance at the plants. There is a *sattvik*, sublime joy in all this. This joy, in fact, is the true and main reward of his work. Compared to it, the material fruit of action is secondary.

When the Gita takes a man's attention away from the fruit of his actions, it increases hundredfold his concentration in his work through this ingenuity. When the doer's mind is free from the desire for the fruit, his absorption in his work attains the character of *samadhi*. Hence his joy is also hundred times more than that of others. Looked at from this angle, it is clear that the desireless action is itself a great reward. Jnanadeva has rightly asked, "The tree bears fruits, but what fruit could the fruit bear?" When the body is used for the desireless pursuit of *swadharma*, such pursuit itself is the beautiful fruit that the body bears. Why then look for any other fruit? The Gita asks us to refrain from such behaviour. It asks us to relish work, to rejoice in it, to be fully absorbed in it and draw life-blood from it. To act itself is everything. A child plays for the joy of playing. He does get the benefit of exercise thereby, but he does not think of this benefit. His joy lies in playing only.

9. Renunciation of the fruit of action : Two examples

16. The saints have demonstrated this in their lives. Shivaji, the king, had great respect for saint Tukaram because of the latter's exemplary devotion to the Lord. Once he thought of honouring him and sent a palanquin to fetch him. But Tukaram was deeply distressed by the arrangements made to honour him. He thought to himself, "Is this the reward for my devotion to the Lord? Is it for this that I worship Him?" He felt that the Lord, by placing this fruit of the worldly honour in his hands, was pushing him away from Him, and said,

'जाणोनि अंतर । टाळिसील करकर ।
तुज लागली हे खोडी । पांडुरंगा बहु कुडी ।।'

– 'O, Lord! This prank on your part is not good. You may be trying to push me away from you by offering this little bribe. You may be thinking of getting rid of me this way. But I am not so naive as to be taken in by this. I shall cling firmly to your feet.'

Devotion (*Bhakti*) is the *swadharma* of the devotee (*Bhakta*). His 'art of living' consists in ensuring that the devotion does not get distracted by the lure of other worldly gains.

17. The life of Pundalik shows us an even more profound ideal of renunciation of the fruit of actions. Pundalik was devoted to the service of his parents. Pleased with this, Lord Pandurang rushed to meet him. But Pundalik refused to give up his duty to welcome the Lord. The service of the parents was, for him, a form of worship of the Lord. Someone may rob others to provide comforts to his parents; or a patriot may seek the prosperity and glory of his own country at the cost of other countries. Such 'worship' of one's parents or one's country is nothing but selfish attachment; it is not true worship. Pundalik was not trapped in such attachment. It was indeed true that the Lord Himself was standing in front of him; but was that His only form? Was the whole creation lifeless like a corpse before He appeared in that form? Pundalik told the Lord, "O, Lord! I fully understand that you have come to bless me. But I believe in the doctrine of 'this also.' I do not think that you alone are God. You certainly are God; but my parents too are God to me. And since I am engaged in their service, I am not in a position to pay attention to you. Please, therefore, forgive me." Saying this, he pushed a brick for the Lord to stand on, and again became engrossed in his work. Saint Tukaram says with loving admiration in a lighter vein —

'कां रे प्रेमें मातलासी । उभें केलें विठ्ठलासी ।
ऐसा कैसा रे तूं धीट । मागें भिरकाविली वीट ।।'

('Why have you become so presumptuous in Love? You made Lord Pandurang stand at your door! How have you become so audacious as to throw a brick for Him to stand on!')

18. The doctrine of 'this also' which Pundalik applied is a part of the ingenuity in the renunciation of the fruit of actions. A man who renounces the fruits of actions is totally absorbed in his work and his outlook is broad, tolerant and balanced. He does not, therefore, get entangled in the web of abstruse academic arguments and remains firm on his own standpoint. He does not argue, 'not that, this alone is true.' He holds, humbly but firmly, that 'this also is true and that also is true, but this alone is for me' – that he should stick to his own *swadharma*.

A man once went to a sage and asked him, "Must one leave one's home – that is, give up one's worldly duties and responsibilities as a householder – in order to attain *moksha*?"[10] The sage said, "Certainly not. King Janaka attained *moksha* while living in the palace, fulfilling his duties as a king; then where is the need for you to leave your home?" Later, another man went to the sage and asked him, "Sir, can one attain *moksha* without leaving the home?" The sage replied, "Who says so ? Had it been possible, were

---

[10] *Moksha* means the liberation of Self from bondage and its unity with the Brahman, whereby it is freed from the cycle of births and deaths. According to the Hindu tradition, it is the ultimate goal of human life for which everybody should aspire and strive for. It is often translated in English as 'salvation'.

persons like Shuka[11] fools to leave their homes – that is, worldly attachments – for the sake of *moksha*?" Later, they met each other and a dispute arose. While one asserted that the sage was in favour of leaving home, the other said that the sage had advised him against it. They again came to the sage. He explained, "Both the advices are correct. What is important is to become detached. Then one can follow different ways in accordance with one's disposition. The answer depends on the way the question is posed. It is true that one need not leave home for *moksha* and it is equally true that one has to leave home for attaining it." This is what the doctrine of 'this also' means.

19. Pundalik's example shows the extent to which one can renounce the fruits of actions. The temptation that the Lord offered to Pundalik was certainly much more alluring than that offered to Tukaram. Still, Pundalik was not carried away by that. Had he succumbed to that temptation, it would have spelled his ruin. Once a certain path (for God-realisation) is chosen for oneself after due deliberation, then it must be pursued till the end. Even if the Lord Himself appears before you, you should not be tempted to leave that path. As long as one is in a body, it is one's duty to follow the chosen path. Seeing the Lord face to face is then in one's hands; His vision is always there for the asking. Why should then one bother about it? 'सर्वात्मकपण माझें हिरोनि नेतो कोण?' ('Who can deprive me

---

[11] Shuka, son of sage Vyasa, is said to have left his home immediately after his birth.

of my oneness with the whole creation?') 'मनीं भक्तीची आवडी' ('The heart longs for the Lord.'). The very purpose of this birth is to fulfil that longing. When the Gita says, 'मा ते संगोऽस्त्वकर्मणि' ('Let there not be any attachment to *akarma*'[12]) the comprehensive meaning is that while doing desireless work, one must not have desire even for the ultimate freedom from action, i.e., *moksha*. *Moksha* means nothing but freedom from all desires. Why should there be desire for it? When the renunciation of the fruit of actions reaches this point, the art of living attains perfection like the full moon.

10. The ideal teacher

20. Thus the science and the art have been explained. Still the whole picture does not stand clearly before our eyes. Science is abstract. Art is not so; but it too has to assume concrete form to become perceptible. Otherwise it too will remain abstract and elusive. Similarly, understanding of the principles of life and the art of living will not be complete unless we have before us their embodiment. That is why Arjuna says, "O, Lord! You have told me the basic principles of life and explained the art of translating them into practice. Still the picture is not clear to me. Please, therefore, tell me the characteristics of one whose intellect and mind are fully anchored in the basic principles of life and who has fully assimilated the *yoga* of renunciation of the fruit of actions. Tell me about such a person who demonstrates the limit upto which the fruit of actions could be renounced, who is steadfast in the

---

[12] Please refer to Chap. 4.4 to 9

contemplation of the Lord while working and who is firm like a rock in his settled conviction – a person who can be called a *sthitaprajna*.[13] How does he speak, how does he sit, how does he walk? In short, how does he live his daily worldly life, and how can one recognise him?"

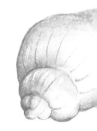

21. In response to this entreaty the Lord has portrayed, in eighteen verses at the end of the Second Chapter, the noble and exalted character of the *sthitaprajna*. These eighteen verses can be said to contain the essence of the eighteen Chapters of the Gita. *Sthitaprajna* is the ideal that the Gita puts before us. In fact, it is the Gita which has coined the word *sthitaprajna*. Later the Gita describes the *jivanmukta* (the liberated one) in the Fifth Chapter, the *bhakta* (the devotee) in the twelfth, the *gunateeta* (one who has transcended the three *gunas*) in the Fourteenth and the *jnananishtha* (one steadfastly committed to the Supreme knowledge) in the Eighteenth Chapter, but the description of the *sthitaprajna* is much more elaborate and lucid. This description highlights the characteristics of both the *siddha* (one who has attained spiritual liberation) and the *sadhaka* (the spiritual seeker). Thousands of

---

[13] *Sthitaprajna* means the one who has attained 'steadfast wisdom', whose intellect is settled in a state of union with the Divine as a result of assimilating the fundamental priciples of life and mastering the art of living in accordance with them. Vinoba was particularly fond of the eighteen verses in the Gita describing the ideal of the *sthitaprajna* and gave discourses on them during his incarceration in 1944. They have been published in the form of a book titled '*Sthitaprajna-darshan*' (The Steadfast Wisdom).

satyagrahi[14] men and women regularly recite these verses in their evening prayers. If these verses could be taken to every home in every village, what a happy thing it would be! But then, they would spread of their own accord if they are first imprinted on our own minds. If the daily recitation becomes mechanical, it would not get imprinted on the mind; it could rather have an opposite effect. But it would not be the fault of regular recitation; it is the lack of accompanying reflection over them that is to be blamed for this. Regular recitation must be accompanied with constant reflection and soul-searching.

22. *Sthitaprajna,* as the term itself tells, means one having steadfast wisdom. But how could there be steadfast wisdom without subduing the senses? Hence the *sthitaprajna* has been described as the embodiment of restraint. Restraint implies that the intellect is anchored in the Self and the mind and the organs are under the control of the intellect. The *sthitaprajna* reins in all his organs and uses them in desireless and selfless action. Just as a farmer uses bullocks for ploughing, the *sthitaprajna* uses his organs for the desireless pursuit of *swadharma*. His every breath is used in the highest pursuit – the spiritual quest.

23. Reining in the organs is certainly not easy. It is, in a way, easier to stop using them altogether. Things like fasting, observing silence etc. are not really very

[14] Participants in the *satyagraha* campaigns led by Mahatma Gandhi against the British colonial rule. *Satyagraha* means holding steadfastly to the truth one has perceived and suffering for it non-violently.

difficult. On the other hand, as is quite evident, is not everybody giving free rein to his organs? But it is most difficult to practise restraint like a tortoise.  It draws in its limbs completely in its shell whenever it senses danger and uses them whenever it is safe to do so. Likewise, one should refrain from using the organs for sensual pleasures and make proper use of them in the spiritual pursuit. This is extremely difficult and requires Herculean efforts, and also wisdom. Even then, one may not always succeed. Are we then to despair? Certainly not. A spiritual seeker should never lose hope. He should try everything in his capacity, use all his ingenuity; and when he reaches the end of his tether, he should seek the love of the Lord – supplement his efforts with devotion. This is the valuable advice the Lord has given while describing the attributes of *sthitaprajna*. This advice is given in just a few words, but these few words are far more valuable than volumes of sermons; for, the element of devotion has been introduced precisely where it is needed. We shall not here go into a detailed discussion of the attributes of the *sthitaprajna*. My intention is to draw your attention to the exact place of devotion in the spiritual pursuit lest we should forget it. God alone knows who would reach the ideal of the perfect *sthitaprajna*; but the figure of Pundalik is ever in my mind as an example of the *sthitaprajna* who is completely dedicated to service.

24. The Second Chapter ends with the description of the *sthitaprajna's* qualities. We can summarise this by the formula —

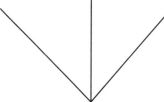

(Nirguna) Sankhya (Comprehension of the principles of life)	+ (Saguna) Yoga Art of applying them in life	+ (Saakaar) Sthitaprajna Personification of those principles and master of the art

together constitute the Whole Science of Life

It is bound to lead to *brahmanirvana*, or *moksha*, i.e. liberation of the Self and its union with the *Brahman*. What else could follow?

(28.2.32)

CHAPTER 3

Karmayoga
(Yoga of selfless and desireless action)

11. Renunciation of the fruit leads to infinite gains

1. Brothers, in the Second Chapter we viewed the whole science of life. The Third Chapter provides further elaboration of that science. We had a look at the principles; now we shall look into the details. In the last talk, *karmayoga* was discussed. Renunciation of the fruit of actions is the thing of distinctive importance in *karmayoga*. The question then is, does any gain accrue to a *karmayogi* or not? The Third Chapter tells us that by renouncing the fruit a *karmayogi* gains it in infinite measure.

Here I am reminded of the story of Lakshmi's *swayamvara.*[1] A whole lot of gods and demons had gathered at her *swayamvara* with the hope of marrying her. Lakshmi had not announced any task for them. Coming to the court where they were seated, she declared that she would marry the one who was not coveting her. But all those assembled there were desirous of marrying her; so all of them were naturally ruled out. Lakshmi then set forth in search of the one having no desire for her. She finally found Lord Vishnu lying serenely on the serpent Shesha. She put the garland around His neck[2] and has been sitting at His feet ever since. As the poet

---

[1] In ancient India, princesses used to choose their spouses. The custom was called *swayamvara*. All those princes wishing to marry the princess used to be invited to the ceremony at which the princess would publicly choose a bridegroom for herself. Often, the princes were made to perform some particularly difficult task.

[2] The act signifies acceptance of the person as the spouse.

puts it, 'न मागे तयाची रमा होय दासी'[3] – 'Lakshmi serves one who does not covet her.' This is the beauty of it.

2. An ordinary man closely guards the fruit of his actions so that none else could have it. But thereby he loses infinite gains that could otherwise have been his. The man attached to worldly affairs toils a lot, but gets little in return. On the other hand, a *karmayogi* receives infinite gains with little effort. It is the difference in their mental attitudes that makes all the difference. Tolstoy has said, "People talk a lot about Jesus' sacrifice, but the ordinary people toil much more than Jesus, carry much more burden, suffer much more. Were they to put in half the labour for the Lord, they would become greater than Jesus!"

3. Worldly people put in arduous labour; but that is in the pursuit of petty gains. We get what we seek; as is the desire, so is the fruit. The world will not pay more for our goods than the price that we ourselves mark on them. Sudama went to Lord Krishna with the offering of a handful of parched rice. It might not have been worth a farthing, but to Sudama it was priceless. It had the stamp of his love and devotion on them[4] which, as it were, had charged them with magical potency. A small, insignificant thing gains in value and potency when it is so charged. What, after

---

[3] Lakshmi is the Goddess of prosperity. So the verse also means that one gets wealth when one does not hanker after it.

[4] Sudama, a childhood friend of Lord Krishna, was a poor *Brahmin*. His wife once coaxed him to meet Krishna, who had become the ruler of Dwarka and could therefore remove their poverty. Sudama visited Krishna with an offering of parched rice as he could afford nothing else. The Lord sensed the feeling of love behind this offering and gave him countless riches.

all, is a currency note? It is just a little piece of paper. If burnt, it would not warm up even a drop of water. But it has the stamp of the government on it, and that gives it value.

This is the whole beauty of *karmayoga*. Action is like the currency note. Stamped with *bhavana* – sentiments and genuine feelings – it acquires value. In a sense, I am revealing here the secret of image-worship. The idea of image-worship is extremely charming. To begin with, an image was just a piece of stone. I put life into it, I poured my devotion into it. These feelings cannot be broken. A stone can be broken into pieces, but not the sentiments. The moment I withdraw my devotion from the image, it once again gets reduced to a mere stone which can easily be broken into pieces.

4. Action is like a stone, or a piece of paper. My mother scribbled just three or four lines on a piece of paper and sent it to me; another gentleman sent me a bundle of fifty pages. Now, which one has more value? The feelings expressed in the few lines from my mother are priceless, they are sacred. The other stuff cannot stand comparison with it. Action must be imbued with the warmth of feelings. We assess a labourer's work and pay him wages accordingly; but *dakshina*[5] is not given like that. Water is sprinkled on it before it is given. The amount of *dakshina* is not important; it is the sentiment of reverence behind it

---

[5] Offering to the priest or the *guru* (master) with reverence and gratitude.

that is important. The touch of water is symbolic of the feelings in the heart of the host. There is a remarkable saying in Manusmriti. In those days, students used to stay with the *guru* (master) for twelve years. The *guru* would teach them, make them human beings in the true sense. Now, what should a student offer to the master? In those days, fees were not collected in advance. The student, after completion of his studies, was supposed to offer what he felt like giving and thought proper. Manu says, "Give the master a flower, a fan, a pair of sandals, or a pitcher of water." Is this a joke? No; the point is that, whatever is offered should be offered as a sign of reverence. A flower in itself has little value, but charged with devotion, its value becomes immeasurable. The poet has sung the praise of Rukmini. She put in the scale a single leaf of Tulsi (the holy basil plant) which equalled the weight of Lord Krishna while heaps of gold ornaments put by Satyabhama proved to be insufficient to weigh Him, because the Tulsi leaf put by Rukmini was full of devotion. It was no longer an ordinary leaf; it was a charged one.[6] This is true of the actions of a *karmayogi* too.

5. Suppose two persons have gone to bathe in the river Ganga. One of them says, "What, after all, is

---

[6] Satyabhama and Rukmini, both queens of Lord Krishna, once had a dispute over who loves Him the most. They thereupon decided to weigh Him. Krishna sat on one of the pans of the balance and Satyabhama put heaps of gold ornaments on the other pan, but they could not equal the Lord's weight. Rukmini then weighed the Lord against just a Tulsi leaf, but the leaf equalled the Lord's weight.

this Ganga that people talk so much about? Combine two parts hydrogen and one part oxygen, and you will have Ganga." The other one says, "This great river emerged from the holy lotus-feet of Lord Vishnu, she dwelt in the matted hair of Lord Shiva. Thousands of seers – both ascetic and royal – have done penance on her banks. Countless holy acts have been performed by her side. Such is this sacred Mother Ganga." He takes a bath with these feelings in mind. The other fellow, for whom Ganga's water is just a compound of hydrogen and oxygen, also bathes in the river. Both get the benefit of physical cleansing; but it is a petty benefit. Even a bullock can get this benefit. Dirt of the body will go. But how to wash out the taint of the mind? One gets the petty benefit of physical cleanliness; the other, in addition, gains the invaluable fruit of inward purity.

A man doing *surya-namaskars*[7] after bathing will certainly get the benefit of physical exercise; but if he is not doing them for the sake of health only, but as a form of worship, he will also have a sharp and radiant intellect in addition to a healthy body. He will get from the Sun-god vigour and creative energy.

6. The act may be the same outwardly; but the difference in the inward feelings makes a world of difference. Action by a spiritually motivated selfless person contributes to his moral and spiritual

---

[7] A form of worshipping the Sun-god, it is also a well-known *yogic* exercise wherein body goes through different motions, thereby getting all-round physical exercise.

development whereas the same action by a worldly person serves to bind him. A *karmayogi* farmer will look upon farming as his *swadharma*. It will, of course, fill his stomach; but he is not farming for that purpose. He will eat only to enable him to perform the *swadharma* of farming. *Swadharma* is the end for him, and food a means therefor. But to another farmer, food is the end and farming a means therefor. These two attitudes are the opposite of each other.

This has been figuratively described in the Second Chapter. It is stated therein that a *karmayogi* is asleep when others are awake whereas he is awake when others are asleep. What does this mean? We are ever mindful about filling our stomachs, while a *karmayogi* is keen about spending every moment in work and does not waste a single moment. While ordinary worldly persons live in order to eat, he eats only because something has to be given to the body to survive to perform selfless service. While ordinary worldly persons enjoy eating, for a *yogi* it is a burdensome task. He would not therefore eat with relish; he would have control over his palate. The attitudes are thus diametrically opposite to each other. What gives pleasure to one is burdensome to the other. This has been metaphorically described as 'the night for the one is a day for the other, and the day for one is the night for the other.' The actions look alike, but what is important is that a *karmayogi* enjoys work leaving aside any attachment to the fruit of his actions. He will eat and sleep like others, but his attitude towards everything will be different. To

impress this point, the ideal of the *sthitaprajna* has been put forth at the outset itself in the Gita, although sixteen Chapters are still ahead.

The similarity and difference between the actions of a worldly man and those of a *karmayogi* are immediately clear. For example, if a *karmayogi* is engaged in the care of the cows, he will do the work with the idea of serving the society by providing it with plenty of milk; and at the same time he will look to it as an opportunity to have a relationship of love with all the lower orders of beings through the service of the cows. He will certainly get his wages, but that is not his motivation. Real joy lies in the divine feelings informing the actions.

7. Every act of a *karmayogi* unites him with the whole universe. There is a custom of watering the Tulsi plant before taking meals. This is for creating a bond of love with the whole world of plants. How can I eat, keeping the Tulsi plant starved? Beginning with the identification with the cow and the Tulsi plant we are to progress till we are one with the whole creation. In the Mahabharata war, fighting used to stop at sunset and everybody would then go for performing religious rites etc. But Lord Krishna would rejoice in actions like unyoking the horses from the chariot, giving them water, gently rubbing them down and nursing their wounds. What a joy the Lord found in such service! Poets never get tired of describing all this. Bring before your mind's eye the picture of the divine charioteer carrying the feed of the horses

in the folds of His lower garment and feeding the horses with His own hands and realise how joyful *karmayoga* is. In *karmayoga*, all actions attain the highest spiritual character. Take *khadi*[8] work. A *khadi* worker hawking *khadi* from door to door carrying the load on his head never feels tired, for he knows that millions of his brothers and sisters are famished and is motivated by the idea of providing a few morsels to them. His work of selling a few yards of *khadi* is linked to *daridranarayan* – God in the form of the poor.

12. Various gains from karmayoga

8. There is extraordinary power in the selfless and desireless *karmayoga*. It richly blesses both the individual and the society. A *karmayogi*, who follows his *swadharma*, does get his daily bread. Besides, his industriousness makes his body healthy and pure. His work also contributes to the well-being and prosperity of the society in which he lives. A *karmayogi* farmer will not cultivate opium or tobacco to earn more money. He links his work to the welfare of the society. Actions done in the pursuit of *swadharma* will confer nothing but benefit on the community. A trader who believes in working for the good of the people will not sell foreign cloth[9]. His business will therefore be beneficial to the society. A society which

---

[8] Handspun, handwoven cotton cloth, popularised by Mahatma Gandhi. For him, it was a symbol of the dignity of labour and of self-reliance and identification with the poor.

[9] The *Swadeshi* movement in pre-Independence India sought boycott of imported cloth to protect the indigenous textile industry.

has in its midst such *karmayogis* who have identified themselves with those around them, forgetting their selfish interests, will be marked with prosperity, order and harmony.

9. Work of a *karmayogi* helps sustain him. It keeps his body healthy and intellect radiant. It results in the welfare of the society as well. It also confers on the *karmayogi* a great gift in the form of the purity of his mind. It is said that work is a means for the purification of the mind – 'कर्मणा शुद्धिः'. But this is true only of the work done by a *karmayogi*, as it is charged with the spirit of selfless service, and not of the work ordinarily done by the people. In the Mahabharata, there is a story of Tuladhar, the grocer. Jajali, a *Brahmin* goes to him seeking true knowledge.[10] Tuladhar tells him, "My dear fellow, what is really required is that the scales must always be held even." The outward action of weighing had straightened and balanced Tuladhar's mind. Whosoever came to the shop, Tuladhar's balance was always true. Actions affect the mind. A *karmayogi's* work is like *japa*[11] – a form of prayer. It purifies the mind and it is only the clean and pure mind which receives true knowledge. A *karmayogi's* work ultimately leads to the attainment of wisdom. Tuladhar learnt equanimity

---

[10] In ancient India, teaching was the vocation of the *Brahmins*. But here a *Brahmin* is shown going to a *Vaishya* (trader) for knowledge.

[11] *Japa* means uttering in low voice or internally the Name of God or a sacred verse. It also implies unremitting mental contemplation of the object of devotion.

53

of mind from the weighing balance. Sena was a barber who cut the hair and cleansed the heads of his customers. While doing this work, a realisation dawned on him. He thought, "I have been cleansing others' heads, but have I cleansed my own head, my own mind?" While removing weeds from the field, it occurs to a *karmayogi* that the weeds of base desires and passions should be removed from one's own mind. Gora Kumbhar, the potter, realised, while shaping and baking earthen pots, that his own life should also be properly moulded and baked in the fire of desireless action. He eventually attained such an exalted status by virtue of his wisdom that he earned the authority to judge the degree of spiritual development in others.[12] *Karmayogis* gained true knowledge through their vocations. To them, they were like schools of the spirit. Their work was imbued with the spirit of worship and service. Although it appeared worldly, it was spiritual in essence.

10. Another great gain that flows from the actions of a *karmayogi* is that a model is placed before the society. In the society, there are persons belonging to different generations. It is the duty of the older generation to set an example to the younger one. It is

[12] Saint Namdeva, when he was still a seeker, once thought that he was quite close to Lord Pandurang, and had thus gained all that he should. To remove his vain misconception, Lord Pandurang sent him to Gora, the potter. Gora was busy testing the strength of his pots by stroking them with his testing implement when Namdeva approached him. Gora then stroked Namdeva's head with the same implement and announced that 'the pot is not yet fully baked', meaning that Namdeva had yet to attain Self-knowledge.

the duty of an elder brother to his younger brother, of parents to their children, of leaders to their followers, of masters to their pupils, to set an example through their actions; and who else but a *karmayogi* is fit to set an example?

As a *karmayogi* finds joy in the work itself, he is ever-absorbed in his work. Hypocrisy does not, therefore, gain ground in the society. A *karmayogi* is happy and content with fulfilment; still he continues to work. Saint Tukaram says, "Should I give up singing *bhajans*[13], now that I have realised God through them? Singing *bhajans* has now become my nature."

'आधीं होता संतसंग । तुका झाला पांडुरंग
त्याचें भजन राहीना । मूळस्वभाव जाईना'

('Earlier, Tukaram used to keep company with the saints. Eventually he became one with Lord Pandurang. Still he cannot help singing *bhajans*. One's original nature does not, after all, change.')

The *karmayogi* reaches the summit of spiritual liberation using the ladder of work. He does not kick off that ladder even thereafter. He just cannot do so. Doing work becomes his nature. He thus continues to impress on the society the importance of service in the form of work enjoined by *swadharma*.

Removal of hypocrisy from the society is extremely important. Hypocrisy spells doom for the society. If

---

[13] Devotional songs.

a *jnani*[14] stops working, others will follow suit. The *jnani*, being ever-content within himself, may sit still in a state of bliss, but others will become inactive even though inwardly unhappy and disgruntled. One is at rest because he is happy at heart; the other is merely passive but unhappy within. This is a horrible situation. It will encourage hypocrisy.

That is why all the saints continued to hold on steadfastly to the means even after reaching the end, the pinnacle of fulfilment. They kept on working till the last breath. A mother actively participates in the children's play with the dolls even though she knows that it is all make-believe. If she takes no part in the play, the children will not enjoy it. Likewise if a *karmayogi* stops working because of contentment, others will follow suit despite being discontented; but inwardly they will continue to be dissatisfied and joyless.

Therefore, a *karmayogi* continues to work like an ordinary man. He does not think that he is exceptional in any way. He exerts himself infinitely more than others. It is not necessary to put a stamp on any action and mark it as spiritual; no action should be publicised as such. If you are a perfect *brahmachari*[15]

---

[14] One who has attained Self-knowledge; a man of wisdom. The term '*Jnana*' is commonly used for knowledge and understanding, but it also means Self-knowledge or saving wisdom. The meaning has to be understood from the context.

[15] *Brahmachari* is one who practises *brahmacharya*. *Brahmacharya* is normally translated as chastity or celibacy, but it is a much wider concept. Etymologically, it means a course of conduct adopted for realisation of *Brahman*. It includes control of all the senses.

your work should have much more zest and vigour than that of others. You should work much more even if you get less to consume. Your service to the society should be greater. Let your *brahmacharya* be reflected in your actions. Let its fragrance, like sandalwood, spread far and wide. This is what should be true for the truly spiritual work.

In short, a *karmayogi,* by renouncing desire for the fruit of his actions, will receive infinite rewards. His body will be sustained and both his body and mind will remain healthy and radiant. The society to which he belongs will also be happy. His mind will be purified and he will attain wisdom. The spread of hypocrisy in the society will be precluded, and the sacred ideal will be revealed to all. Such is the glory of *karmayoga,* which is testified by experience.

13. Obstacles in the way of karmayoga

11. A *karmayogi*'s work is much better than that of others. For him, work is worship. I perform *pooja*[16] and receive *prasad* thereafter. But is the *prasad* a reward for the *pooja*? If one performs *pooja* for the sake of *prasad*, one will, of course, get it. But a *karmayogi* seeks to see God face to face through performance of *pooja*. He does not think that the value of his *pooja* is so trivial as to have the *prasad* as its only reward. He is not prepared to underestimate

---

[16] *Pooja* is a form of worshipping the image of the Lord. After completion of the same, sweets, fruits etc. are offered to the Lord. These eatables, called *prasad*, are then distributed to the devotees, as a mark of God's grace.

the value of his work. He does not measure the value of his work in gross terms. The fruits of actions depend on the outlook behind them. A person with a gross outlook and gross aim will receive reward in gross terms. There is a saying among the farmers : 'Sow deep, but sow in moist soil.' It is not enough to sow deep; there should also be moisture in the soil. Then only the yield will be high. There should thus be depth, that is, thoroughness and excellence in the work and there should also be the moisture, that is, devotion and surrender to God, dedication to God. A *karmayogi* has depth in his work and he then dedicates that work to God.

We have developed some absurd ideas about spirituality. People feel that a spiritual seeker need not do any work. They wonder how a farmer or a weaver could be a spiritual seeker. But they do not raise the question how one who feeds his body could be a spiritual seeker! The Lord of the *karmayogis* – Lord Krishna – rubbed down horses, mopped the floor after people had their meals at the time of Pandava's *Rajsooya Yajna* and grazed the cattle. The ruler of Dwarka (Lord Krishna) would play flute and graze the cattle whenever he visited Gokul, his childhood abode. The saints have sketched the picture of such a *karmayogi* Lord; and the saints themselves have attained liberation while working as a tailor, or a weaver, or a gardener, or a potter, or a grocer, or a barber, or a tanner.

12. A person slips from the observance of such a divine *karmayoga* on account of two reasons. We should keep in mind the peculiar nature of our senses. They always get caught in the duality of likes and dislikes. We are attached to or fond of what we want and are averse to what we do not want. Love and hate, desire and anger pounce upon a man and prey on him. How beautiful and infinitely rewarding *karmayoga* is! But desire and anger are always after us, driving us to hanker after something and reject something. The Lord is warning us, at the end of this Chapter, to shun them. A *karmayogi* should also become an embodiment of self-restraint like the *sthitaprajna*.

(6.3.32)

CHAPTER 4

Vikarma:
The key to *Karmayoga*

14. *Karma needs vikarma*[1] *to complement it*

1. Brothers, in the last chapter, we discussed the *yoga* of desireless action. It is impossible to attain desirelessness if we give up *swadharma* and embrace the *dharma* which is not ours. It is a trader's *swadharma* to sell indigenous goods. But when he gives it up and starts selling foreign goods imported from distant lands, his motive is nothing but to earn more profit. How can such work be free from desire? Pursuit of *swadharma* is therefore indispensable for desireless work. But *swadharma* could also be pursued with an eye on the gains. Take the case of non-violence. For a votary of non-violence, violence is taboo; but he could be one steeped in violence within while being non-violent in outward appearance. For, violence is an attribute of the mind. The mind would not be non-violent merely by giving up outward violence. A sword in hand is a sure sign of a violent mind; but one does not become non-violent merely by throwing the sword away. The same is true about *swadharma* also. To have desirelessness, one must definitely avoid the *dharma* which is not one's own; but that is only the first step towards desirelessness. That itself does not mean attainment of the goal.

Desirelessness is a state of the mind. Pursuit of *swadharma* is necessary but not sufficient for acquiring that state. Other means must also be used towards this end. To light a lamp, oil and wick are necessary

─────────────

[1] See p. 72

63

but not sufficient. It is also necessary to have a flame. Darkness disappears only when we light a flame. How to light a flame? For this one must purify one's mind. The mind should be thoroughly cleansed through intense soul-searching. The Lord has given this important advice at the end of the Third Chapter. The Fourth Chapter has its genesis in this advice.

2. The Gita uses the word *'karma'* (action) in the sense of *swadharma*. We eat, drink, sleep; these are all actions. But these are not the actions that the Gita refers to when it talks of *karma*. *Karma* refers to the performance of *swadharma*. But in order to attain desirelessness through such *karma*, an important aid is necessary. One must overcome desire, attachment and anger. One cannot have desirelessness unless and until the mind has become pure and calm like the waters of the Ganga. The actions necessary for the purification of mind are called *'vikarma'* by the Gita. *Karma*, *vikarma* and *akarma* – these three terms are important in the Fourth Chapter. *Karma* means the outward actions done in the pursuit of *swadharma*. *Vikarma* means total involvement of the mind therein. We may bow to somebody, but that outward action is meaningless without inner humility. There should be unity between the inner and the outer. I may worship the image of the Lord; but that act is worthless if it is not accompanied with devotion. In the absence of devotion, the image is just a piece of stone and so am I; and the worship then means nothing; it is just the case of a stone facing another stone! Desireless, selfless *karmayoga* is attained only when outward

actions are complemented with the inward action of the purification of mind.

3. In the term 'desireless action', the adjective 'desireless' is more important than the word 'action', just as in the phrase 'non-violent non-cooperation', the adjective 'non-violent' is more important than the word 'non-cooperation'. Non-cooperation without non-violence could be a terrible thing. In the same way, it could be dangerous if performance of *swadharma* is not complemented with *vikarma* of the mind.

Those engaged in social service today are certainly pursuing their *swadharma*. When people are poor and destitute, it is a natural duty to serve them and make them happy. But all social workers cannot be called *karmayogis*. Social service without pure motives in the heart of the workers could have disastrous consequences. Such a social service can generate in equal measure the vanity, hatred, envy and selfishness that we generate when we serve our families exclusively. This is clearly evident in the realm of social work today.

15. *Karma + Vikarma = Akarma*

4. The mind should be fully in tune with and involved in work. '*Vikarma*' is the word that the Gita uses for this involvement and application of the mind in work. '*Vikarma*' means the special *karma* which varies with the needs of each individual mind. Many kinds of *vikarma* have been mentioned in the Fourth Chapter. They have been further elaborated from the

Sixth Chapter onwards. Only when we perform this special *karma*, only when the mind is in tune with the outward action, will the flame of desirelessness be lighted. Desirelessness is gradually developed when *karma* and *vikarma* come together. The body and the mind are distinct entities; so the means to be employed for their growth are bound to be different. The goal is reached when they are in tune with each other. To achieve harmony between them, the authors of the scriptures have prescribed a two-fold path. In *bhaktiyoga* (the *yoga* of devotion) they have prescribed penance and austerities without and *japa* within. If such *japa* does not accompany outer forms of penance like fasting, the latter would be in vain. One should never forget why one is doing penance; the motive, the spirit should always be alive in the mind like a burning flame. The word '*upavas*' (fasting) etymologically means 'to dwell close to God'. In order that our mind and heart may dwell close to God, sensual pleasures are to be abjured. But if we give up such pleasures and do not think of God, of what value is the physical act of fasting? If, instead of thinking of God, we think of things to eat and drink while fasting, that 'fast' would be worse than a feast! In fact, there is nothing more dangerous than thinking about sensual pleasures. *Tantra* (technique) must be accompanied by *mantra* (spirit). *Tantra* in itself is not important; and *mantra* without action too has no value. True service can be rendered only when the hands are engaged in service and there is spirit of service in the heart.

5. Performance of *swadharma* will be a dreary affair without the warmth of feelings in the heart. It would not then blossom forth and bear the fruit of desirelessness. Suppose we undertake the work of nursing the sick. If there is no compassion in the heart, it would be a burdensome drudgery for us. To the patient too it will be a burdensome obligation. If the mind is not absorbed in service, it will boost the ego. Expectations will then arise in the mind : "I am helping him today; tomorrow he should help me. He should praise me. People should admire me." Or else, we may get fed up and complain that the patient is peevish and irritable even though we are taking so much care of him. Sick men are usually in a depressed and irritable mood. Without the spirit of service, we would get tired of nursing them.

6. If the mind is in tune with the work, the work is transformed into something unique. When *vikarma* joins *karma,* desirelessness comes into being. When a spark touches the gunpowder, it explodes. *Karma* is like the gunpowder. It works wonders when the flame of *vikarma* ignites it. *Karma* in itself is inert and lifeless; it is the spark of *vikarma* that makes it indescribably powerful. We may keep a packet of gunpowder in our pocket or handle it with impunity; but if ignited, it would blow up the body into pieces. The infinite power in *swadharma* is likewise dormant. Combine it with *vikarma,* and then see what transformation it can bring about! The resultant explosion would reduce to ashes ego, desires, passions and anger, and then supreme wisdom will be attained.

7. Action is that which can kindle the fire of knowledge. When you ignite a log of wood, it turns into embers. How different are they from the log! But it is, after all, the log which has undergone this transformation. When *vikarma* is united with *karma*, *karma* attains a divine radiance. A mother's action of caressing her child is apparently insignificant; but who can describe the upsurge of emotions it gives rise to in the hearts of both the mother and the child? It would be utterly nonsensical if one were to say that such emotions would result if a hand of such weight and such softness is moved up and down such a back. Yes, the action is insignificant; but the mother has put her whole heart into it, and it is this *vikarma* that gives unparalleled comfort and joy. There is an incident described in the Ramayana written by saint Tulsidas. The *vanaras*[2] had come wounded and bleeding after a battle with the demons. They were in great pain. Lord Rama just looked at them with love, and all their pain vanished. It would be ridiculous if someone else were to try to bring about such a result by looking at them in an outwardly similar way.

8. When *Vikarma* is combined with *karma*, there is a powerful explosion of energy, resulting in *akarma*. A big log of wood, when burnt, turns into just a handful of harmless ash. In the same way *karma*, ignited by *vikarma*, results in *akarma*. Is there any relation between the properties of wood and that of

---

[2] *Vanara* (commonly believed to be monkeys) was probably an aboriginal community living in the forests of south India. They formed Lord Rama's army which vanquished the forces of Ravana, the demon king of Lanka.

the ash? Absolutely nothing. You can collect the ash in your hands and merrily smear it all over your body without harm. But there is no doubt that the ash has come out of the burning of that log of wood.

9. When *vikarma* is united with *karma*, *akarma* results. What does it mean? It means that one does not then have the feeling of having done anything. Action does not weigh on the mind of the actor. We act, but still we are not the doers. As the Gita says, you are not the slayer even if you slay somebody. A mother may give a thrashing to her child, but the child will still turn to her for solace. He would not do so if you were to thrash him. It is so because the mother's heart is pure. Her action is totally devoid of any self-interest. *Vikarma*, or the purity of mind, erases the 'action-ness' of the action. Infused with the inner *vikarma*, Lord Rama's action of looking at the *vanaras* became a sheer outpouring of healing love. And it did not tire Rama a bit. Action performed with pure heart is free from any attachment. There is, therefore, no question of any sin nor merit remaining as a residue after that action is over.

Otherwise, an action puts great burden and pressure on the mind and the heart. Suppose, the news breaks out now that all the political prisoners are going to be released tomorrow. Imagine the resulting commotion! We are always agitated and strained with anxiety by the actions, good or bad. Action engulfs us from all sides. It catches us by the scruff of our neck. Just as the sea-waves dash against the shore and make channels into it, the forceful waves of *karma* enter the mind and agitate it. Dualities of pleasure and pain are created. Peace of mind is lost. Even after the action is over, its momentum remains. It takes hold of the mind and makes it restless.

But if *karma* is coupled with *vikarma*, any amount of action does not tire. The mind remains calm, peaceful and radiant. When *vikarma* is poured into *karma*, it results in *akarma*. It is as if *karma* gets erased after it is over.

16. Art of akarma should be learnt from the saints

10. How does *karma* become *akarma*? From whom can we learn this art? From the saints, of course. The Lord says at the end of this Chapter, "Go to the saints and learn from them." Language fails in describing how *karma* is transformed into *akarma*. To gain an understanding of this, one has to sit at the feet of the saints. The Lord is described as 'शांताकारं भुजंगशयनम्' – He is fully at peace even though He is lying on Shesha, the thousand-headed cobra. The saints too do hundreds of actions, but do not allow even a little ripple of commotion to arise in the still waters of their minds. This remarkable thing can never be understood unless the lives of saints are observed at close quarters.

11. Nowadays, books have become quite cheap. There is no dearth of teachers. Education is widespread and cheap. Universities are liberally doling out knowledge. But nobody seems to have assimilated it. In fact, the more one looks at the heaps of books, the more one realises how necessary it is to sit at the feet of the saints. The knowledge encased within the thick covers of the books does not step out of those covers. I

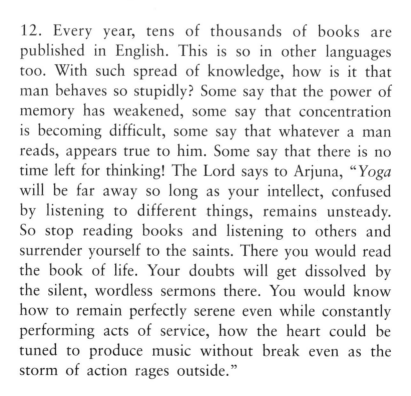

am always reminded of an *abhang* (devotional poem) in this context : 'काम क्रोध आड पडिले पर्वत, राहिला अनंत पैलीकडे ॥' ('The high mountains of desires, passions and anger bar the way to the Lord.') Similarly, the way to knowledge is barred by the heaps of books. Although libraries are everywhere, man still seems to be an ape – ignorant and uncouth. There is a big library at Baroda. Once a gentleman was carrying a thick volume with a lot of pictures, thinking it to be an English book. When I browsed through it, I found it to be a French book! The gentleman must have thought that as the book was in the Roman script, had nice pictures and good binding, so it must be full of knowledge!

12. Every year, tens of thousands of books are published in English. This is so in other languages too. With such spread of knowledge, how is it that man behaves so stupidly? Some say that the power of memory has weakened, some say that concentration is becoming difficult, some say that whatever a man reads, appears true to him. Some say that there is no time left for thinking! The Lord says to Arjuna, "*Yoga* will be far away so long as your intellect, confused by listening to different things, remains unsteady. So stop reading books and listening to others and surrender yourself to the saints. There you would read the book of life. Your doubts will get dissolved by the silent, wordless sermons there. You would know how to remain perfectly serene even while constantly performing acts of service, how the heart could be tuned to produce music without break even as the storm of action rages outside."

(13.3.32)

Vikarma is normally translated as wrong or forbidden action. Vinoba has given the term a different meaning. He had once explained the logic behind it in 1957. The prefix '*vi*' has three different meanings : (1) opposite, as in *viyog* (2) different types, as in *vijnana* and (3) special, as in *vidhwams*. Vinoba says that one has to see the context while determining the meaning of any term. "It has been said in the 4th Chapter that one should understand *karma*, *vikarma* and *akarma*; only then one can grasp the meaning of the principle of *karma*. This means that it is an introductory remark; the 4th Chapter is going to explain them. But there is no mention of opposite *karma* (If *vikarma* is to mean opposite *karma*, such actions should have been mentioned there). Rather, different special actions (which aid the performance of *swadharma*) have been mentioned from verse 25 to 32.

"And what does our experience say? Actions have been said to purify the mind, but do we find that actions alone lead to such purification? They have to be complemented with other things.

"Thus, taking into account the tenor of the Gita and our general experience, I have held that *vikarma* means special *karma*.

"When I understood the process of *Karma-vikarma-akarma*, the meaning of the Gita became clear to me.

"But one need not entangle oneself in a debate over the meaning of words. If one takes *vikarma* to mean opposite *karma*, one should shun such *karma* and if one takes it to mean special mental actions which help in the performance of *karmayoga*, one should take up such actions. Then there will be no place for debate and the truth will be revealed to us."

CHAPTER 5

Two-fold state of *akarma*: Yoga and *Sannyasa*

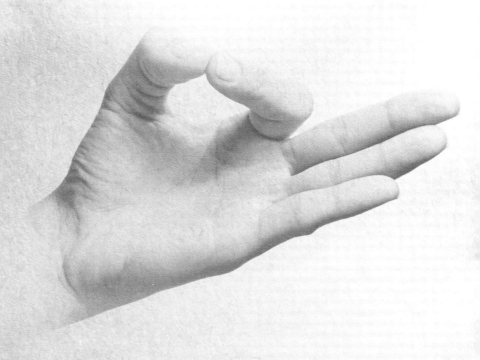

17. Outward action : a mirror of the mind

1. *Samsara*[1] is something very terrible. It is often compared to an ocean. In the midst of an ocean, you see water wherever you look. Same is the case with *samsara*. It has surrounded us from all the sides. Even if a man leaves his home and devotes himself to public service, *samsara* does not leave his mind. Even if one retires to a cave to lead a hermit's life, his few possessions become the centre of his attachment and *samsara* engulfs him there too. Just as a currency note can hold one thousand rupees, a loin-cloth too can hold unlimited attachment. There is, therefore, no attenuation of *samsara* simply through reduction in the involvement in worldly business and/or reduction in one's possessions. You may say 10/25 or 2/5, it means the same. One may be in the midst of family or alone in a forest, attachment does not leave one's mind. A *yogi* retired to the Himalayan caves for doing penance may burn with envy if he happens to hear another *yogi* praised. The same thing happens in the realm of social service.

2. *Samsara* has thus engulfed us and is ever tormenting us. It does not leave us even if we decide to remain within the bounds of *swadharma*. Even if we curtail our activities, engagements and affairs, attachment to 'I and mine' remains the same. It is said that the

---

[1] *Samsara*, in fact, is untranslatable in English. It includes the whole of man's this-worldly life and affairs in the material world in which he is totally immersed and to which he is attached. The term has to be understood with reference to the context.

demons could become small or big at will. *Samsara* too is like a demon. And a demon remains a demon, whatever be his size. You may live in a palace or in a hut, *samsara* is equally inescapable. Even if we limit *samsara* by choosing to remain within the bounds of *swadharma*, there would still be conflicts and you will feel, 'Enough of it!' Therein too you will have to deal with a whole lot of individuals and institutions and that will exasparate you; you would become disgusted. But then that is the time of trial for your mind. Detachment does not automatically result from the performance of *swadharma*. Curtailing activities does not result in detachment.

3. How can then one have detachment? For this, the mind must cooperate fully. Nothing can be achieved without the cooperation of the mind. Parents sometimes keep their wards in a residential school. There the boy leads a disciplined life. He wakes up early, takes exercises regularly and is generally away from bad habits. But as soon as he comes home, he abandons all the good habits. A man is not like a lump of wet clay to which you can give the form you like. He has a mind of his own, which must be ready to assume that form. If there is no cooperation on the part of his mind, all efforts to educate him would be in vain. Cooperation of the mind is, therefore, extremely necessary irrespective of the means adopted.

4. Outward performance of *swadharma* and the inward mental *vikarma* – both are necessary. Outward work is, of course, necessary. The mind cannot otherwise

be tested. In the stillness of early morning, we feel that our minds have become calm. But the moment a child cries, we lose our calm and it becomes clear that the peace of mind is illusory. There is, therefore, no point in avoiding outward work. The true nature of our minds, the real quality of our minds is revealed through such work. Water in a pool may appear clear, but the moment you throw a stone in it, the dirt settled at the bottom will immediately rise up. That happens with our minds too. There are heaps of dirt at the bottom of the mind's lake. They come to the surface when disturbed by an external agent. When a man gets angry, it is not that the anger comes from without; it was already there within him. Otherwise it would never have shown itself.

People say that coloured cloth gets dirty; white cloth does not. But coloured cloth too gets dirty, although it does not appear to be so. White cloth says, "I have become dirty; wash me please." People do not like such 'talking' cloth. Our action too talks. It proclaims whether we are given to selfishness or to anger or something else. Action is the mirror that reflects our true nature. We should, therefore, be grateful to it. If the mirror shows that our face is unclean, would we smash the mirror? No. We would rather thank it and wash our face. Likewise, should we avoid action because it reveals the dirt in our minds – our defects and weaknesses? Is the mind going to be pure simply by avoiding action? We should rather continue to act while trying continually for the purification of mind.

5. A man living alone in a mountain cave, cut off from all human contact, may imagine that he has attained perfect peace of mind. But let him leave the cave and go for meals to somebody's house and let a child playfully rattle the bolt of the door there. The innocent child may be absorbed in the music of that sound, but the recluse will find it jarring and curse the child in his mind. His stay in the isolated cave has made his mind too weak and over-sensitive to stand even the slightest disturbance. His peace of mind may get disturbed by just a little rattling noise. It is not good that one's mind should be in such a weak state.

6. To sum up, *karma* is very much needed to enable us to understand the state of our minds. We can remove our defects only when we become aware of them. Without such awareness, all efforts for progress and growth will come to naught. It is while doing work that we become aware of our defects. *Vikarma* is then to be employed to get rid of those defects. With ceaseless inward *vikarma*, we will gradually come to know how to remain detached while performing *swadharma*, how to remain beyond desires and passions, anger, greed, temptations and delusions. When there is a constant endeavour to purify *karma*, pure *karma* will follow naturally and effortlessly. When detached and passionless action begins to take place frequently and effortlessly, we would not even be aware of its occurrence. When *karma* becomes effortless and burdenless, it is transformed into *akarma*. *Akarma*, as we have seen in the Fourth Chapter, means effortless, burdenless, natural *karma*. The Lord has also told at

the end of the Fourth Chapter that one could learn how *karma* is transformed into *akarma* at the feet of the saints. This state of *akarma* cannot be described in words.

18. The nature of the state of akarma

7. Let us take a familiar example to understand the naturalness of an action. When a child first learns to walk, what effort does he put into it! We encourage him, appreciate his efforts. 'Hey, he has learnt to walk!', we say with delight. But later, walking becomes natural; the child can then walk and talk at the same time. It is the same with eating. When a child is given solid food for the first time, we celebrate the occasion, as if the act of eating is something great.[2] But in the course of time, it becomes quite natural. How hard it is to learn swimming! In the beginning, one finds it tiring; but later one goes for swimming to relax, to shake off fatigue. Swimming is then no longer a tiring activity; the body floats over water effortlessly. The mind is in the habit of getting tired; it gets tired when it is consciously engaged in work. But when actions flow naturally, no strain is felt. *Karma* then becomes *akarma*. It is then full of joy.

8. Such transformation of *karma* into *akarma* is what we want to achieve. It is for this purpose that we should perform *karma* in accordance with our *swadharma*. In doing so, our defects will come to light. To remove

---

[2] Reference is to a custom named '*ushtavan*' prevalent in Maharashtra.

them, we should take recourse to *vikarma*. If all this is constantly practised, the mind reaches a stage where it is no longer perturbed by actions. It remains calm and clear even though we are doing thousands of actions. If we ask the sky whether it gets scorched by the sun and drenched in the rain and shivers with the cold in winter, what reply will we get? Will it not say, "You can settle what happens to me; I know nothing." 'पिसें नेसलें कीं नागवें लोकीं येऊन जाणावें ।' – It is for others to see whether a mad man is naked or clad; he is totally unaware of it.

In short, when we go on performing actions in the pursuit of *swadharma* with the help of *vikarma*, they gradually become detached and purified, and eventually become natural and effortless. Such actions then become second nature. Even the most trying situations are not then felt to be daunting. Such is the key of *karmayoga*. Our hands will simply get bruised in trying to force open a lock without a key; with the key we can open it in no time. The key to *karmayoga* makes all the actions light and without any bother. This key can be secured by conquering the mind. There should, therefore, be continuous effort to subdue desires and passions in the mind. Whenever we become aware of any impurities in the mind in the course of action, we should try to cleanse the mind. Outward actions then cease to be troublesome. The egoistic feeling that 'I am the doer' vanishes. The powerful forces of desires, passions and anger subside. There is then no feeling of anguish. Even the awareness of performing an action is no longer there.

9. Once a gentleman wrote to me, "We have decided to recite *Ramanama* (Lord Rama's Name) a certain number of times. Please join us and inform us how much *japa* you are going to do daily." The gentleman was acting according to his light. I would not disparage him. But should we count how many times we have taken the Name of the Lord? *Ramanama* is not a thing to be counted. A mother cares for her child. Does she publish the report on it? Were she to do so, we could just say, 'Thank you', and be free from our obligations to her. But she does not submit any report. She rather says, "What have I done? I have done nothing. Is this a burden to me?" *Karma* ceases to be *karma* when one does it with full dedication and with the aid of *vikarma*. *Karma* then becomes *akarma*. There is then no question of any strain or tensions or anything untoward.

10. It is impossible to describe this state. One can at best give a rough idea. The sun rises daily. But does it rise to remove darkness, urge the birds to fly and set men working? It just rises and that is all. Its very existence makes the entire world go round. But it is not aware of it. If you thank him for dispelling darkness, he would be at a loss to understand what you are saying. He will say, "Have I really done so? Please bring a little darkness. If I could dispel it, then only I would claim any credit for doing so." Can we carry darkness to the sun? The existence of the sun dispels darkness and brings light. Some may read good books in that light and some may read bad ones; some may harm others while some may help others;

the sun is not in any way responsible for the merits or sins committed in his light. He will say, "Light is my nature. What else but light could there be in me? I am not conscious of giving light. For me, to be means to shine and give light. I do not feel any strain in it. I do not feel that I am doing anything."

Giving light is natural to the sun. It is the case with the saints also. Their very existence is enlightening. If you praise a man of wisdom for his truthfulness, he would say, "If I adhere to the truth, what is so special about it? What else can I do?" Untruth just cannot exist in such a man.

11. This is what *akarma* means. Actions become so much a part of one's being and nature that one is not even aware of their happening. The sense organs are then naturally disposed to what they should be doing; right action flows from them of its own accord. 'सहज बोलणें हितउपदेश' – Counsel of wisdom flows out without any self-conscious deliberation and effort. When this happens, *karma* has become *akarma*. For a man of wisdom, performance of good actions becomes as natural and effortless as singing is to the birds. Just as a child thinks of his mother naturally, the saints think of God. Another example of such a natural action is the crowing of a cock in the early morning. Panini[3] has given this example while explaining *swaras* (musical notes). The cocks have always been crowing every morning. But has anybody presented

---

[3] A great grammarian of ancient India.

them scrolls of honour? Crowing is a cock's natural action. Similarly, it is natural for a sage to speak the truth, to have compassion for all the living beings, not to find fault in others, to serve everybody. He cannot, in fact, live without this *karma*. Do we honour anybody for having taken his food? Just as eating, drinking, sleeping are normal and natural actions for worldly persons, serving others is natural to a man of wisdom. Helping others is his second nature. Even if he were to decide not to help others, it is impossible for him to do so. *Karma* of such a sage can be said to have become *akarma*. Such a state has also been given the sacred term '*sannyasa*'. *Sannyasa* is nothing but the blessed state of *akarma*. It can also be called *karmayoga*. It is *karmayoga* since the man of wisdom goes on acting; and it is *sannyasa* since there is no feeling of doing anything even while actions are done. The man of wisdom acts with such ingenuity that the actions do not bind; hence it is *yoga*; and as nothing is done even while doing everything, it is *sannyasa*.

19. Yoga : one aspect of akarma

12. What, after all, does *sannyasa* mean? Does it mean renunciation of some actions, while doing others? No. *Sannyasa* has, in fact, been defined as renunciation of all actions, freeing oneself absolutely from all actions. But what does 'not acting' mean? How can we give up all the actions? Action is a queer thing. It pervades the whole life. Even sitting is an action : 'To sit' is a verb. Sitting is not only an action in grammatical sense, but also in physical sense. If one sits for quite a long time, the legs begin to ache. There is strain

in sitting also. When such is the case, how can there be renunciation of all the actions? The Lord showed 'vishwaroop'[4] to Arjuna. That all-encompassing vision terrified Arjuna and he closed his eyes. But even then the vision did not disappear; the vishwaroop appeared before his mind's eye. How can one escape from a thing which continues to be visible even after closing one's eyes? How can one avoid action when it takes place even when we are doing nothing?

13. There is a story of a man who had a lot of precious gold ornaments. He thought of keeping them safely locked up in a box. His servant got a big iron box made for them. He looked at it and said, "You idiot! Don't you have a sense of beauty? Should these valuable ornaments be kept in this ugly iron box? Go and get a good gold box." The servant did as he was told. The master then ordered, "Now bring a gold lock. Only a gold lock would suit the gold box." The fellow wanted to hide his gold from others' eyes. But what was the result? There was then no need for the thieves to search for the gold; just taking away the box was enough. When not doing is also a form of doing, how to renounce action which is all-pervasive?

14. The way to renounce such action is to do all the actions in such an ingenuous way that they are shed as soon as you complete them. Only then sannyasa can be attained. How to do an action without letting

---

[4] Chapter 11 of the Gita describes the transfiguration of Lord Krishna into vishwaroop, i.e. the Supreme, divine, cosmic form.

it stick to you? Look at the sun. It is working continually; even during the night it is working in the other hemisphere. Still one can say that it does not act at all. That is why the Lord says in the Fourth Chapter, "I taught this *yoga* first to the Sun, and from him the thoughtful and contemplative Manu learnt it." The sun does no work even while working all the time. This is truly a wonderful state.

20. *Sannyasa : the other aspect of akarma*

15. But this is only one form of *sannyasa*. To act, and still not be the doer, is one aspect; while the other aspect is to make the whole world act without doing anything oneself. In this state there is immense power to impel others to act. This is the beauty of *akarma*. It is packed with power that is capable of infinite work. It is like steam which, when compressed, does enormous work. It can then easily move big trains. The sun also does no work outwardly, but still works round the clock and is not aware of doing anything. Working day and night and still not doing anything outwardly is its one aspect and setting in motion an infinite number of actions without doing anything outwardly is another aspect. This is the two-fold splendour of *sannyasa*.

Both the aspects are far from the ordinary. In one aspect, the action is manifest and the state of *akarma* is hidden. In the other aspect, the state of *akarma* is manifest, yet endless activity is continuously going on. In this state, *akarma* is packed with power, resulting in enormous work. This state of *akarma* is diametrically different from laziness. A lazy man easily gets tired and bored; but a *sannyasi*, in the state of *akarma*, concentrates his energy inside him. He does no work physically, but still he inspires work in enormous measure.

16. Suppose someone gets angry with us. If it is because of our fault, we go to pacify him. But he refuses to talk to us. How great is the effect of his keeping mum, of this renunciation of the action of speaking! Another man in the same situation may pour abuse on us. Both are angry, but one keeps mum and the other speaks out. Both the reactions express anger. Keeping mum is also an expression of anger and it too works. When a mother or a father stops speaking to the child, its impact on the child is far more decisive than that of any action. Silence can have an effect which speaking can never have. Such is the state of a *jnani*. His *akarma*, his being still, accomplishes much; it generates great power. While being in the state of *akarma*, he does work that no activity can accomplish. This is another type of *sannyasa*.

In such type of *sannyasa*, all enterprise, all frenetic efforts cease. Saint Tukaram describes such a state :

'उद्योगाची धांव बैसली आसनीं
पडिलें नारायणीं मोटळें हें ।
सकळ निश्चिंती झाली हा भरंवसा
नाहीं गर्भवासा येणें ऐसा ।
आपुलिया सत्ते नाहीं आम्हां जिणें

अभिमान तेणें नेला देवें ।
तुका म्हणे चळे एकाचिये सत्ते
आपुलें मी रितेपणें असें ।।'

('Now all enterprise, all activity has ceased. The body is lying like a little sack at the feet of the Lord. All care is over; I now feel assured that I shall not be born again. I have not to live now on my own strength, as the Lord has emptied me of my ego. I am no more master of my life; it is His power that moves me. I have been reduced to zero.')

Tukaram is empty – his sense of 'I' has dissolved. But there is tremendous power in that emptiness. The sun gives call to no one; yet, when it rises, birds soar in the sky, lambs begin to prance around, cows head for grazing, shopkeepers open their shops, farmers start out towards their farms. The whole world is on the move as the sun makes its appearance on the horizon. Its mere existence is enough; that gives rise to innumerable activities. Its state of *akarma* has potentiality to stimulate those activities; it is packed with power. Such is the wonder of *sannyasa*.

21. To compare the two is beyond the power of words

17. In the Fifth Chapter, these two forms of *sannyasa* are compared with each other. In one form, nothing is done while doing work twenty four hours a day – there is inaction within – and in the other, there is no actual action even for a moment, but still everything is done – it is caused to be done. The former shows

how one could speak while being silent within, and the latter shows how one could be outwardly silent and still communicate. Now, there is a comparison between the two. To have a look at them, think over them, ruminate over them – there is sheer bliss, rare joy in doing so.

18. In fact, this whole matter is incomparably novel and noble. The idea of *sannyasa* is indeed grand and sacred. How thankful should we be to him who first thought of such a sublime idea! This idea, one may say, is the highest point reached by human imagination and reason, although man has been, and is even now, trying for higher and higher flight. As far as I know, it is the highest point reached by man's intellect and his power of thought. There is a rare joy in the very contemplation of this idea. The joy recedes when one steps into the domain of speech and of everyday life. One then feels like having fallen down. I am never tired of talking to my friends about this idea. For years, I have been meditating over it. Words fail in describing it. It is clearly beyond the reach of words.

19. Doing everything without action, and doing nothing while ceaselessly acting – how noble, enchanting and poetic the idea is! What more can poetry offer? Compared with the joy, ardour, inspiration and exaltation embodied in this idea, the most highly praised poetry pales into insignificance. The Fifth Chapter has thus been raised to a very high plane. *Karma* and *vikarma* have been explained upto the Fourth Chapter and then the Fifth Chapter has soared

sky-high. In this Chapter two forms of the state of *akarma* have been directly compared with each other. Language falls short in this attempt. Who is greater : a *karmayogi* or a *sannyasi*? It is impossible to say who works more. In fact, remaining inwardly inactive while doing everything and doing everything while outwardly remaining inactive, both are forms of *yoga*. But for the purpose of comparison, one is called *yoga* and the other is called *sannyasa*.

22. Two analogies : Geometry and Mimamsa[5]

20. How are we to compare the two? It will have to be done with the help of some analogies. While doing so, one does have a feeling of falling down from the high altitude of these ideas, but it cannot be helped. In fact, absolute *karma-sannyasa* and absolute *karma-yoga* are ideas too magnificent to be manifested in a living person. These ideals cannot be fully realised when one is confined within the body. An attempt to live these ideals here in this world would shatter the body. Hence we have to take illustrations from the lives of great men who had realised these ideals to the extent possible. Analogies are never perfect, but for the time being one has to assume that they are.

21. It is said in geometry, 'Let ABC be a triangle.' Why is the word 'let' used here? Because the lines forming the triangle are not really lines according to the definition of a line. A line, by definition, has

---

[5] One of the six systems of Indian philosophy. It is divided into two parts : Poorvamimamsa and Uttaramimamsa. The former is usually referred to as Mimamsa. It deals mainly with the interpretation of the rituals in the Veda.

length but no breadth. How to draw such a line on a blackboard? Breadth invariably accompanies length whenever one attempts to draw a line. Hence one has to use the word 'let'. One has to assume that what has been drawn is a line. Is not the same thing applicable in the science of *bhakti* (devotion)? There too the devotee says, 'Let this tiny image be the Lord of the universe.' If someone calls it idiocy, you may ask him, "Is there idiocy in geometry? We are seeing quite a thick line and you are asking us to assume that it has no breadth!"

22. Just as certain postulates are made in geometry, certain postulates are made in *bhaktishastra* too. It asks us to assume that there is God in an image. If one says that God is indestructible, but the image could break on being hit, it would not be a thoughtful statement. If postulates are valid in geometry, why cannot they be so in *bhaktishastra*? Geometry asks us to assume a point also. Definition of a point is akin to that of *Brahman*. A point is defined as having neither length, nor breadth, nor thickness. It is without any dimension; still we try to draw it on a blackboard. What we draw is practically a circle, but it is assumed to be a point. A true triangle and a true point exist only in definitions. Yet we have to proceed on the assumption that they actually exist. In *bhaktishastra* too, we have to postulate the existence of the indestructible all-pervading God in an image.

23. What the *mimamsakas* (adherents of the system of *Mimamsa*) have done in this context is striking.

Vedas refer to different deities like Indra (the king of the deities), Agni (the god of fire) and Varun (the god of rain and water). While on the subject of these deities a question is asked, 'What does Indra look like, what is his nature, where does he reside?' The *mimamsakas* answer, the word 'Indra' is itself the form of Indra; he resides in the word 'Indra'. Same is true about Varuna, Agni etc. The words, made up of certain syllables arranged in certain order, are the forms of the deities; the deities are not apart from the words. This concept of the deities having the form of words is indeed fascinating. In fact, the concept of the deities cannot be contained in any form; it cannot be adequately described. Letters comprising the words may therefore be taken as adequate representation. What is God like? The answer is, 'It is like the word God containing the letters G, O, D.' The most striking example of this is the letter ॐ (Om). ॐ means God. A term for God has thus been coined. It is necessary to coin such terms for great ideas which cannot be contained in any concrete material form. It is man's strong and earnest desire which makes him invent symbolic forms for them.

23. *The sannyasi and the yogi are one like Shuka and Janaka*

24. *Sannyasa* and *yoga* represent the highest flights of the human spirit. *Sannyasa* and *yoga* are ideals which are impossible to attain in their fullness within the confines of the body, but human thought can rise to such heights. A true *yogi* and a true *sannyasi* will exist only in definitions; the ideals will always be beyond

our reach. But we have to take as examples persons who have approximated the ideals, and say, on the lines of geometry, 'Let so and so be taken as a perfect *yogi* and so and so be taken as a perfect *sannyasi*.' While talking about *sannyasa*, the names of Shuka and Yajnavalkya are usually mentioned. As examples of *karmayogis*, Janaka and Krishna have been mentioned in the Gita itself. Lokmanya Tilak has listed a number of *yogis* and *sannyasis* in his treatise 'Gita-Rahasya.' He has written that King Janaka, Lord Krishna etc. took the path of *karmayoga* while Shuka and Yajnavalkya took the path of *sannyasa*. But these two paths are not mutually exclusive. Janaka, the *karmayogi* was a disciple of Yajnavalkya, the *sannyasi* and Shuka, a disciple of Janaka took the path of *sannyasa*. What this means is that *yogis* and *sannyasis* are parts of the same chain; *yoga* and *sannyasa* constitute a single order; they are not mutually exclusive paths.

25. Vyasa told Shuka, his son, "Shuka, my son, you have certainly attained Self-knowledge, but it lacks the seal of confirmation from a *guru* (religious preceptor). So, I would like you to go to Janaka, the King for this purpose." Shuka thereupon proceeded to meet King Janaka. On the way to the palace, he passed through the capital city, observing the urban scene which was unknown to the young hermit. When he reached the palace and met the King, the following conversation took place —

Janaka: Why have you come here, young man?
Shuka: To gain knowledge, sir.

Janaka: Who has sent you?

Shuka: Vyasa, my father, has asked me to meet you.

Janaka: Wherefrom have you come?

Shuka: From the *ashram*.[6]

Janaka: While coming here from the *ashram*, what did you observe in the market?

Shuka: I observed sweetmeats made of sugar piled up everywhere.

Janaka: What else did you see?

Shuka: I saw sugar-statues walking on the streets and talking with each other.

Janaka: What did you see next?

Shuka: I then saw the palace steps, made of sugar.

Janaka: And what thereafter?

Shuka: Everywhere I found pictures made of sugar.

Janaka: What are you seeing now?

Shuka: A sugar-statue is talking to another sugar-statue.

Janaka: Well, you may go now. You have indeed attained Self-knowledge.[7]

Thus Shuka got what he wanted: a certificate from Janaka. The point is that Janaka, the *karmayogi*, accepted Shuka, the *sannyasi* as his disciple.

---

[6] *Ashram* here means a hermitage, a dwelling of the ascetics.

[7] A man who has attained Self-knowledge sees that all things in the world are different forms of the same single substance. Shuka has used the word 'sugar' to indicate that substance.

There is another interesting story about Shuka. King Parikshit had been cursed that he would die after seven days. He wanted to prepare himself for the impending death; he wished to be instructed by a *guru* as to how to be so prepared. He sent for Shuka. Shuka came and sat in cross-legged position, narrating the Bhagavata[8] to him continuously for full seven days. He never changed his sitting position. What was remarkable was that he felt no strain although he was made to exert himself so much. Though he was constantly working, it was as if he was not doing anything. There was no feeling of fatigue. Thus it is clear that *yoga* and *sannyasa* are not mutually exclusive.

26. That is why the Lord says, 'एकं सांख्यं च योगं च यः पश्यति स पश्यति' ('He truly sees who sees both *sankhya* and *yoga*, that is, knowledge and selfless action as one'). He who realises that *yoga* and *sankhya* are one understands the true secret. Let a true *sannyasi*, with mind completely pure and still, dwelling in the divine consciousness, stay amongst us for just a few days. Imagine how much he will illuminate and inspire our lives! His mere sight, mere presence will achieve what good works accumulated over years cannot. Even a look at a photograph can cleanse the mind, pictures of departed persons can arouse devotion and love in the heart and purify it. Imagine then the inspiration one can derive from being in the presence of a living *sannyasi*!

---

[8] A great religious and spiritual epic, said to be written by Vyasa.

27. Both the *sannyasi* and the *yogi* do *loksamgraha*.[9] In the case of *sannyasi* action appears to have been renounced, but the apparent inaction is full of action. It is packed with infinite inspiration. A *jnani sannyasi* and a *jnani karmayogi* are on the same plane. Terms differ, but the meaning is the same. *Yoga* and *sannyasa* are two modes of the same reality. A wheel in rapid motion seems at rest. This is the case with a *sannyasi*. Mahavira, Buddha, Nivrittinath[10] were such realised souls. Although the activity of a *sannyasi* appears to have come to a standstill, he is doing immense work. Thus, a *yogi* is a *sannyasi* and a *sannyasi* is a *yogi*. These terms are synonymous and interchangeable.

24. But still yoga is better than sannyasa

28. Nevertheless, the Lord has given a little more weight to *yoga*. He says that *karmayoga* is superior to *sannyasa*. Why does He say so when there is no difference between them? What does it mean? When the Lord says so, it is from the standpoint of a seeker. Doing everything without being active is possible for a realised soul, not for a seeker. But it is possible for a seeker, at least to some extent, to follow the way of doing everything without getting attached to work, i.e. acting outwardly but remaining inactive within. Working without outward action will be a riddle for a seeker; he will be at a loss to understand it. For a seeker, *karmayoga* is both the way and the goal.

---

[9] *Loksamgraha* means bringing the people together, holding them together and guiding them along the path of virtue and righteousness.

[10] Elder brother and *guru* of saint Jnanadeva.

But *sannyasa* is only the goal; it cannot be the way. Hence, from the standpoint of the seeker, *karmayoga* is superior and preferable to *sannyasa*.

29. By the same reasoning the Lord has, in the Twelfth Chapter, said that *saguna* is preferable to *nirguna*.[11] All the organs can be put to use in *saguna sadhana*;[12] it is not so in the *nirguna sadhana* where there is no work for the organs. This is difficult for a seeker to follow. In *saguna sadhana*, eyes can behold the Lord's form, ears can hear His praise, hands can worship Him (in the form of an image) and serve the people, feet can be used to go on a pilgrimage. In this way, all the organs can be given some work; and putting them to such use, they can be gradually saturated with the divine consciousness. This is possible in *saguna sadhana*, not in the *nirguna* one where there is no use for any organ; there is, as it were, a ban on the use of all the organs. Such a blanket ban could very well frighten a seeker. How can then *nirguna* get imprinted on his mind? If he sits still, his mind will get filled with all sorts of useless and untoward thoughts. The

---

[11] '*Saguna*' means 'with attributes' while '*nirguna*' means 'without attributes'. These are two aspects of *Brahman*, or God, who could be *saguna* (Personal God with attributes) as well as *nirguna* (Impersonal, Unmanifest and Absolute). *Saguna sadhana* or *bhakti* includes service and image-worship. *Brahman* can also be '*saakaar*' (with form) as well as '*niraakaar*' (formless). Different religions and traditions believe in one or more of these aspects. For example, for an image-worshipper, God is *saguna* as well as *saakaar*. In Islam, God is *saguna* but *niraakaar*.

[12] Sadhana means spiritual pursuit, i.e. efforts for Self-realisation or attainment of Self-knowledge.

nature of the sense organs is such that they invariably tend to do what they are told not to do. Do not the advertisements exploit this very fact? They start with the headline : 'Don't read this'. So the reader is intrigued and invariably reads what follows. That is the very purpose of the advertisements – to induce the people to read their contents attentively. In *nirguna sadhana*, the mind will wander aimlessly, while in *saguna bhakti* it will be engaged in something or the other. In *saguna bhakti*, there is place for worship, service, compassion. The organs have something to do in it. If the organs are so engaged, the mind will not go anywhere even if given freedom to do so; it will get interested in the activities and will automatically get concentrated without even being aware of it. But if you try to concentrate the mind forcibly, it will run away in no time. It is, therefore, better to engage the organs in some good work and let the mind go anywhere; it will not do so. But if you try to force it to be still in one place, it will invariably run away.

30. *Saguna* is superior to *nirguna* for a man encased in the body, because it is easier. The ingenuity in seeing that the actions leave no trace on the mind is better than doing work without acting, because it is easier. In *karmayoga* there is scope for efforts and practice. In it one can control the organs and then try to withdraw the mind from all the activities gradually. This effort can succeed some day, even if it is not immediately possible. *Karmayoga* is thus easier to follow : It is its special plus point. Otherwise *karmayoga* and *sannyasa* are one and the same in their perfect states.

In *karmayoga,* hectic activity appears on the surface but there is perfect peace within, while in *sannyasa* there is power of moving the whole world without doing anything. Thus both are not what they appear to be. Perfect *karmayoga* is *sannyasa* and perfect *sannyasa* is *karmayoga;* there is no difference. But *karmayoga* is easier for a seeker to follow.

31. Changdeva sent a letter to Jnanadeva. It was nothing but a piece of blank paper, as he could not make up his mind on how to address Jnandeva; Jnanadeva was much younger in years but superior in wisdom. Should he address him respectfully as one addresses an elder, or as one addresses a younger person? Unable to decide, he sent the blank letter. It first reached the hands of Nivrittinath. He 'read' it and passed it on to Jnanadeva who too 'read' it and passed it on to Muktabai, their youngest sister. 'Reading' the letter, Muktabai exclaimed, "Hey, Changdeva, you are so old, but still you are blank[13]!" Nivrittinath had read something different in that letter. He said, "Yes, Changdeva is blank, which means that he is pure and innocent, and therefore deserves to be taught." So he asked Jnanadeva to send a reply to this letter. Jnanadeva sent a letter comprising 65 small stanzas. This letter is therefore called 'Changdeva Pasashti'.[14] Such is the charming story of this letter. It is easy to read written words, but difficult to read what is not written. There is no end to reading it. A *sannyasi*

---

[13] Implying thereby that he had yet to acquire true knowledge.

[14] *Pasasht* means 65.

appears to be empty and blank, but he is full of infinite work.

32. Although *sannyasa* and *karmayoga* are of equal worth in their perfect states, *karmayoga* has an additional practical value. A currency note and a gold coin of the same denomination have the same value as long as the government is stable; but if the government collapses, the currency note is reduced to a piece of paper whereas the gold coin will have some worth under all circumstances as it is, after all, made of a precious metal. In the perfect state, *karmayoga* (action) and renunciation of action have the same value as Self-knowledge is there in both of them. Value of Self-knowledge is infinite. In mathematics there is a principle that you may add any quantity to infinity, the total remains equal to infinity. *Karmayoga* and renunciation of *karma* are of equal value when coupled with Self-knowledge, but when Self-knowledge is deleted from both the sides, *karmayoga* is preferable for a seeker. Action through inaction is a riddle beyond the understanding of the seeker. *Karmayoga*, as already stated, is a path as well as the destination while *sannyasa* is only the destination. In the terminology of the scriptures, *karmayoga* is a means as well as the *nishtha* while *sannyasa* is only the *nishtha*, that is, the ultimate state.

(20.3.32)

CHAPTER 6

Control of the mind

25. Aspiration for redemption of the self

1. In the Fifth Chapter, we could conceive and visualize the highest possible flight of the human spirit. *Karma*, *vikarma* and *akarma* together complete the *sadhana*. *Karma* is gross in nature. There should be full cooperation from the mind in the work done in the pursuit of *swadharma*. *Vikarma* is the work done to educate the mind for this purpose. It is a special kind of *karma*, a sort of subtle *karma*. *Karma* and *vikarma*, both are necessary. While doing them, ground is prepared for *akarma*. We have seen in the last Chapter that *karma* and *sannyasa* become one in the state of *akarma*. It has been restated at the beginning of this Chapter that *karmayoga* and *sannyasa*, although their standpoints appear different, are one and the same. Difference lies only in the way of looking at things. The Chapters that follow deal with the means to reach the state described in the Fifth Chapter.

2. Many people have a misconception that spirituality and spiritual texts like the Gita are meant only for the ascetics. I once heard a gentleman commenting that he was 'not an ascetic', which implies that ascetics belong to a particular species of animals like horses, lions, bears, cows etc. and spirituality is meant only for them; others engaged in mundane affairs belong to a different category with thoughts and ways of their own! This distinction has led to a hiatus between ascetics and the worldly men. Lokmanya Tilak has drawn our attention to this in his 'Gita Rahasya'. I

wholeheartedly endorse Tilak's view that the Gita is for ordinary people engaged in worldly life. In fact, the Gita is for the whole world. All the practices and means adopted in the course of the spiritual pursuit are meant to be followed by everyone. Spirituality, in fact, teaches how our daily life can be purified, leading to contentment and peace of mind. The Gita is meant to teach us how worldly life can be purified. At whatever level you may be engaged in the world of practical affairs, the Gita comes to you. But it does not want you to remain there. Holding your hand, it will take you to the ultimate destination (Self-realisation). There is a famous saying that 'If the mountain will not come to Mohammed, Mohammed must go to the mountain'. Mohammed is anxious to see that his message reaches even an inert mountain. The moutain is inert; so Mohammed would not keep waiting for it to come to him. This is also true of the Gita. The Gita will come to the lowliest of the low, to the poor and the weak and the ignorant, not to keep them in that state, but to grasp them by their hands and lift them up. Its only desire is that man should purify his daily life and reach the ultimate state, the final destination. In fact, this is the very aim and object of the Gita.

3. Therefore, never consider yourself a mundane ordinary being caught up in *samsara*, never raise a fence around you confining yourself to where you are. Do not say with despair, 'What can I do? This body measuring three and a half cubits is all that I am.' Do not remain in the prison of your own making

and lead a beast-like existence. Gear up your spirit to move ahead, to rise higher and higher. 'उद्धरेदात्मनात्मानं नात्मानमवसादयेत् ।' ('Let a man raise himself by his own Self, let him not debase himself.') Have confidence that you would certainly raise yourself to great heights. Do not weaken the power of your mind by thinking that you are a worthless worldly creature. Do not clip the wings of imagination; spread them out. Look at the skylark. Early in the morning, as the sun rises, the skylark sees the sun and boldly says, 'I will soar high in the sky and reach the sun.' That should be the spirit. Can the skylark ever reach the sun with its weak wings? But its imagination can certainly take it there.' Our behaviour, however, is just the opposite. We cripple our imagination and erect a fence around us. We therefore do not rise even to the extent we can; not only that, we become the cause of our own downfall. By underestimating our strength, we lose whatever strength we have. When imagination is crippled, we are sure to fall; what else can happen? Therefore, we should always aspire to rise higher and higher. It is aspiration that ensures man's progress in life. Do not, therefore, throttle it. Do not whine, 'One should never leave the beaten track of worldly life and wander here and there.' Do not insult your Self. A seeker can persevere in his course only if he has vision and confidence. That is the key to liberation. Do not think that *dharma* is only for the saints, and that one may go to them only to get a certificate from them that 'under the given circumstances, what you are doing is right for you.' Do not entertain such ideas and bind yourself. One cannot take a single step forward without high aspirations.

If you have this vision, this aspiration, this exalted spirit, then only the question of appropriate means arises; otherwise, everything will reach a dead-end.

We saw that *vikarma* coupled with *karma* leads to the divine state of *akarma*. We dealt with the divine state of *akarma* and its types in the Fifth Chapter. From this Chapter onwards, various types of *vikarma*, the varieties of *sadhana* have been outlined. Before embarking on this exercise, the Gita exhorts us to have divine aspirations, to keep the mind free and wings strong, so that the *jiva* (the individual self) can become one with God, i.e., unite with the Supreme Self. Devotion, meditation, development of virtues, enquiry and analysis, discrimination between the Self and the not-Self – all these are different types of *vikarma* or spiritual discipline. This Chapter discusses the *yoga* of meditation.

26. *One-pointedness of mind*

4. The *yoga* of meditation consists chiefly of three important components : (i) One-pointedness of mind, (ii) Moderation and regulation in life to help attain one-pointedness, (iii) Equanimity and evenness in outlook. A true spiritual quest is not possible without these three.

One-pointedness of mind requires that the mind be restrained and its fickleness controlled. Moderation and regulation in life implies doing everything in a measured way and within proper limits. Equanimity and evenness in outlook means having a positive and constructive outlook. These three together make up the *yoga* of meditation. There are two means to achieve these three – *abhyasa* (constant practice) and *vairagya* (non-attachment). Let us discuss these five in brief.

5. Let us first take one-pointedness of mind. It is indispensable for any work. Even in worldly affairs, one needs concentration. It is not that the qualities needed for worldly success are different from those needed for spiritual progress. Spirituality means nothing but purification of worldly life. Business, scientific research, politics, diplomacy – in fact, take any activity, concentration of mind is the key to success. It is said of Napoleon that after chalking out the strategy and deploying the troops on the battlefield, he would lose himself in solving mathematical problems. Amidst heavy shelling and dying soldiers, he would sit absorbed in those problems. I am not suggesting that Napoleon's concentration was of the highest degree; one can give examples of even higher concentration. I just want to draw your attention to the level of his concentration. The same thing is said about Caliph Omar. Even when the battle was in progress, he would steady his mind, kneel down and start praying on the battlefield at the appointed hour. He would then totally unaware of what was happening around. It was because of such devotion and one-pointedness of mind of the early Mohammedans that Islam spread far and wide.

6. The other day, I heard a story about a Muslim ascetic. An arrow had pierced his body and stuck

into it. The pain was unbearable. But any attempt to pull out the arrow resulted only in greater pain. Anaesthetic agents like chloroform were not available in those days. Everybody was perplexed. Some persons who knew the ascetic well said, "Forget about the arrow for the time being. We shall pull it out when he starts his prayers." In the evening, at the appointed hour, the ascetic started his prayers. In a moment, his mind was so concentrated that he did not know when the arrow was pulled out. What a wonderful degree of the concentration of mind!

7. Thus, success is hard to come by, in temporal as well as in spiritual pursuits, without one-pointedness of mind. If you could make your mind one-pointed, you will never be short of strength. Even if you are an old man of sixty, you will have enthusiasm and strength of a young man. The mind should, in fact, go on getting stronger as one gets older. Look at a fruit. In the beginning it is raw, then it ripens, then decays; but the seed within gets harder and harder. The shell deteriorates and falls off; but that is not the essential part of the fruit. Its essential part is the seed. Similarly, memory should grow stronger and intellect should become sharper and more radiant as one ages. But this does not happen. People complain of failing memory and attribute the cause to their old age. But knowledge, wisdom, memory are like one's seed, one's essential part. Even as the body grows older and becomes infirm, the soul should become stronger. One-pointedness of mind is necessary for this purpose.

27. How to attain one-pointedness of mind?

8. But how to attain it? What should be done for it? The Lord says, one should fix the mind in the Self and think of nothing else. 'न किञ्चिदपि चिन्तयेत् ।' But how to do this? To still the mind is extremely important. Concentration will always elude us if we do not forcefully stop the revolving wheels of thought. The 'outer wheel' may perhaps be stopped somehow – we may put a stop to worldly activities – but the 'inner wheel' continues to revolve. As we go on employing different means for the concentration of mind, the 'inner wheel' revolves all the faster. You may sit in this or that posture and fix your gaze; by itself it will not achieve concentration of the mind. The important thing is that one must be able to stop the 'inner wheel'.

9. The mind is crowded with the thoughts of limitless *samsara* – affairs and happenings in the outside world. Concentration of the mind is impossible until all those thoughts are put out. We dissipate the Self's boundless potential power of knowing in brooding over worldly trifles. This must not happen. A man who has become rich, not by robbing others but through his own hard work, will never squander his money. We too should not waste the Self's power in gross and petty matters. This power can lead us to enlightenment. It is our priceless treasure. But look, how we waste this power! If we find at the dining table that there is not enough salt in the vegetable, we grumble and complain about it. Is it that important? This is misuse

of our faculty of cognition. The children are taught within the four walls of the classroom. We are afraid that they would get distracted by the crows and the sparrows if they are taught in the open. Poor little children! Their minds can get concentrated if they do not see a crow or a sparrow. But what about us? We are grown-ups! We have lost our innocence and have become worldly-wise, and therefore cannot concentrate our minds even if we are kept within a seven-walled fortress. We go on discussing merrily, each and every trivial matter in the world. We go on expending our power of thought, which can lead us to the Lord, in discussing the taste of vegetables and pat ourselves on the back for this feat!

10. Day and night, this frightening *samsara* is always surging around us, within and without. Even our prayers are for some material gain. There is no longing to become one with the Lord, forgetting *samsara* at least for a moment. Our prayer is nothing but a show. When such is the mental state, sitting cross-legged and closing the eyes is bound to be in vain. As the mind is disposed to get distracted all the time by the things without, a man's strength is completely sapped. He loses any kind of discipline and controlling power. We are witnessing this state of affairs at every step in our country. Truly, India is a land of spirituality. It is believed that her people live at the high altitude of spirituality. Still, how pitiable is our condition! It is painful to see us engaged in hair-splitting over trivial matters. Our minds are always immersed in such matters.

'कथा पुराण ऐकतां । झोपें नाडिलें तच्चतां
खाटेवरी पडतां । व्यापी चिंता तळमळ
ऐसी गहन कर्मगति । काय तयासी रडती'

('While listening to the narration of epics and stories from mythology, sleep overtakes us; but when in bed, anxieties keep us awake. Such is the inscrutable way of *karma* – actions accumulated in the present and the earlier lives. What is the use of shedding tears over it?')

The mind is either focused on nothing or is focused on too many things at the same time, but it is never fixed on one single object. Man is such a slave to the senses. Once a gentleman asked me, "Why is it said that the eyes should only be half-open while meditating?" I replied, "I give you a simple answer. If the eyes are fully closed, one is likely to go to sleep and if they are kept wide open, attention would be diverted and there would be no concentration. Proneness to sleep when the eyes are closed is *tamas* and the diversion of attention when the eyes are open is *rajas*. Therefore, an intermediate state has been prescribed."

In short, there cannot be concentration of mind without change in its disposition. The disposition of mind should be pure. This cannot be attained merely by sitting in particular postures. All our worldly activities should be purified for this purpose. This requires a change in the goal of those activities. We should not engage in them for our own personal gains or for satisfying baser instincts and desires, or for any material purpose.

11. The whole day, we are engaged in doing some or other worldly activity. What is the purpose of all this toil? 'याजसाठीं केला होता अट्टाहास । शेवटचा दिस गोड व्हावा ॥' ('All my persistent efforts were to make the last moment happy.') All the toil in this life is to be done to make the last moment happy. Throughout the life bitter poison is to be swallowed – suffering and hardships are to be endured – to have a calm, serene and holy end. The last moment of the day comes in the evening. Had the activities throughout the day been carried out with a pure heart, then the night prayer would be sweet, bringing a sense of contentment and fulfilment. If the last moment of the day is sweet, it means that the day's work has been fruitful. Then the mind can easily get concentrated.

Purity of life is essential for concentration. Mind should never be preoccupied with worldly matters. A man's life is not long, but even in the short span of life he can experience the eternal, divine bliss. Two men may appear to be cast in the same mould, but one of them becomes God-like while the other sinks to the level of a beast. Why does it happen? When all are the children of God – 'अवघी एकाचींच वीण' – why is there such a difference? Why does one 'nara'[1] become 'Narayan' whereas the other becomes 'vanara'?

12. There have been men in the past who have shown what great heights man can scale. Such men are there

---

[1] There is pun on the world 'nara' meaning man. Narayan means God, and vanara means monkey.

even now in our midst. This is a matter of experience. The saints have shown what a man can achieve even while remaining caged within the body. If some men can do miraculous deeds while remaining within the body, why should it not be possible for me? Why should I set bounds to my imagination? I too possess the same human body, dwelling in which others have done heroic deeds. Then why should I be in such a sad plight? There must be something wrong with me. My mind is all the time focused on things outside. It is too preoccupied in finding faults in others. But why should I judge others? 'कासया गुणदोष पाहों आणिकांचें । मज काय त्यांचें उणें असे ॥' ('Why should I be concerned with the virtues and vices of others when I myself have them in abundance?') If I remain busy in observing and criticising the faults in others, how could I have concentration of mind? Then I am bound to be caught between *rajas* and *tamas* – the mind will either wander aimlessly or it will go to sleep – it will go blank.

It is true that the Lord has given suggestions about the sitting posture, the fixing of gaze etc. for attaining one-pointedness of mind. But they could be useful only when one has realised the need of having one-pointedness of mind. Let one realise this need; then one will seek and find for oneself the means to attain it.

28. Moderation and regulation in life

13. One more thing that aids concentration is to set bounds to one's life. All our actions should be measured and weighed. This is an essential characteristic of mathematics and it should be there in all our actions.

As we take medicine in measured doses, so should be the case with our food and sleep and, in fact, with everything. All the sense-organs should be under strict vigil. We should be ever alert lest we should eat too much or sleep too much, or see what we need not. All our activities should thus be continuously examined with meticulous care.

14. I once heard of a gentleman who, within a minute of entering a room, would note what things are kept in it and where. I said to myself, "O Lord! May I never have such a faculty!" Am I somebody's personal secretary to keep in my mind an inventory of his possessions, or am I a thief? How does it concern me where he keeps his soap or his watch? Why do I need such information? We should prevent waywardness of our eyes; and of our ears too. Some people seem to feel that it would have been wonderful to have ears like a dog's that could be turned in any direction at will. 'God has not provided man with this faculty,' they rue. But no, excessive curiosity must not be there. The mind of a man is a very powerful thing. It is wayward too; it gets distracted by the slightest disturbance.

15. Therefore, there should be regulation and moderation in life. Let us never look at bad things. Let us never read bad books. Let us never listen to anybody's slander or even praise. Let us turn away not only from bad things, but also from the excess of good things. Indulgence in any form should be avoided. Things like liquor, sweetmeats or fried

eatables should no doubt be positively shunned, but even fruits should not be taken in excess. A fruitarian diet is certainly pure and healthy. But the fruits too should not be taken in excessive quantities. The Master within should never allow the tongue to have its own way. The sense organs should feel awe for the Master within; they must ever be on guard and realise that if they misbehave, they will be punished. Moderation and regulation in life means having a disciplined and regulated life.

29. Equanimity and evenness in outlook

16. The third thing is to have equanimity and evenness in outlook. It means having an outlook infused with goodwill, a disposition to look at the positive side of men and matters. It implies faith in the goodness and order in the universe. There cannot be concentration of mind without it. The lion is the mighty king of the forest and yet he does not take four steps forward without looking behind. How can the lion, which lives by violence, attain concentration of mind? Tigers, crows and cats are always looking here and there with apprehension. This is bound to be so with the beasts of prey. One should look at the world with a sense of equanimity. One should feel that everything in the world is good, friendly and auspicious. Just as we trust ourselves, so should we trust the whole world.

17. What, after all, have we to fear here? Everything is good and sacred. 'विश्वं तद् भद्रं यदवन्ति देवाः' – The universe is full of goodness, as God is looking after it and protecting it. The poet Browning has said in the

similar vein : 'God's in His heaven, all's right with the world!' Nothing is really wrong with the world. If there is something wrong at all, it is my vision. As is my vision, so is the world. If I put on red-coloured glasses, the world is bound to appear red and aflame.

18. When Saint Ramdas was writing the Ramayana, he used to read it out to his disciples. It is said that Hanuman[2] used to come incognito to hear the same. Once Ramdas read out, "Hanuman went to Ashokvan[3]. There he saw white flowers." Hearing this, Hanuman came forward and said, "I did not see white flowers. What I saw were red flowers. Please correct what you have written." Ramdas insisted, "No, what I have written is correct. The flowers you saw were white." Hanuman said, "I myself was there. How could I be wrong?" Finally the dispute was taken to Lord Rama. He said, "The flowers were indeed white, but Hanuman's eyes were red with anger; hence they appeared red to him." The point of this charming story is that what the world appears to us to be, depends on the way we look at it.

19. So long as we are not convinced that the world around us is good, our mind will not become one-pointed. As long as we think that the world around us is bad, we are bound to look around with suspicion.

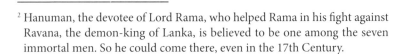

[2] Hanuman, the devotee of Lord Rama, who helped Rama in his fight against Ravana, the demon-king of Lanka, is believed to be one among the seven immortal men. So he could come there, even in the 17th Century.

[3] The ashoka-grove where Sita was confined by Ravana.

Poets eulogise the freedom of birds. Let them become birds for a while; they would then know the worth of that freedom. A bird is never calm. Its neck is always moving back and forth. It is always afraid of others. If you put a sparrow on the seat for meditation, will its mind attain one-pointedness? If I try to go near a sparrow, it will immediately fly away, fearing that I may hurt it. How can those who entertain the frightful idea that the whole world is out to destroy them can ever have peace of mind? So long as a man thinks that he is his sole protector and everybody else is an enemy, he cannot attain one-pointedness of mind. An outlook that treats everybody with equality and fairness is the best means for attaining one-pointedness of mind. When you see goodness and benevolence all around, the mind will automatically attain peace.

20. Take an anguished man to a running stream. The sight of clear, pure and peacefully flowing water will assuage his sorrow. He will forget his troubles. What gives the stream such healing power? It is because of the manifestation of the benign power of God in that stream. There is a beautiful description of the streams in the Veda: 'अतिष्ठन्तीनां अनिवेशनानाम्' – The stream flows without break, it has no resting place, no home of its own. It is like a *sannyasi* in this respect. Watching the flow of such a sacred stream concentrates the mind in a moment. Should that stream not motivate me to create a spring of love and wisdom within me?

21. If the flowing water which is, after all, part of the material world can bring such peace to my mind,

imagine the peace if the stream of divine consciousness, devotion and wisdom begins to flow through the valley of mind. Once a friend of mine was travelling in the Himalayas in Kashmir. He used to write to me about the holy mountains and the beautiful streams there. I wrote to him, "Those holy mountains and the streams and the winds blowing there give you immense joy. I can see and feel all that within my heart. I daily view such marvellous scenes in the inner recesses of my heart. Even if you invite me, I would not come there, leaving the great and divine Himalaya within me. The Lord has said, 'Among the fixed and immovable things, I am the Himalaya.'[4] The Himalaya is the symbol of steadfastness and should, in fact, be worshipped to imbibe that quality. Why should then I forsake my duty and head for the Himalayas, enamoured by the description of its beauty?"

22. So, calm the mind a bit. Look at the world with a positive and friendly eye. Then an infinite number of springs will begin to flow within your heart. Your inner firmament will be illuminated with the stars of noble ideas. If auspicious objects made of stone or clay can bring peace to the mind, would not the vision of the inner world have this effect? I had once been to Travancore (Kerala). One evening I was sitting on the beach, silently listening to the majestic roaring of the boundless sea. I was just still, full of peace, lost in myself. My friend brought fruits for me. Absorbed in another world, I felt distaste even for such a pure

---

[4] Gita, 10.27.

sattvik food. The sea was as it were chanting ॐ, ॐ (Om, Om) reminding me of the Gita's exhortation, 'Remember Me and fight on.'[5] That was what the sea was doing; it was ceaselessly doing *karma*. Its waves were surging back and forth without a moment's rest. That sight had made me lose appetite for anything. What was there in that sea to have such an effect? If my heart could overflow with joy at the sight of waves of salt-water, how ecstasically would I dance when the waves of wisdom and love surge in my heart? Vedic seers had this experience in their hearts.

'– – अंत:समुद्रे हृदि अंतरायुषि
– – घृतस्य धारा अभिचाकशीमि – –
समुद्रादूर्मिर्मधुमानुदारत् – –'

('I am witnessing all around the streams of *ghee*[6] ... in the sea, within the heart, in all the living beings ... waves of sweetness are arising in the sea ...')

Such divine language has nonplussed the commentators. What is meant by the streams of honey and *ghee*? But, how can there be streams of salt-water in my heart? It is bound to have waves of milk and *ghee* and honey surging within it.

30. A child as preceptor

23. Learn to behold the surging waves of the sea within. Look up at the clear blue sky outside and

---

[5] Gita, 8.7.

[6] Clarified butter, obtained after heating the butter.

make your mind pure and unsullied like it. In fact, attaining one-pointedness of mind is child's play. It is the occupation of the mind in umpteen matters that is unnatural. Look into the eyes of a child intently. He looks with a constant gaze, while you blink every few seconds. A child's mind easily becomes one-pointed. If you show the greenery outside to a child, four or five months old, he will be absorbed in observing it. Women, in fact, believe that such an intent observation of the greenery causes the children's stools to be green. It is as if all their senses come together in their eyes when they see. Any small thing can make a deep impression on the minds of children. Educationists say that what the children learn within the first three to four years is what is firmly imprinted on their minds. You may open any number of schools or colleges or any other institutions to educate them; it is during the early years that real learning takes place. I have been associated with education and I am getting increasingly convinced that only the impressions formed in the early years prove to be indelible; subsequent formal education has little effect. That is nothing but outer polish. A soap can remove a stain; but can it wash out the dark colour of the skin? The impressions of the early years are likewise hard to remove.

Why are these impressions strong and indelible and the subsequent ones weak? It is because a child's mind gets concentrated effortlessly. Such is the wonderful power of the concentration of mind. Nothing is impossible for those who have achieved it.

24. Today our whole life has become artificial. We have lost childlike innocence. Life has become dull and joyless. Our behaviour lacks any rhyme or reason. It is not Darwin who proved that human beings are the descendants of apes; we ourselves are daily proving that through our actions!

A child is trustful. He believes in everything that the mother tells. He never questions the truth of even the fairy tales wherein crows and sparrows speak like human beings. His mind can quickly become one-pointed because of such an attitude.

31. Abhyasa (constant practice), vairagya (non-attachment) and faith

25. In short, the *yoga* of meditation needs one-pointedness of mind, regulation and moderation in life and a friendly, fair and positive outlook. Two other aids have also been suggested : *vairagya* (non-attachment) and *abhyasa* (cultivation through constant practice). One is negative in nature while the other is positive. *Vairagya* is akin to uprooting weeds from a field. It is negative in nature. *Abhyasa* is akin to sowing the seeds. To sow seeds is a constructive work. *Abhyasa* is constructive. It involves rumination upon pure thoughts.

26. How could one imbibe *vairagya*? We say that a mango is sweet. But is sweetness really a quality of the mango? No. Sweetness is really an attribute of the Self, and a particular thing tastes sweet when it is infused with that sweetness. One should, therefore,

121

learn to taste the sweetness within. Sweetness is not in things themselves; it is in the Self which is an ocean of sweetness. As this realisation sinks deep within us, *vairagya* will become ingrained in us. Sita gave Hanuman a pearl necklace. Hanuman cracked every pearl to see whether Lord Rama was within it. In no pearl could he find Rama. So he threw away all the pearls. Rama was there in his heart. Fools would have gladly paid millions of rupees for that necklace.

27. While explaining the *yoga* of meditation, the Lord has made one important point at the very outset. One should make a firm resolve, 'I want to redeem myself, I shall go ahead, I shall scale great heights, I shall not remain within this human body for ever, I shall have the courage to make efforts to realise God.'

Listening to all this, Arjuna had a doubt. He said, "I am no longer in the prime of my life and am destined to die soon. What is then the use of spiritual pursuit?" The Lord replied, "Yes, you will die. But death is nothing but a long sleep. We sleep daily. Are we afraid of it? On the contrary, we are worried if we do not get sleep. Death is as necessary as the daily sleep. We resume our daily work after waking up; likewise, we resume our spiritual pursuit in the next birth from the very point we had reached at the time of death. We do not lose what we have already gained. No spiritual pursuit ever goes waste."

28. Jnanadeva appears to be referring to his own life when he writes in 'Jnaneshwari' on the relevant

verses of the Gita e.g. 'बालपणींच सर्वज्ञता । वरी तयाते', ('All knowledge comes to him in the childhood itself'), 'सकल शास्त्रें स्वयंभें । निघतीं मुखें।' ('Words of spiritual wisdom come out of his mouth of their own accord.') *Abhyasa* in the previous birth pulls you onward. That is why some persons are not drawn to the objects of senses. They are not tempted by them. This is because of their *sadhana* in the previous birth. The Lord has given an assurance at the end, 'शुभकारी कुणी बापा दुर्गतीस न जातसे ।' ('No well-doer ever meets with a sad end.') Good done is never wasted. One should have faith in this assurance. What remains incomplete in this life will be completed in the next one. Understand the essence of this teaching and attain fulfilment in life.

(27.3.32)

CHAPTER 7

Prapatti or Surrender to God

32. *The magnificent vision of bhakti*

1. Brothers, Arjuna, deluded by the sense of 'mine' and 'not mine', was seeking ways to evade *swadharma* when the situation demanded adherence to it. The First Chapter describes his vain delusion. The Second Chapter sets out to remove it. It states three basic principles : the Self is imperishable and has an all-encompassing presence, the body is transient and mortal, and *swadharma* should never be given up. It also spells out the idea of renunciation of the fruit of actions as a key to realise these principles. While expounding this *karmayoga*, three concepts have emerged – *karma*, *vikarma* and *akarma*. In the Fifth Chapter, we have seen two types of *akarma* which result from the confluence of *karma* and *vikarma*. From the Sixth Chapter onwards different types of *vikarma* are being explained. The Sixth Chapter tells about one-pointedness of mind necessary for spiritual pursuit.

Today, we are going to deal with the Seventh Chapter. This Chapter opens before us the gallery of a magnificent new *vikarma*. Moving through an extensive forest, the temple of the Goddess of nature, we are enthralled by a great many captivating scenes. It is the same with the Gita. It now unfolds before us a new vista.

2. Even before unfolding this vista, the Lord reveals the secret of the structure of this world which creates illusions. An artist paints a variety of pictures on

the same type of canvas and with the same brush. A sitarist[1] creates different *ragas*[2] out of the same seven notes. In literature, a variety of thoughts, ideas and feelings are expressed through the letters of the alphabet. Same is the case with the creation. We find in it innumerable objects and propensities. But all of them are products of only two things – the eternal Self and the eight-fold *prakriti*.[3] The anger of the angry man, the love of the lover, the agony of the sufferer, the happiness of the happy one, the drowsiness of the idler, the activity of the industrious man – all these are manifestations of one and the same Cosmic energy. These different emotions and urges, often contrary to each other, spring from the same source. As the Cosmic energy within is one and the same in all, the outer bodily cover of all is also the same in nature. The Lord is telling at the very outset that the Self, full of consciousness, and the insentient *prakriti* are the twin source from which all the creation has come into being.

3. The Self and the body, the higher and the lower *prakriti* are the same everywhere. Why should man be deluded then? Why should he see differences instead

---

[1] Sitar is a stringed Indian musical instrument.

[2] Modes of Indian classical music.

[3] 'Earth, water, fire, air, space, mind, reason and ego – these are the eight-fold divisions of My Nature' – Gita. 7.4. The *Sankhya* philosophy believes in two eternal principles : *Prakriti* and *Purusha*. *Prakriti* is the primordial matter or material Nature which consists of three *gunas* or constituents viz *sattva*, *rajas* and *tamas*. *Purusha* is the inactive, Pure conscious Being and it is without *gunas*.

of unity? The face of someone whom we love attracts us, whereas that of someone whom we dislike is found repulsive; we desire to meet one person and shun the other. Why is it so? Different pictures drawn by the same artist with the same brush on the same canvas evoke different feelings. Therein lies the skill of the artist. The artist and the sitarist have such a skill in their fingers that they make you laugh or cry. In their fingers lies a magical power.

We welcome someone while we shut the door to another's face. We embrace someone and push aside another. Such feelings arise in the mind and, at times, deflect us from the path of duty. All this is because of delusion. If we are to escape this, we should understand the marvellous skill in the Creator's fingers. Brihadaranyaka Upanishad gives the analogy of a drum. A drum produces a variety of sounds. Some frighten us, some make us dance. If we are not to be swayed this way or that and remain in full control of all such emotions, we must catch hold of the drummer. Then all the sounds of the drum would be under our control. The Lord declares, "Those who want to cross the river of *maya* should take refuge in Me.[4]" In the words of Jnanadeva —

'येथ एक चि लीला तरले । जे सर्वभावें मज भजले ।
तयां ऐली चि थडी सरलें । मायाजळ' (7.97)

---

[4] Gita, 7.14. *Maya* is the creative power of the Lord which creates illusions. It is the *maya* which makes us forget that we are Divine. It is the veil that hides the Real from us.

('Only those who worship me single-mindedly and with unswerving devotion can cross this river of *maya*. In fact, they need not have to cross it at all; for them the water of *maya* dries up while they are at this bank itself – that is, the mirage created by *maya* disappears for them here and now.')

What is this *maya*? It is the Lord's creative power, His art and His skill. He created this world out of the single eternal Self and the eight-fold *prakriti*, or what the Jain terminology calls *jiva* and *ajiva*. The Lord has created this variegated world out of these two elements; out of them He is ever creating all sorts of things. They evoke different sentiments and responses. If we want to go beyond them and attain true inner peace, we should reach out for the creator of them all. We should know Him. Only then can we get rid of the delusion that gives rise to divisions, antipathies and attachment.

4. In this Seventh Chapter, the Lord has thrown open the beautiful mansion of *bhakti*, a singularly effective means, a great *vikarma* for knowing Him. To attain purity of mind, many *vikarmas* like *yajna* (sacrifice), *dana* (sharing, charity), *japa* (prayer, repeating God's Name), *tapa* (penance), meditation and concentration are prescribed. I would liken them to washing soda or soap, while *bhakti* is like water. Soap and washing soda are useful only in conjunction with water; by themselves they are of no use. Water, on the other hand, can cleanse even without them, although their aid does result in better cleansing. It is like adding

130

sugar to milk. How can there be purity of mind if the heart and soul are not there in *yajna*, meditation, penance etc.? *Bhakti* is nothing but such involvement of the heart and soul.

All the *vikarmas* stand in need of the aid of *bhakti*. It is the sovereign means. It is no doubt advisable that a man trained in nursing and having knowledge of different remedies should be deputed to take care of a patient; but if he lacks genuine empathy and compassion, he cannot render true service. A bullock may be strong and stout, but it would not pull a cart if it does not wish to. It will then refuse to step ahead and may even land the cart in a ditch. Work without involvement of heart and soul – without heartfelt empathy and concern – can give neither satisfaction nor strength.

33. Bhakti results in pure and unalloyed bliss

5. If we have *bhakti*, we would see the art of that great artist; we could see the brush with which He paints. Once we have reached the source of all creation and have tasted the rare sweetness of water from the spring at the very source, we cannot but find all other things insipid and worthless. A man who has tasted a real banana would appreciate the beauty of a painted wooden banana for a moment, and then will put it aside. He will not be much enamoured by it. A man who has tasted true joy would not be taken in by external pleasures in the material world.

6. Once, some people told a philosopher, "Sir, there is festive lighting of lamps in the city today. Let us go and watch it." The philosopher said, "What is it after all? Only an arrangement of a lot of lamps in rows, is it not? I can visualize it from here itself." In an arithmetical progression like 1+2+3 ... , figures can be written upto infinity. But there is no need to write all the numbers if the difference between two succeeding numbers is known. Likewise one can visualize the arrangement of lamps in rows. What is there to be so excited about it? But man does enjoy such things. He squeezes a lemon in water, adds sugar, sips the drink and smacks his lips in delight! The tongue has, as it were, nothing else to do than to taste different things. From different ingredients man creates a variety of food products and finds all the pleasure in eating them! When I was a child, I once went to see a movie. I had taken a mat with me so that I could go to sleep whenever I wanted. I could watch the dazzling pictures barely for a few moments. My eyes got tired and I went to sleep, asking my companion to wake me up when the show was over. Instead of going out in the open and watching the moon and the stars and enjoying the peace and serenity of nature, people go to congested theatres and excitedly applaud the dance of the bright moving pictures there. I just failed to understand that!

7. Why is man so devoid of joy that he seeks and finds some sort of momentary and illusory joy in the dance of those lifeless figures? Evidently, there is no real joy in life; that is why people go in for such

artificial amusements. Once I heard drums beating next door. On enquiry, I learnt that it was to celebrate the birth of a son. Now, what is there so special about it that it should be announced to the world with the beat of drums? People even dance with joy and invite singers on such occasions. Is it not childish? It is as if the world is famished of joy. Just as in famine people rush in frenzy at the sight of a few eatables, they jump at the slightest opportunity like the birth of a child or a cinema or a circus show, because they are starved of joy.

But is this true joy? Waves of music enter the ears and strike the brain. Different forms enter the eyes and strike the brain. The impact of such sensations is the only source of joy for the poor fellows. Some stuff their noses with snuff, some smoke tobacco, and the kick they get thereby is a source of tremendous joy to them. Their joy knows no bounds when they lay their hands on a cigarette butt! Tolstoy has written that a man may even commit murder under the influence of tobacco. It too is a kind of intoxication.

Why does man lose himself in such pleasures? Not knowing the real thing, he is infatuated with the shadows. His pleasures are confined to those derived from the five senses. Had he got a sense-organ less, he would have thought that there are only four types of pleasures. If tomorrow a man with six sense-organs comes down from Mars, such people would feel dejected at the thought that they can have pleasure only from five sense-organs instead of six and envying the man from Mars they would exclaim, "What a handicap we human beings on the earth suffer from!"

How can man, with just five senses comprehend fully the meaning of creation in all its aspects? Restricted to five senses, he makes his choices within those limits and derives joy from what the senses offer him. He considers the braying of a donkey inauspicious. But is it not possible that an encounter with a man could be equally inauspicious for a donkey? You think that its braying will spoil or harm something that you are going to do. But is it not true that you could also be causing harm to others? When I was a student at Baroda, a group of European singers once came to our college. They were good singers and were trying their best. But I, being thoroughly bored, was waiting for an opportunity to slip out. I was not used to listening to that sort of music. I could not appreciate it. Singers from our country may face similar response in Europe. What is sweet music to the ears of one is just noise for the other. It means that the joy it gives is not real joy; it is an illusory joy. Until we experience real joy, such illusory joy would enthrall us. So long as he had not tasted real milk, Ashwatthama[5] used to drink water mixed with grain flour, believing it to be milk. Once the true nature of things is revealed to you and you experience the true joy therein, everything else will pale into insignificance.

---

[5] Ashwatthama was the son of Dronacharya, the teacher of Kauravas and Pandavas in the Mahabharata. On account of acute poverty, his mother used to give him, in the name of milk, grain flour mixed with water.

8. *Bhakti* is the best way to discover true joy. As we advance on this path, we shall discover the ingenuity of the Creator. Once we have grasped that divine vision, attraction for other fancies will recede. Then nothing trivial will attract us. The whole world will then be found filled with one undifferentiated joy. There may be hundreds of sweetmeat shops, but the sweets they sell are of the same kind. So long as we have not tasted the real thing, we go on pecking a sweetmeat here and a sweetmeat there like restless sparrows, and still remain unsatisfied. Once I was reading Tulsidas' Ramayana in the early morning hours. Moths had gathered near the lamp. A house-lizard came there. What interest could it have in the Ramayana? It was happy at the sight of the moths. I waved it away when it was about to pounce on a moth, but its attention was still riveted on that moth. I asked myself, "Would you eat a moth? Does your mouth water at its sight?" The sight of a moth was not mouth-watering for me; and the house-lizard had no inkling of the great joy in the Ramayana. It could not taste the sweetness of the Ramayana. Our condition is like that of the house-lizard. We are engaged in a multitude of enjoyments; but how nice will it be if we could taste the true joy! The Lord has shown us the way of *bhakti* as the means to taste the true joy.

34. Bhakti for gains too has value

9. The Lord has mentioned three kinds of devotees *(bhaktas)*: (i) one who has desire for some worldly gains. (ii) one who is desireless, but whose *bhakti* has

not blossomed fully. (iii) *Jnani*, or the man of wisdom, whose *bhakti* has blossomed fully. The second type consists of three sub-types: (i) one who is restless and impatient for God's grace (ii) the seeker of knowledge (iii) the seeker of the well-being of all. These are different branches of the tree of *bhakti*.

A devotee with desires in mind prays for some gains. I would not despise such *bhakti*, considering it inferior. Many people take to social service to earn name and fame. What is wrong in it? Give them honour unreservedly; there is no harm in it. That honour would eventually settle them in social service. They would begin to find joy in their work. Why, after all, does a man desire recognition and honour? It is because he is thereby convinced about the utility and excellence of his work. One who has no inner yardstick to judge the worth of his service depends on such external yardsticks. When a mother pats her child, the child gets enthused to do more work for her. This is also true for this type of *bhakti*. Such *bhakta* would straightway go to the Lord and ask Him to give what he wants. To make demands on God for everything is no ordinary thing; it is something rare. Jnanadeva asked Namdeva, "Will you accompany me on a pilgrimage?" "But why go on a pilgrimage?", asked Namdeva. Jnanadeva replied, "We can thereby meet a number of saints and ascetics." Namdeva said, "Let me ask the Lord." He went to the temple and stood before the Lord. With eyes riveted on the Lord's feet and tears flowing down his cheeks, he asked, "O Lord! Should I go on a pilgrimage?" Would you call

Namdeva an idiot? Not a few people are anguished by separation from their wives, but a *bhakta* who weeps at the idea of going away from the Lord is out of the ordinary. Because of ignorance, he does not seek what he ideally should; but even then his *bhakti* is not to be dismissed out of hand.

10. Women take a number of vows with the idea of accumulating merit so that they can have God's grace after death. This may be a silly idea, but they do undergo hardships willingly for that purpose. Great men are born in families with such traditions of piety and devotion. Swami Ramatirtha, a descendent of Tulsidas, the great scholar and poet, was well-versed in the Persian language, but had no knowledge of Sanskrit. Someone commented, "You are a descendent of Tulsidas; how is it that you have no knowledge of Sanskrit?" This comment went straight to Ramatirtha's heart. Reminder of ancestry had a powerful effect. It impelled Ramatirtha to take up the study of Sanskrit. We should not, therefore, make fun of the women's ways of *bhakti*. The children born in families where tradition of *bhakti* is built up have a rare brilliance. That is why the Lord says, "Even if my *bhakta* is desirous of some gains, I shall make his faith steadfast. I shall not create confusion in his mind. If he earnestly prays for getting cured of his disease, I shall cure him, supporting his will to health. Whatever may bring him to Me, I shall lovingly encourage him." When the child prince Dhruva was pushed aside from his father's lap by his stepmother, his mother asked him to seek from the Lord a place from which nobody

could push him aside. Dhruva started penance in all earnestness. Pleased with his penance, the Lord granted him a permanent abode from which he could never be dislodged.[6] The mind may not be desireless; so what? Whom you approach, to whom you pray is important. It is important to have the inclination to beseech the Lord for something rather than prostrating before the world.

11. Whatever be the ground, do enter the temple of *bhakti*. It will mark a new beginning for you. Even if the desires are initially there, they will eventually fade away. In *khadi* exhibitions the organisers urge people, "Please come and just have a look at the fine specimens of *khadi* available now." People visit the exhibition, get impressed and start thinking about wearing *khadi*. Similar is the case with *bhakti*. Once you enter the temple of *bhakti*, you will discover its power and beauty for yourself.

When Dharmaraj reached the gate of heaven, there was only a dog with him. All of his brothers – Bheema, Arjuna et al – had died on the way while walking to heaven.[7] Dharmaraj was told at the entrance, "You are welcome; but not the dog." Dharmaraj said, "If

---

[6] Dhruva, according to this mythological story, became the pole-star which is still shining in the sky.

[7] Dharmaraj or Yudhishthir was the eldest among the Pandavas. After the great Mahabharata war, Pandavas ruled for a few years and then proceeded to heaven. Lord Yama joined them on the way in the form of a dog. During the journey, other Pandava brothers and queen Draupadi died on the way, as they were not fit to enter the heaven.

my dog is not allowed to enter, I too will not enter." Even a despised creature like a dog is superior to those who have inflated egos, if it is faithful and serves with total devotion. The dog proved to be superior even to Bheema and Arjuna. Even an insect that moves towards God is greater than the worthies who have not turned towards Him. In the Shiva temples, there are images of Nandi, the bull. Everybody bows before the Nandi also. It is not an ordinary bull; it is the Lord's bull sitting in front of Him. Hence it is superior to the most intelligent amongst men. Even an idiot with God in his heart deserves respect and adoration from the whole world.

12. Once I was travelling by a train. When it was passing over a bridge across the river Yamuna, a passenger, visibly charged with emotions, threw a coin in the river. A rationalist sitting nearby commented, "The country is poor; still these people waste money in this way!" I said, "You have not understood the motivation of that man. Look at the feelings with which he threw that coin. Are they not worth even a farthing? We may grant that the coin could have been utilized for a better purpose. But this devout man felt that God's compassion itself was flowing in the form of the river and threw the coin as a mark of sacrifice. Has this feeling any place in your economics? Emotions welled up in that man's heart at the sight of a river in the country. If you could appreciate this sentiment, I would rate you as a true lover of the country." What, after all, does patriotism mean? Does it have to do with material betterment

only? In fact, it is the height of patriotism to feel impelled to offer one's entire wealth to a great river in the country. What we call money or wealth – the pieces of yellow and white metal and the so-called precious stones produced from the secretions of the insects – is, in fact, only worthy of being thrown into the river. Consider all that wealth as mere dust before the feet of the Lord. You may ask, 'What is the relation between the river and the Lord's feet?' Has God a place in your scheme of things? For you, river-water is nothing but the combination of oxygen and hydrogen; the sun is nothing but a bigger-sized gas burner. You find nothing worthy of reverence therein! Should one then bow only before the bread and butter – things of limited economic utility? But what is a bread after all? It is nothing but a sort of white clay. Why do you then relish it so much? If divine presence is not felt in the rising sun or in a flowing river, where else could it be? The poet Wordsworth laments : 'I used to dance at the sight of a rainbow. My heart used to overflow with joy at that sight. Why does this not happen now? Have I lost the sweetness of my early life?'

In short, even *bhakti* rooted in the desire for gains has great value. The feeling of devotion even in an ignorant man has a value of its own. That is why it can generate great power. No matter what sort of a person, of whatever worth, one who enters the portal of the Lord's mansion is redeemed. No matter what sort of wood is thrown into the fire, it burns. *Bhakti* is an extraordinary way of *sadhana*. The Lord

encourages *bhakti* even if it is accompanied with desires. In due course it will become desireless and move towards perfection.

35. *Desireless bhakti : Its varieties and fulfilment*

13. *Sakaam bhakta* (a *bhakta* who has desire for some worldly gains) is one type of *bhakta*. Now let us have a look at the *nishkaam bhakta* i.e. desireless *bhakta*. As we have seen, his *bhakti* could either have blossomed fully or not. The latter type of *bhaktas* can be further categorized into three sub-types.

The *bhakta* of the first sub-type craves for the love of the Lord and cries for Him like Namdeva. He is restless and desperate to embrace the Lord and lay himself at His feet and have His love showered on him. He examines every action of his to find out whether there is sincere yearning and love therein.

14. The *bhakta* of the second sub-type is a seeker of knowledge. Presently such seekers are rare in our country. Persons of this type will risk their lives in trying again and again to climb Mount Everest and may perish in the attempt. Some may go on an expedition to North Pole, note down their observations and findings on a piece of paper and keep that piece in a bottle for the posterity before embracing death. Some may descend into the womb of a volcano to learn more about it. But the Indians are so scared of death! Taking care of the family is for them the greatest achievement; they have nothing better to do. The *bhakta* who is a seeker of knowledge has an

irrepressible and insatiable curiosity. He tries to know the nature and properties of everything. He too would eventually unite with the Lord.

15. The *bhakta* of the third sub-type has been called '*artharthi*' – one who seeks *artha*. *Artha* is commonly translated as money or wealth; but it really means welfare or well-being. *Artharthi bhakta* judges everything in terms of the good of society. Whatever he writes, whatever he speaks, whatever he does, he sees to it that it is for the good of the world. He dislikes useless or harmful activities. He is indeed a great soul who is always concerned for the good of the whole world! His joy lies solely in the welfare of the world.

Thus, the outlook of the first sub-type of the partly-blossomed *nishkaam bhakta* is marked with love, that of the second sub-type with quest for knowledge and that of the third sub-type with concern for the well-being of all.

16. All those belonging to these three sub-types are no doubt desireless, but their approach is not holistic. They approach God either through work or through love or through knowledge.

Lastly, about the fully-blossomed *bhakta*. He is a man of wisdom. Whatever he sees are nothing but different forms of the Lord. In the handsome and the ugly, in the prince and the pauper, in men and women, in birds and beasts – everywhere he has the sacred vision

of God. Saint Tukaram's prayer to the Lord was, 'नर नारी बाळें अवघा नारायण। ऐसें माझें मन करीं देवा।।' ('O Lord! Orient my mind in such a way that I find You alone in men and women and children.')

In Hinduism, there is worship of serpents, worship of an elephant-headed God[8], worship of even the trees. All this may appear silly. But we find the height of such 'madness' in the pefect *bhakta*. He sees God in everything, right from an insect or an ant to the sun and the moon, and his heart overflows with joy. 'मग तया सुखा अंत नाहीं पार । आनंदें सागर हेलावती ।' ('Then the bliss knows no bounds. The ocean of joy surges within the heart.')

You may say, if you like, that this magnificent divine vision is an illusion; but such an illusion is the height of bliss and happiness; it is a treasure of joy. In the serenity and majesty of an ocean, the man of wisdom sees the glory of the Lord. In a cow, he sees His tenderness. In the earth, he sees His forgiveness and the capacity to bear. He finds His purity in the clear sky, His grandeur and splendour in the sun and the moon and the stars, His delicateness in flowers. Even in an evil man, he sees the Lord testing and trying him. Thus he is constantly seeing Him everywhere. Doing so, one day, he ultimately merges into the Lord.

(3.4.32)

---

[8] Ganapati, the elephant-headed God, the son of Lord Shiva, is the God of knowledge.

CHAPTER 8

Sadhana for a happy end:
The Yoga of constancy

36. Accumulation of good samskaras[1]

1. Human life is full of various *samskaras*. Innumerable actions are being continually done by us; there is really no end to them. Even if we take a superficial look and count the activities done during twenty-four hours of a day – eating, drinking, sitting, walking, working, writing, speaking, reading – they would make a long list. Besides these, in life there are various dreams, sentiments and perceptions like love and hate, honour and insult, joy and sorrow. All these make their impact on the mind and shape a man's personality and behaviour. Therefore, if somebody asks me to define life, I would say that life means an aggregate of accumulated *samskaras*.

2. *Samskaras* are good as well as bad, and both of them influence human life. We hardly remember our childhood days. *Samskaras* from the former births are so completely erased that one wonders whether one had any previous birth at all. When we cannot remember even the childhood days, why talk of previous births? Let us, therefore, leave them aside and think only of this birth. Even here we do not remember all the actions. Many are the things done and many the things known. In the end, most of them get erased leaving behind only a few *samskaras*. If we try to recollect at bedtime all that we did during the day, we fail to do so. Only the most prominent incidents come before the

---

[1] *Samskaras* mean the imprints of actions, associations and experiences that remain indelibly engraved on our mind and mould our behaviour, our personality and our world-view.

mind's eye. For example, if we had a serious quarrel, we remember only that at night. That quarrel is the only thing of the day that is carried forward in the account book of our life. Important and conspicuous events leave strong impressions; the rest fade away. When we write a diary, we note therein only a few important things. When we review the week, we note even less. While reviewing the month, only the most important happenings therein are remembered. Many of those would also be forgotten while reviewing the year. Thus very few things remain in memory, and they form the *samskaras*. Most of the innumerable actions and much of what we have learnt ultimately fade away leaving only a small residue in the mind. Those actions and the information and knowledge have done their work and disappeared. Only a few *samskaras* remain, and these *samskaras* are our capital. That is our net gain from the business of living. A trader keeps daily, monthly and annual accounts of income and expenditure and arrives at the figure of profit or loss. It is exactly the same with life. Addition and deletion of *samskaras* go on throughout the life, resulting finally in a particular net balance. When the end of life comes near, the self begins to think of the gains in life. Looking back, it finds that they are few. This does not mean that all that one did and all that one learnt have proved to be futile. They have certainly done their work. There could be thousands of transactions in a trader's business, but a single final figure of either profit or loss is the net result. If there is a loss, his heart sinks. If there is a profit, he is happy.

3. We too are in a similar position. If at the time of death the mind craves for food, it is a clear indication of having spent the entire life in indulging the palate. Craving for food is then the only 'achievement' in life; it is the only capital that has been accumulated in this life. If a mother thinks of her child at the time of death, it shows that her attachment to her child is the strongest *samskara* she has acquired in her life; whatever else she did was secondary. In arithmetic, there are problems of fractions where addition, subtraction, multiplication and division of big figures ultimately result in a small figure or even zero. Likewise, the entire life of a man is an arithmetical exercise wherein addition, subtraction, multiplication and division of numerous *samskaras* go on continuously and finally one strong *samskara* remains. That is the final answer of the equation of life. The thought that arises at the last moment in this life is the essence of the whole of one's life; it signifies what has been gained in this life.

This essence should be sweet; the last moment should be happy. A person should experience inner peace and fulfilment at the time of death. It is for this that one should endeavour throughout one's life. All is well that ends well. We should fix the mind on this final answer while solving the problem of life. We should plan the life with this aim in view. In a mathematical exercise, we have to keep the problem in mind and employ the appropriate method to solve it. Our life should be oriented in such a way that, at the last moment we will have the *samskara* we want. Day and night, our whole attention should be turned in that direction.

37. Living with the awareness of death

4. The Eighth Chapter puts forward a thesis that the thought uppermost in mind at the time of death prevails over others in the next birth. When we start a journey, we carry provisions with us for our sustenance. The thought uppermost in mind at the time of death, which is the essence of what has been earned in this life, is the provision with which we start our journey in the next birth. We begin a new day with the previous day's gains in hand. Death is like a long sleep, after which we begin a new life with the gains of the previous birth. End of this life is the beginning of the next one. Hence one must always be aware of the inevitability of death, while conducting oneself in this life.

5. This is necessary also to enable us to face the dread of death and find ways and means to counter it. There is a story about Saint Eknath. A gentleman once asked him, "Sir, your life is so simple and pure. Why is ours not so? You never lose temper or quarrel with anybody. How serene, pure and kind-hearted you are!" Eknath said, "Leave me out for the time being. Let me tell you that I have come to know something about you. In seven days from now, you are going to die." Who would disbelieve Eknath's words? Only seven days of life left! The gentleman rushed home. He could think of nothing else. He started entrusting his affairs to others and making preparations for the end. He was taken ill and took to his bed. Six days passed. On the seventh day, Eknath went to him and

enquired, "How are you?" The man replied, "Sir, I am about to leave this world." Eknath asked, "Well, how many sins did you commit in these six days? How many evil thoughts came into your mind?" The gentleman replied, "Sir, where was the time for that? Death was always there before my eyes." Eknath said, "Now you know the reason why the lives of people like me are sinless." How can mind entertain evil thoughts when death is standing before you, ready to pounce on you like a tiger? Even for committing sin, mind has to be relaxed. Constant awareness of death is the means for avoiding sin. If death is staring in the face, who can muster up courage to commit sin?

6. But man always evades the thought of death. The French philosopher Pascal has written a book titled 'Pensees' (Thoughts). It contains his stray thoughts. He observes therein that although death is always looking over our shoulders, we continually try to forget it; how to live with the awareness of death in mind is never our concern. Man detests even the very mention of the word 'death'. If somebody utters this word while taking meals, he is immediately admonished. Nevertheless, we are continually moving towards death. Once you board a train to Mumbai, it is bound to take you there even if you just keep sitting. The moment we are born, we have booked a ticket to the destination of death. Whether we run or keep sitting, death is bound to come. Whether you think of it or not, you cannot avoid it. Whatever else may be uncertain, death is certain. The sun sets everyday, taking away a portion from our life. Life is continually

being gnawed at. It is continually withering away. Still man takes no notice of it. Jnanadeva exclaims, 'कौतुक दिसतसे' (How curious)! He wonders how man could be so thoughtless and unperturbed in such a situation. Man is so frightened of death that he cannot even bear the thought of it, and tries to evade it like an ostrich burying its head in the sand. Soldiers going to the front play, dance or sing or smoke to avoid the thought of death. Pascal wonders how they lose themselves in eating and drinking, singing and dancing in order to forget death even when they see death everywhere.

7. We are all like those soldiers. We try to keep a smiling face, apply creams to hide wrinkles, dye our greying hair. We are ceaselessly trying to brush aside the thought of death even though it is just around the corner. We talk about anything but death. Ask a boy who has done his matriculation about his future plans. He will reply, "Don't ask me now; I have just joined the college." If you put the same question next year, he will reply, "Let the second year of college pass. I shall think of the future thereafter." So it goes on. But should not one think of the future in advance? One should plan the next step beforehand; otherwise, one will land oneself in a ditch. But the student shirks this task. The education that the poor fellow receives is so full of darkness that he has little idea of what is in store for him. He refuses to visualize the future, since he sees only darkness ahead. But there is no escape from the future; it is bound to catch him by the neck.

8. The Professor of logic teaches in the college, "Man is mortal. Socrates is a man. Therefore, Socrates is mortal." Why does he not give his own example? The Professor too is mortal. But he would not say, "All men are mortal. Therefore I, the Professor, am mortal and dear students, you too are mortal." He gives the example of Socrates, since Socrates is already dead and is not there to protest howsoever we use his name! Students and teachers talk of the mortality of Socrates, but conveniently keep mum about their own. Perhaps they feel that they are fully secure from death!

9. In this way, people everywhere are continually making deliberate efforts to forget death. But does that ward off death? It makes its presence felt when someone dear to us passes away. But still man does not think of death fearlessly and summon courage to overcome its challenge. A deer chased by a tiger finally gets exhausted, although it is swift and agile. Death in the form of the tiger continues to pursue it. Imagine the condition of that poor creature. It cannot look at the tiger. It closes its eyes and buries its antlers and face in the ground and helplessly waits for death. We too cannot dare to look at death. But howsoever we may try, it is bound to pounce on us.

10. And when death finally comes, man begins to take stock of what he has on balance at the end of his life. A dull and lazy student in the examination hall just looks here and there and whiles away his time. Dear chap, is Saraswati, the Goddess of knowledge, going to come down from heaven to write answers for

you? He keeps the answer-book blank or at the most scribbles a few lines and submits it when the time is up. Our condition is no different. But, keeping in mind that life ultimately ends in death, we must constantly practise throughout our life the means by which we can make the last moment pure, sacred and happy. From this very moment, we should be concerned with having the best of the *samskaras*. But who cares? On the contrary, we are constantly training ourselves in bad ways; we are constantly teaching our sense organs to behave in a perverse and wayward fashion. Mind must be trained in a different way. It should be led to what is good and should be encouraged to get absorbed in it. The moment we realise that we have erred, we should start taking corrective steps. Once we realise that we have made a mistake, should we go on repeating it? The moment you come to realise your error is the moment of your rebirth. It should mark a new beginning in your life. Look at it as the dawn of your new life. You are now truly awake. Now you should critically examine your life day and night. You should become alert lest you should slip again; lest you should go back to practising bad ways.

11. A few years ago, I had gone to meet my grand-mother. She had grown quite old. She would say, "Vinya, I don't remember things these days. I go to fetch the *ghee* but return empty-handed." But she could vividly describe an incident about her gold ornaments that had occurred fifty years ago. She could not remember what had happened before five minutes, but the strong *samskara* imprinted on the mind fifty

years ago was still fresh. What could the reason be? She must have narrated the incident again and again, whereby it clung to her memory and became a part of her being. I said to myself, "O God! Let grandma not remember her ornaments at least at the time of her death!"

38. 'Ever absorbed in that'

12. How could something that is practised day and night not stick to us? Do not delude yourself by the story of Ajamila[2]. To all appearances he was a sinner, but there was an undercurrent of virtue in his life. It surfaced at the moment of death. Do not, therefore, delude yourself by imagining that you could continue your sinful ways and still the Name of the Lord will be on your lips at the last moment. The mind has to be trained and disciplined by strenuous practice right from childhood. It has to be carefully ensured that good *samskaras* are imprinted on the mind one by one. Never have a careless and casual attitude. Do not ask, for example, why one should always get up early in the morning. If you give free rein to your mind, you are bound to be caught in a snare. Then good *samskaras* would surely elude you. Just like wealth and knowledge, *samskaras* have to be acquired bit by bit without wasting a moment. Therefore, see to it that the *samskara* that is imprinted on the mind at every moment is good. The moment you utter a foul

---

[2] Ajamila, who led a life of sin, had on his lips the name of his son Narayan (which is also a Name of Lord Vishnu) at the time of death. Lord Vishnu, hearing His Name, rushed to Ajamila and redeemed him.

word, a bad *samskara* gets immediately imprinted on your mind. Every act of ours is like the stroke of a chisel shaping the block of stone of our life. Even if the day passes off well, evil thoughts surface in the dreams. It is not that only recent thoughts surface in the dreams; bad *samskaras*, got imprinted on the mind inadvertently, may surface any time. Hence one must be ever vigilant even over little things. A drowning man clutches even at a straw. We are drowning in the ocean of *samsara*. Utterance of a few good words too can prove to be the lifeline to save us. No good deed is ever wasted; it will save you. Even the slightest of bad *samskaras* has be prevented. Always strive not to see anything that could leave a bad *samskara*, never give an ear to abuse and revilement and keep the speech free from foulness. Only when you are so conscious and alert, you will be rewarded at the last moment. You shall become the Master of life and death.

13. To inculcate good and pure *samskaras*, one must always ruminate over noble thoughts. Let the hands be busy in doing pure and good deeds. Remembrance of God within and performance of *swadharma* without, hands engaged in service and *vikarma* in the mind – all this should continue day in and day out, without any lapse. Look at Gandhiji. He spins every day on his *charkha* (spinning wheel). He insists that everybody should spin daily. Why? Will it not do if we spin for the cloth we need whenever it suits us? But then that spinning would be an activity for a practical purpose, whereas there is spirituality in daily spinning. It reflects

an urge to do something for the country. That yarn daily links us to *Daridranarayan* – God in the form of the poor. Daily spinning is an affirmation of one's fellowship with *Daridranarayan*.

14. The doctor has prescribed medicine in particular doses. Will it serve the purpose if we gulp it down all at once? It will be plain stupidity. The body should be restored to health through daily *samskara* of the medicine. The same holds good for life. Take the example of gradual *abhishek*[3] on the image of Lord Shiva. It is my favourite illustration. I used to watch it everyday when I was a child. Two buckets of water might be trickling down the image in twenty four hours. Why not pour two bucketfuls of water all at once on it? I got the reply to this at that time itself. Water must not be poured at once; it should trickle down drop by drop uninterruptedly. That is what makes it an act of worship. There should be continuous flow of the same *samskara* twenty four hours a day, every day, every year; even throughout the cycle of births and deaths. Each moment and each hour, each day and each night, each month and each year – even in each birth, the same good *samskara* should be there. The divine stream of good *samskaras* should flow in this way throughout life, for ever without interruption. Then only we can reach our destination and hoist our flag there. The stream

---

[3] Ceremonial bathing of the Lord's image. In the temples of Lord Shiva, a pot with a hole at the bottom is filled with water and hung over the image of the Lord. Water trickles down the image drop by drop and bathes it uninterruptedly.

of *samskaras* must flow in one single direction only. If the rainwater falling on a hilltop flows down the hill in several different directions, it does not form a river; but if it flows in one single direction, it becomes a stream which gradually grows in size, eventually becoming a river that finally reaches the sea. Water which takes one single direction reaches the sea while that which takes many directions soon dries up and is lost. This also happens in the case of good *samskaras*. If they come and go, of what use are they? It is only when the stream of good *samskaras* flows continually through the life in one single direction, that death will be found to be a source of supreme bliss. A trekker who does not unduly linger in the way, does not yield to the temptations in the way and continues to walk along the path doggedly reaches the mountaintop, throws off his backpack and experiences the fresh breeze blowing there. The joy that he experiences is beyond the imagination of others.

39. 'Day and night, the fight goes on'

15. In short, death will be a matter of joy when there is continuous performance of *swadharma* outside while inwardly the mind is being purified through devotion etc., when the streams of *vikarama* and *karma* flow within and without. That is why the Lord says, 'म्हणूनि सगळा काळ मज आठव झुंज तूं'[4] ('Remember Me all the time and fight'). He also refers to one who is 'ever

---

[4] Gita, 8.7.

absorbed in That' – 'सदा त्यांत चि रंगला ।'[5] When love for the Lord pervades your whole being, when your whole life is informed with that love, you will then always rejoice in things sacred. Evil urges and tendencies would never appear before you. Noble resolves and noble thoughts would germinate in the mind and good deeds would follow naturally and effortlessly.

16. It is true that good deeds become natural when one always remembers the Lord. But the Lord's command is to keep on striving. Saint Tukaram says, 'रात्री दिवस आम्हां युद्धाचा प्रसंग । अंतर्बाह्य जग आणि मन ।।' ('Day and night, we are required to fight with the world without and the mind within.') This conflict is going on relentlessly. It is not that you will win every battle. One has to persevere till the end to win the war. It is the final result of the war that counts. During this war we shall win and lose many a time. But loss is no cause for dejection. When a stone breaks at the twentieth blow, it does not mean that the previous nineteen blows had been in vain. In fact, they were preparing ground for the success of the twentieth blow.

17. To feel dejected means to lose faith in God. God is always there to support and protect you. Have faith in Him. To develop self-confidence in the child, the mother lets him wander here and there, but she keeps watch. She does not let him fall. If he starts tottering, she is there to lift him up in her arms. God too

---

[5] 'Thinking of whatever state a man in the end casts his mortal frame aside, to that state does he accede, being ever absorbed in the thought thereof.' – Gita 8.6.

is watching you. He holds in His hands the string of your life's kite. Sometimes He pulls it taut while sometimes He lets it loose; but be assured that He Himself is holding the string in His hands. To teach swimming in a river, one end of a rope is tied to a tree on the bank and the other end is tied to the learner's waist, and then he is thrown into the water. Trainers are there in the river to take care of him. The novice struggles initially but, in the end, masters the art of swimming. God is teaching us the art of living in this way.

40. Uttarayan and Dakshinayan

18. So, if you continue striving day and night with all the resources of the body and the mind at your command, with faith in the Lord, the last moment will be extremely happy. You will have all the gods – that is, divine powers – on your side when the hour of death comes. This has been said at the end of this Chapter using a metaphor. Understand this metaphor properly. If at the time of one's death fire is burning, the sun is shining, the moon is waxing and there is beautiful and cloudless sky of *Uttarayan* (six months of the northern course of the sun), then one unites with the *Brahman*. But if at that time there is dense smoke, there is darkness within and without, the moon is waning and there is cloudy and dull sky of *Dakshinayan* (six months of the southern course of the sun), he again gets caught in the cycle of births and deaths.

19. This metaphor is puzzling to many. It tells that the grace of the gods of fire (Agni), sun, moon and sky is necessary for a holy death. Fire symbolises *karma* and *yajna* – work and sacrifice. The sacrificial fire must be burning even at the time of death. Justice Ranade used to say, "Blessed is the death which comes while one is performing one's duties. I shall be happy to die while reading, writing or doing something." This is what the burning of sacrificial fire means. Working till the last breath signifies the grace of Agni, the god of fire. Grace of the sun-god keeps the intellect bright and radiant till the end. Grace of the moon is indicated by the growth of pure and sacred feelings in the heart at the time of death, as the moon is the god of the heart. Sacred feelings like love, devotion, enthusiasm, altruism, compassion etc. should wax and grow to fullness in the mind like the moon in the bright half of the month. The grace of the sky means having the heart completely free from the clouds of attachment. Gandhiji once said, "I am always talking of the spinning wheel. I consider it sacred. But I must not have attachment even to it at the last moment. He who led me to the spinning wheel is fully capable of taking its care. Now the spinning wheel has been taken up by many leading figures. I should now cease to worry about it and be ready to meet the Lord." *Uttarayan* thus means freedom of the heart from the clouds of attachment.

20. If death comes when a man's body is engaged in service till the last breath, pure sentiments have grown to fullness, there is no trace of attachment in the heart and intellect is sharp and radiant, he becomes one with God. To have such a supremely auspicious end, one must ever be alert and continue to strive day and night. No impure and evil *samskara* should be permitted in the mind even for a single moment. One must pray constantly to the Lord to have the necessary strength to achieve this. Again and again, one should remember His Name and meditate over His nature and essence.

(10.4.32)

CHAPTER 9

The sovereign science of service to humanity: Yoga of surrender

41. Knowledge through direct experience

1. Brothers, I have a sore throat today and I doubt whether my voice would reach you. I am reminded here of an anecdote from the life of Peshwa Madhavrao. That saintly man was on his death-bed. His lungs were full of phlegm. It is said that phlegm can be converted into dysentery. Madhavrao told his physician, "Please convert my phlegm into dysentery, so that I would be able to utter the Name of the Lord." I too was praying to God today and He told me to speak to the extent the throat permits. My intention in delivering these talks on the Gita is not to preach anyone, although those who want to profit from them may surely do so. When I talk on the Gita, I do so to have the Lord's Name on my lips.

2. What I am telling here has connection with the Ninth Chapter. This Chapter tells about the wonderful greatness of the Lord's Name. It is at the centre of the Gita, which itself is at the centre of the Mahabharata. For many reasons, this Chapter is considered particularly holy. It is said that when Jnanadeva bid farewell to the world and entered into *samadhi*,[1] he was reciting this Chapter. Whenever I think of this Chapter, tears well up in my eyes and my heart dances with divine joy. How great is this gift that Vyasa has given to us! Not only India but

---

[1] Saints and sages used to voluntarily end their life when they thought that they had accomplished what they should have. They would then concentrate all the energies and merge into the Absolute, ending worldly existence. This is called *samadhi*. This is the sense in which the word is used here. See also footnote on p. 6.

all mankind is indebted to Vyasa for this gift. In fact, what the Lord told Arjuna was not something that could be expressed in words; but Vyasa, moved by compassion, put it into Sanskrit verse. He clothed in words the secret wisdom.

3. At the very outset, the Lord says that this unique wisdom is the supreme secret; it is the highest and the purest. And this is something to be directly experienced. This Chapter describes something that cannot be put into words, but which has stood the test of experience. That is why it has become exceedingly endearing. Saint Tulsidas has said, 'को जानै को जैहै जमपुर को सुरपुर पर-धाम को; तुलसिहिं बहुत भलो लागत जग जीवन रामगुलाम को l' – What is the use of the stories of heaven where one can go after death? Who knows who will go to heaven and who to hell? We are here to live only for a few days. Tulsidas says that he is happy in spending these few days in the service of the Lord. This Chapter describes the beauty and the sweetness of living in the service of the Lord. It tells about things which can be directly experienced in this body, seen directly with the eyes, enjoyed here and now in this life. When one eats jaggery, one can directly experience its sweetness. This Chapter gives a taste of sweetness in life that is totally surrendered to the Lord. It deals with the supreme knowledge that enables us to experience directly the sweetness in the life on this earth. This knowledge is otherwise most difficult to grasp, but the Lord has revealed it here to all, made it accessible and comprehensible to all.

42. The easy way

4. The Gita is the essence of the Vedic religion – the religion that originated from the Vedas. The Vedas are considered to be the oldest among the ancient scriptures in the world. That is why the devout consider them *anadi* (which have no beginning, which have always been in existence). The Vedas are, therefore, held in great reverence. Even from the historical point of view, they are the oldest recorded expression of our ancient social mind. This written record is far more valuable than the copper and stone inscriptions, coins, pots and pans or animal fossils. The Vedas are the oldest historical documents. The religion that was in the form of a seed in the Vedas grew gradually into the tree which finally bore the sweet divine fruit of the Gita. What else can we have from a tree to eat than a fruit? It is only when the tree bears fruit that we can have something to eat. The Gita is the twice-distilled essence of the Vedic religion.

5. The ancient Vedic religion prescribed various rites and rituals, *yajnas*, austerities and penances, different practices and various types of spiritual discipline. All these were not useless, but they called for certain fitness; they were not open to all. Suppose I am hungry, and there is a coconut high up on the tree. How can I get it if I cannot climb the tree, pluck the coconut and break it open? Can the mere sight of the coconut satisfy my hunger? That coconut is of no use to me until I can have it in my hands. The Vedic rites and rituals were based on subtle and significant ideas.

How could the common folk comprehend them? It was laid down that the Vedic path was essential for attaining *moksha* (spiritual liberation), but only a few were entitled to follow it. How could others redeem themselves? That was a predicament.

6. Hence the saints, overflowing with compassion for the masses, came forward and said, "Let us extract the essence of the Vedas and give it to the whole world." That is why Saint Tukaram said, 'वेद अनंत बोलिला । अर्थ इतुकाचि साधिला ।' – 'There are innumerable teachings in the Vedas. But all that boils down to this.' To what? To the Name of the Lord. That is the essence of the Vedas. The saints proclaimed that the Lord's Name can lead one to *moksha*. The door to *moksha* was thus thrown wide open to all – to the women and the children, the workers and the peasants, the weak and the ignorant, the sick and the handicapped. *Moksha* that lay locked up in the Vedas was brought within the reach of everybody, thanks to the Lord Himself. A simple and easy way became available. Why cannot one's ordinary day-to-day life, what one does as *swadharma*, one's acts of service be infused with the spirit of *yajna*? Where is the need for other complicated and elaborate *yajnas*? Let your daily work itself be a *yajna* – let it be sacrificial in nature.

7. This is the highway. 'यानास्थाय नरो राजन् न प्रमाद्येत कर्हिंचित् । धावन्निमील्य वा नेत्रे न स्खलेन्न पतेदिह ।।' – 'Even if you run on this road with closed eyes, there is no risk of stumbling or falling.' The other way is like the edge of a sharp razor: 'क्षुरस्य धारा निशिता दुरत्यया ।'

– The Vedic way is sharper than a sword's edge and is thus extremely arduous. The way of devotion, the way of surrender and service to the Lord is easy. An engineer designs a road to the hilltop in such a way that we have no feeling of having climbed such a height till we reach the top. Therein lies his skill. This highway too is designed with such skill. By this way one can reach God, while remaining where one is, through performing one's *swadharma*.

8. Is God hiding somewhere in a cave or in a river or in heaven? Is He hidden somewhere just as diamonds and gold are in the womb of the earth and pearls are in the depths of the sea? Have we to dig Him up from somewhere? Not at all. All that is around us is nothing but God; He is standing before all of us all the time. Everyone here is His image. The Lord is urging us, "Please do not look down upon My manifestations in human forms." It is the Lord, and the Lord alone, who appears in everything animate and inanimate. Where is then the need for devising artificial methods to seek and find Him? The way is straight and easy. Whatever work you do, do it in the spirit of service and as a service to the Lord. Surrender totally to the Lord and be His devoted and humble servant. The arduous Vedic path with its complex rites and rituals and the numerous *yajnas* will no doubt take us towards *moksha*; but the problem there is that the question of fitness arises there. Let us have none of it. Just dedicate to Him whatever you do. Relate to Him every act of yours. This is what the Ninth Chapter tells us. Hence the *bhaktas* are extremely fond of this Chapter.

43. No question of entitlement

9. In the life of Lord Krishna, His childhood is particularly charming. Balkrishna (the child Krishna) has always been the object of special adoration and worship. He would go along with the cowherds to graze cattle; He would eat and laugh and play with them. When they set out to worship Indra[2], He asked them, "Has anybody seen Indra? What do we owe him? On the other hand, this Govardhan hill is here before our eyes. Cows graze on its slopes. Streams flow from it. It is better to worship it."[3] Such things He taught them. To His cowherd companions, to their womenfolk, to the cows and the calves whose company He enjoyed, to them all He opened the door of spiritual liberation. Lord Krishna has thus shown through His own life an easy way to *moksha*. He moved with cows in His childhood and with horses when He grew up. On hearing the music of His flute, cows would go into raptures. The horses would get thrilled as He stroked their backs. Those cows and horses, belonging to the so-called lower species, would as it were become one with Him and attain spiritual liberation. Lord Krishna has thus shown that such liberation is not a prerogative of human beings only; even the birds and the beasts can attain it. The story of His life is a testimony to this fact.

---

[2] The presiding deity of the heaven.

[3] Indra thereupon became furious and caused incessant rains. The child Krishna then lifted the Govardhan hill on his little finger, asking the cowherds to join with their staffs supporting the hill. All the people and the cattle in the village took shelter under the hill.

10. Vyasa too had the same experience. In fact, there is an identity between Vyasa and Krishna. The quintessential message of their lives is the same. *Moksha* depends neither on scholarship nor on performance of rites and rituals. Plain, simple devotion is sufficient. Innocent and devout women have surpassed learned egotists in spiritual progress. If there is pure heart, innocence and faith, *moksha* is not difficult to attain. In the Mahabharata, there is a Chapter narrating a conversation between King Janaka and Sulabha, an ordinary woman. Vyasa has depicted the incident wherein King Janaka goes for Self-knowledge to Sulabha. You may go on discussing whether women have the right to study Vedas or not, but here we find Sulabha, an ordinary woman, imparting the knowledge of the *Brahman* to Janaka, the great Emperor and scholar. Janaka was a learned man, but he was far from securing *moksha*. For that, Vyasa had made him fall at the feet of Sulabha. The story of Tuladhar, the grocer, gives the same message. Jajali, a *Brahmin* goes to him for Self-knowledge. Tuladhar tells him, "All my knowledge consists in holding the scales perfectly even." There is also a story of a hunter who used to kill animals and sell their flesh. That was his way of serving the society. An egotist ascetic was told by his *guru* (teacher) to go to that hunter for Self-knowledge. The ascetic wondered how a hunter could teach him. When he went to the hunter, the latter was busy cutting up meat and cleaning the pieces to be put up for sale. He told the ascetic, "I am doing my best to infuse my work with *dharma* to the extent possible. I pour my soul into this work to the best

of my capacity, and also serve my parents." In the form of that hunter, Vyasa has put before us an ideal.

11. The Mahabharata narrates such stories about women and men of humble occupations specifically to make it abundantly clear that the doors of *moksha* are open to all. The Ninth Chapter affirms the same point. The joy in serving the Lord can be found in that hunter's life. Tukaram was a votary of non-violence, but he has fondly described in appreciative terms the story of Sajan who attained *moksha* through his work as a butcher. Elsewhere he has exclaimed with distress, "O God ! What could be the fate of those who kill animals?", but he has also described how the Lord helped Sajan : 'सजन कसाया विकूं लागे मांस' – The Lord helped Sajan the butcher in selling meat. Tukaram is telling that the Lord who honoured Narsi Mehta's[4] *hundi*, who fetched water for Eknath's household, who became an untouchable servant for Damaji[5], who helped Janabai, the maidservant, in household work, helped Sajan the butcher too with the same love. The moral is that all our activities should be linked to

---

[4] Narsi Mehta was a poet-saint of Gujarat in the mediaeval period. In those days, people on pilgrimage used to deposit excess money with some merchant and get from him *hundi* (a sort of demand draft) in the name of a merchant of another place, which the latter would honour. Once some mischievous persons suggested Narsi's name for the purpose to some pilgrims. Narsi gave them *hundi* on Dwarka in the name of Lord Krishna.

[5] Damaji, a devotee of Lord Pandurang, was a government official. Once, during a famine, he threw open the doors of the government granary to the people. The ruler, on knowing it, got furious and ordered Damaji to deposit the necessary amount. It is said that the Lord thereupon took the form of an untouchable servant, went to the royal court and deposited the money.

Him, dedicated to Him. Acts of service done with pure heart and noble thoughts are essentially a form of *yajna*.

44. Dedication of the fruit of actions to the Lord

12. This is the special teaching of the Ninth Chapter. In this Chapter, there is a fascinating confluence of *karmayoga* and *bhaktiyoga*. *Karmayoga* means doing work and renouncing its fruit. Work should be done with such an ingenuity that the mind remains untouched by attachment to its fruit. It is like planting a walnut tree. The walnut tree takes twenty five years to yield fruit. One who plants it may not be able to eat its fruits. Still one must plant the tree and take care of it lovingly. *Karmayoga* means planting the tree without expecting anything in return. *Bhaktiyoga* means getting attached to God with love and devotion. *Karmayoga* and *bhaktiyoga* combine together in *rajayoga*. *Rajayoga* has been defined by different people in diffferent ways. I would like to define it as a beautiful blending of *karmayoga* and *bhaktiyoga*.

Work has to be done, but its fruit is not to be thrown away; it should be dedicated to God. To throw away the fruit would be to reject it. But dedication of the fruit of actions to the Lord is something very different. It indicates an extremely beautiful state of the mind. Even if we renounce the fruit, it is not that nobody will have it; somebody is bound to get it. Questions like the recipient's fitness may then arise. If a beggar comes to our door, we say, "You are strong and stout. It does not behove you to beg. Get lost." We sit in judgement over the justification for his begging. The poor fellow feels ashamed. There is no trace of fellow-feeling in our hardened heart. How can we then have the right judgement about the fellow?

13. When I was a child, I had expressed the same doubt to my mother. Her answer is still ringing in my ears. I had told her about a beggar, "This beggar seems to be strong and stout. To give alms to such a person will encourage indolence and bad habits." I also quoted a verse from the Gita, 'देशे काले च पात्रे च।'[6] She said, "That beggar was the Lord Himself. Keep it in mind and then judge His worthiness. Would you rate God as undeserving? In fact, what right have we got to judge his worthiness? I see no need to think any more. To me, he is the Lord and that is all." I have not yet found a fitting reply to what she said.

We judge the worthiness of others when it is a question of feeding others, but when it comes to filling our own bellies, the thought of fitness never crosses our mind. Why should we regard the man coming to our doors as just a wretched beggar? Why should we not look upon him as the Lord Himself?

14. *Rajayoga* says, "Isn't it true that somebody is bound to enjoy the fruit of your actions? So better offer it to the Lord. Dedicate it to Him." *Rajayoga* points out the proper recipient. Here, there is no

---

[6] 'Charity should be given at the right place, at the right time, and to the right person, as a matter of duty, without expecting any return. Such charity is said to be *sattvik*.' – Gita 17.20.

negative action of giving up the fruit; and as it has to be dedicated to the Lord, the question of judging the fitness of the recipient is also eliminated. Whatever is offered to the Lord is always pure. Even if your actions have impurities, they will become pure the moment they reach His hands. However hard we try to make our actions perfect, there will still be some flaws. Nevertheless, we should try our best to act with the utmost possible purity. Intellect is God-given. It is our duty to keep it as pure as possible. Not to do so is a crime. So we must judge the fitness of the recipient. But if we look upon the world as a manifestation of God, it is easier to make the right judgement.

15. The fruit of action should be utilized for purifying the mind. Dedicate the actions to God irrespective of their quality, as and when they take place. The mind should thereby be continuously purified. The fruit of work is not to be thrown away; it should be dedicated to Him. Dedicate to the Lord your desires and longings; even the passions and tendencies like anger that arise in the mind, and then have nothing to do with them. 'कामक्रोध आम्हीं वाहिले विठ्ठलीं ।' ('We have dedicated to the Lord our passions and anger.') Here is no question of torturing oneself in the fire of self-control; no need for any suppression or straining oneself to the breaking point. Surrender totally and find freedom. Nothing else needs to be done. 'रोग जाय दुधें साखरें। तरी निंब कां पियावा ।' ('If milk and sugar can cure the disease, why should one take bitter *neem* juice?')

175

16. The sense organs too are means (for realizing Him). Dedicate them to the Lord. People complain that they have no control over what they hear. Should we then refuse to hear anything? Not at all. We must hear. But let us hear only the edifying stories of the Lord. It is difficult to give up hearing altogether, but it is easier, and moreover more desirable and beneficial, to turn the ears to something worth hearing. Lend your ears to the Lord. Use your mouth to chant His Name. The sense organs are not your enemies. They are good and useful. They possess great capabilities. The best way is to take work from them in a spirit of dedication to the Lord. This is what *rajayoga* means.

45. Dedicate all the activities

17. It is not that only some particular actions are to be dedicated to the Lord. All our actions are to be dedicated to Him. Lord Rama gladly accepted the fruits offered by Shabari.[7] One need not retire to a cave to worship the Lord. Whatever you do, wherever you do it, just dedicate that to Him. A mother waiting on her child waits on God. Giving the child a bath is like performing *abhishek* over the Lord. She should regard the child as His gift and bring it up with reverence. Sages and saints like Shuka, Valmiki and Tulsidas consider themselves blessed while portraying how tenderly did Kaushalya care for Rama and Yashoda

---

[7] Shabari, an old tribal woman and a devotee of Rama, invited him to her place. As she had nothing to offer to Him, she picked jujube fruits from the forest and bit them to find out whether they were sweet, and therefore worthy of being offered to the Lord. Rama gladly accepted those wild fruits, that too bitten by her.

for Krishna. They describe it with fond admiration. Such service by a mother is indeed noble. The child is an image of God. What greater fortune could one have than having an opportunity to serve the Lord in the form of a child? Imagine the transformation that will take place in our actions if we were to serve each other with this attitude! Let each one of us consider the work that has fallen to our lot as service of the Lord Himself.

18. A farmer looks after his bullock. Is that bullock to be despised? No. The bull that sage Vamadeva describes in the Veda as pervading the entire universe in the form of energy, is present in the farmer's bullock too.

'चत्वारि शृंगा त्रयो अस्य पादाः
द्वे शीर्षे सप्त हस्तासो अस्य
त्रिधा बद्धो वृषभो रोरवीति
महो देवो मर्त्यों आ विवेश ।'

('The bull which has four horns, three legs, two heads and seven hands and is tied to three posts is roaring. The Great God has pervaded all the mankind in every way.') That greatly effulgent bull, radiating vigour and energy, immanent in all the mortal beings in the universe is roaring. It is the same bull which the farmer worships inwardly while taking care of his bullock. Commentators have interpreted this verse in different ways. This bull is indeed strange. The bull that roars in the sky and causes rainfall, is also present in the farmer's bullock which litters the field with dung and urine and fertilises it to yield abundant crop. If the bullock is looked upon with this feeling, then the ordinary work of taking care of the bullock would become the worship of the Lord.

19. The lady of the house keeps the kitchen spotlessly clean and cooks pure and wholesome food for the family. Her earnest desire is to give nourishment and contentment to all the family-members. All that work of hers is a form of *yajna*. The fire in the kitchen stove is verily the *yajna* fire. Imagine how pure and holy the food will be if it is cooked for the Lord! If the lady has such noble feeling in her mind, she would verily join the august band of the wives of the sages described in the Bhagavata. Many such women must have redeemed themselves through such service, surpassing self-centred scholars.

46. The whole life can be infused with God

20. The moments of our daily life may appear commonplace, but they are not really so. They have deep significance. The whole life is like a great *yajna* – a continual sacrificial performance. Your sleep is also a kind of *samadhi* – an experience of oneness with the divine consciousness. If we surrender all that we did and all that we experienced to the Lord before going to sleep, will not that sleep be a kind of *samadhi*? There is a custom of reciting the Purusha-sukta, a Vedic hymn, while taking bath. What is the connection between the bath and the Purusha-sukta? You will discern it if you wish to. What connection

does the great, all-pervading *Purusha* (the cosmic Person) having thousand hands and thousand eyes have with your bath? The connection is that, there are thousands of drops in the water you pour over your head. They wash your head and clean it, ridding it of your sins. They are the Lord's blessing showering on you. The Lord Himself is washing off your sins through those thousands of water drops. Let your bath be infused with such an exalted sentiment; then it will be an altogether different thing. It will then have boundless power.

21. Any work, howsoever ordinary or commonplace, assumes sanctity if performed in the spirit that it is God's work. You can experience it yourself. Just look upon a guest as the Lord Himself and then see the difference it makes. When some distinguished guest is expected in our house, we clean the house thoroughly and prepare special dishes. Imagine the difference it will make if we look upon the guest as the Lord Himself! Saint Kabir was a weaver. While weaving, he would lose himself in spiritual bliss and sing ecstasically. He was as it were weaving the sheets to drape the Lord. The sage in RigVeda says, 'वस्त्रेव भद्रा सुकृता वसूयु:' – 'I am draping the Lord with my hymns.' It is for the Lord that a poet should compose hymns, and it is for Him that a weaver should weave cloth. How stirring the idea is! How purifying and moving the thought is! How pure our life would become if this feeling informs it! A flash of lightning removes darkness in an instant. Is the removal of darkness gradual? The transformation is instantaneous and total. Likewise,

life is instantly charged with wonderful energy when
every action is linked to the Lord. Every action will
then become pure. Life will be full of zest. Today our
life is devoid of any zest or purpose. There is no joy,
no happiness in it. We are alive only because we are
yet to die. But just think of linking your actions to
the Lord, and then your life will be full of charm; it
will be worthy of veneration.

22. There is no doubt that the Lord's Name brings
about instantaneous transformation. Never doubt the
efficacy of His Name. Give it a try and see what
happens. Suppose a farmer is coming home in the
evening and he meets a stranger on the way. Let him
say to the stranger, 'चाल घरा उभा राहें नारायणा' – 'O
Brother! O Lord! Soon it will be night. So please come
and spend the night in my house.' These words will
transform the stranger. Even if he were a robber, he
would undergo a change and become pure. It is the
attitude that makes the difference. It is the attitude
that really matters in life. One welcomes a young man
and gives him one's daughter in marriage and bows
before the bridegroom much younger in age. Why?
The act of giving away the daughter is so sacred that
the young bridegroom is regarded as the Lord Himself.
This very sentiment has to be further developed and
elevated.

23. Some may object, "Why make such false
assumptions?" But one should not brand anything
true or false beforehand. One should first give it a
try, see what happens, and only then one would know

what is true and what is false. Do not just address the bridegroom as the Lord as a matter of ritual; regard him so in your heart of hearts, and see the difference. That sentiment will bring about a total transformation. Even if the man concerned is not worthy, he will become so. Even if he is evil-minded, he will become good. Did not this happen in the case of Valya Koli[8]? He had never before come across a man with the Lord's Name on his lips while playing *veena*,[9] and remaining not only calm and unruffled even when he (Valya) was about to attack, but also continuing to look at him with love. He had till then seen only two types of people. They would either run away or make counter-attack. But Narada did neither and just stood unperturbed without even blinking his eyes; his singing did not stop for a moment. Valya's axe stopped in the air. Narada asked, "Why has your axe stopped?" Valya replied, "Because you are so calm." Narada brought about transformation in Valya. Was that transformation unreal?

24. After all, who is to decide whether somebody is evil? Even if you come across a wicked man, look upon him as the Lord. That will transform him into a saint. Do not ask, "Why should we make unreal suppositions?" Who can be certain that the man is really wicked? It is said that 'good men, being good,

---

[8] Valya Koli, a bloodthirsty dacoit, was transformed by Narada. He then undertook penance and realized God. He came to be known as sage Valmiki, who later wrote Ramayana.

[9] A stringed musical instrument.

find goodness everywhere, but that is not true.' Should it then be accepted that only what you see is true? Are we to suppose that only bad men have the means to know the true nature of the creation? Why not say that there is nothing wrong with the world, but it appears bad to you as you yourself are bad? Look, the creation is but a mirror. You will see in it your true image. It is the eye of the beholder that determines the nature of the world. Therefore, look upon the world as good and sacred. Let this attitude inform even your ordinary actions. Then you will witness a miraculous change. This is what the Lord intends to convey : 'जें खासी होमिसी देसी जें जें आचरिसी तप । जें कांहीं करिसी कर्म तें करीं मज अर्पण ।'[10] ('Whatever you do, whatever you eat, whatever you offer as sacrifice or gift, whatever austerity you perform, dedicate all that to Me.')

25. When I was a child, my mother used to tell me a story. It is an amusing story, but it contains a profound truth. There was a lady who had resolved to dedicate everything she did to Lord Krishna. After meals, she would wipe the floor with cow-dung[11] and throw the lump of cow-dung out of the house saying, "*Krishnarpan.*" ('I dedicate it to Lord Krishna.') The lump would then reach the image in the temple and stick to it. The priest got tired of cleaning up the image again and again. At last he discovered that it

---

[10] Gita, 9.27.

[11] This was a common practice at that time, and is even now widely prevalent. People take meals sitting on the floor. Thereafter the floor is cleaned and smeared with cow-dung.

was all due to that lady; as long as she was alive, it was impossible to keep the image clean. One day she fell sick. Death seemed round the corner. She dedicated death also to the Lord. At that very moment, the image of the Lord cracked and fell to pieces. A heavenly chariot came to take her to the heaven. She dedicated even that to the Lord. That then dashed against the temple and was smashed up. The moral of the story is that heaven is of no value before the love for the Lord.

26. The import of all this is that, unusual power is generated when whatever good or bad that we do is dedicated to the Lord. A jowar[12] grain is reddish yellow, but when you parch it, you have a nice pop-corn. Put that white, beautiful and nicely shaped pop-corn near a grain and you will find absolutely no resemblance between them. But there is no doubt that it is the grain that has turned into the pop-corn. It is the fire that brings about such a change. If you grind that hard grain, it will turn into soft flour. Fire turns the grain into popcorn and grinding turns the grain into flour. Likewise, infuse your ordinary and seemingly unimportant actions with the devotion for the Lord and then your actions will be transformed beyond recognition. It is the spirit that enhances the value of actions. Do not consider worthless even the leaves and the flowers; they become sacred when they are offered to the Lord. 'तुका म्हणे चवी आलें । जें कां मिश्रित विठ्ठलें ।' ('Tukaram says, whatever is mixed with

---

[12] A type of coarse grains.

the Lord becomes delicious.') Add God to everything and experience the outcome. Which spice can equal the Lord in making things delicious? Add this divine spice to every action, and then everything will become good and delicious.

27. Imagine, it is the night time. The *pooja* is going on in the temple. The incense smoke is rising. Its fragrance is in the air. Lamps have been lit. In such an ambience we really feel God's presence. All day the Lord was awake; now is the time for Him to go to sleep. The devotees sing, 'आतां स्वामी सुखें निद्रा करा गोपाळा ।' ('O Lord! Now you may happily go to sleep.') Sceptics ask, "Does the Lord sleep?" But why can't the Lord sleep? O fool, if the Lord does not sleep and wake up, who do you think does so – a stone? It is the Lord who sleeps and keeps awake, it is the Lord who eats and drinks. As the day dawns, Saint Tulsidas wakes up Lord Rama with gentle pursuasion, 'जागिये रघुनाथ कुंवर पंछी बन बोले ।' ('O Prince Rama! Please wake up. The birds have started chirping in the woods.') He is, in fact, waking up the people, looking at them as the images of the Lord. What an enchanting idea! Contrast it with what happens in a hostel. There the boys are woken up by rude shouts. Is this proper in the auspicious morning hours? There is an incident in Valmiki's Ramayana. Rama is asleep in the *ashram* of sage Vishwamitra. Vishwamitra is waking him up. Valimiki describes,

'रामेति मधुरां वाणीं विश्वामित्रोऽभ्यभाषत ।
उत्तिष्ठ नरशार्दूल पूर्वा संध्या प्रवर्तते ॥'

184

(Vishwamitra is saying softly to Rama, "Arise, O lion among men; the sky is brightening in the east.")

How sweet and loving the action is! And how harshly the boys are woken up in a hostel! The poor sleeping lad feels that the fellow waking him up must be his arch-enemy for ages! One should first call in a low, soft tone. If the boy does not wake up, call him in a little louder voice. But never be rough or rude. If he still does not wake up, you may try again after a few minutes. If even that fails, hope that he will surely get up in time the next day. Sing to him melodious songs, the songs of sunrise, or the hymns. The ordinary action of waking up can thus be made poetic, tender and beautiful when it is done with the feeling that we are waking up the Lord Himself. To wake up somebody too needs the right technique.

28. Let this idea inform all your actions. It is all the more important in the sphere of education. A teacher should feel that the pupils are the Lord incarnate and he is serving Him through teaching them. He would not then act upon the axiom 'Spare the rod and spoil the child.' He will not scold the pupils right and left and hurt them with disparaging remarks. Instead of rebuking them, for example, for wearing dirty clothes, he would wash their dirty clothes. If the teacher does so, what a deep impact such loving care will have on the pupils' minds! Can caning ever have any good effect? The pupils should also look upon the teacher with the same reverence. If the pupils and the teachers regard each other as images of the Lord and behave accordingly, then the knowledge that the pupils gain

will have a rare lustre. If the pupils feel that they are being taught by the Lord Himself, you can imagine how they would behave.

47. *The Lord's Name destroys the sins*

29. Once the sentiment that the Lord is present everywhere is deeply rooted in the mind, we will naturally know how to behave with each other. There will be no need for any rules and canons of ethics. The vices will disappear on their own, sins will flee and the evil would vanish in thin air.

Tukaram has said,

'चाल केलासी मोकळा । बोल विठ्ठल वेळोवेळां
तुज पाप चि नाही ऐसें । नाम घेतां जवळीं वसे'

('You are free to do whatever you like. Just chant the Lord's Name again and again. Once you recite His Name, no sin will remain near you.')

Well, you are free to sin now. You can now commit as many sins as you can. Let us see whether you get tired of sinning or the Lord's Name gets tired of reducing them to ashes! Is there any evil stubborn and belligerent enough to pit itself against the Lord's name? 'करी तुजसी करवती' – Sin as much as you can. Let the Lord's Name and your sins fight it out. The Lord's Name is powerful enough to burn down in an instant the sins committed not only in this life but in countless births in the past. A cave may be full of darkness since ages, but the moment you light a candle, darkness disappears. In fact,

the older the sins, the more quickly they get destroyed, just as old wooden logs are more easily and quickly reduced to ashes.

30. No sin can ever exist in the presence of *Ramanama* (the Lord's Name). Don't the children say, "Ghosts vanish when you take *Ramanama.*" In my childhood, we children used to challenge each other to go to the cremation ground at night and drive in a peg there. There used to be snakes and thorns in the way, and darkness all around. Still I would fearlessly go there. I never came across ghosts. Ghosts, after all, are creations of the mind. How could they appear before us? Wherefrom did a ten-year-old boy gather such courage? From *Ramanama.* It was the power of the Lord who is Truth. If a man feels that the Lord is ever by his side and surrenders himself to Him, then he will not be afraid even if the whole world turns against him. Which demon can devour him? A demon may destroy the body; but never the truth. No power on earth can destroy the truth. Sin can never stand before the Name of the Lord. Hence seek His grace. Dedicate all actions to Him. Surrender completely to Him and be totally devoted to Him. Let the urge to dedicate all the actions to Him become more and more intense. Then this trivial life will become divine. The soiled life will become beautiful.

48. Not what but how you offer is important

31. 'पत्रं पुष्पं फलं तोयम्' – Leaves, flowers, fruits, water, anything can be offered to Him. What is important is that it should be offered with *bhakti*. The spirit

and sentiment with which you offer is important. Once I was having a discussion on education with a professor. There was a difference of opinion between us. In order to clinch the issue, he said, "I have been teaching for eighteen years." He should have convinced me of the correctness of his standpoint; he instead flaunted his experience. I said in a lighter vein, "If a bullock pulls an oil *ghani* (oil expeller) for eighteen years, will it become an engineer?" An engineer is an engineer and a bullock is a bullock. An educationist is different from a teacher who goes on doing his job in a routine and mechanical manner. An educationist will gain much more insight and experience in six months than a labourer working for eighteen years. The Professor boasted of his years of experience. But it proves nothing. Likewise, the volume and value of the offering is of no significance. What is important is the spirit in which you make the offering. What is important is not what or how much you offer, but how you offer. The Gita contains only seven hundred verses. There are some other books containing thousands of verses. But a bigger thing need not necessarily be better. You should judge the intrinsic quality, the intrinsic strength in anything. The number of activities in life is not important; even a single action with dedication, with surrender to the Lord, will make your life richer. A single sacred moment can give experience that cannot be acquired in years.

32. Thus, the point is that even the ordinary actions in life should be dedicated to the Lord. The life would then acquire a new vigour. *Moksha* would come within our grasp. *Rajayoga,* which asks us to work and offer its fruit to the Lord instead of giving it up, is a step ahead of *karmayoga. Karmayoga* asks you to work without desires and give up the fruit of the work. Here *karmayoga* stops. *Rajayoga* tells, "Do not renounce the fruit of the actions. Dedicate all the actions themselves to the Lord. The actions are a means that help you in making spiritual progress. They are like flowers which should be offered at the feet of the Lord. Conjoin your actions with devotion and go on enriching your life. Do not throw away the fruit, dedicate it to the Lord." The fruit that is cut off from the actions in *karmayoga* is linked to the Lord in *rajayoga.* There is a difference between throwing seeds and sowing them. You reap in abundance what you sow; what you throw is wasted. The work that is dedicated to the Lord gets sown, and therefore life gets infused with infinite bliss and sanctity.

(17.4.32)

CHAPTER 10

Contemplation of God's manifestations

1. Friends, we have come halfway through the Gita. It will be worthwhile to recapitulate before we proceed further. In the First Chapter, it is stated that the Gita is for overcoming delusions and inducing us to follow *swadharma*. In the Second Chapter, the basic principles of life are stated and the concepts of *karmayoga* and *sthitaprajna* are spelt out. Chapters 3, 4 and 5 explain the concepts of *karma*, *vikarma* and *akarma*. *Karma* means the actions done for the performance of *swadharma*. *Vikarma* means inner mental action that needs to be done to aid such performance. When *karma* and *vikarma* fuse together, mind is completely purified, passions and cravings die out, distinctions vanish, and then the state of *akarma* is reached. This state is of two kinds. In one, hectic activity goes on unceasingly but still the doer has no sense of doing anything. In the other, one is outwardly inactive but is still acting ceaselessly. The state of *akarma* attains fruition in both the ways. Although these two ways appear different, they are completely identical. These ways are called *karmayoga* and *sannyasa* respectively. Although they are known by different terms, they are the same in essence. The state of *akarma* is the ultimate goal, which is also called *moksha*. Thus, in the first five Chapters of the Gita, the philosophy of life has been fully spelt out.

2. To attain the state of *akarma*, there are various types of *vikarma*. There are several means for the purification of the mind. Important among them have

been described from the Sixth Chapter onwards. The Sixth Chapter tells about the *yoga* of meditation to have one-pointedness of mind and about the supplementary means of *abhyasa* and *vairagya*. The Seventh Chapter is about the great and noble means of *bhakti*. You may go to the Lord either with love or with the quest for knowledge or with passion for the well-being of all, or even with desire for personal gains; the important thing is to enter into the presence of the Lord. I call it *prapattiyoga* or the *yoga* that asks us to surrender to God. The Eighth Chapter puts forward *satatyayoga* (the *yoga* of uninterrupted pursuit). You will not find these terms in other commentaries; I have coined these terms as they help me in comprehending the Gita. *Satatyayoga* means continuing the *sadhana* – the spiritual quest – till death. One should never leave the chosen path; one should go on advancing along that path without break. If one vacillates, there cannot be any hope of reaching the goal. One should never despair or get tired and complain, "How long am I to go on doing *sadhana*?" *Sadhana* should continue till it attains fruition.

3. After explaining this *satatyayoga*, the Lord tells in the Ninth Chapter something very simple, yet capable of transforming the life totally. That is *rajayoga*. This Chapter asks us to dedicate all the actions to the Lord as and when they take place. All the means enjoined by the scriptures, all the *karma* and *vikarma* – everything gets dissolved in *rajayoga*, the *yoga* of surrender. Nothing else is needed. Surrender of everything to the Lord is an all-encompassing and powerful idea.

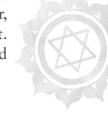

It appears simple and easy, but still it turns out to be exceedingly difficult. This *sadhana* is easy because anybody, from an illiterate villager to a great scholar, can practise it wherever he is, without much effort. But although easy, it requires extraordinary moral and spiritual merit.

'बहुतां सुकृतांची जोडी । म्हणुनी विठुलीं आवडी'

('It is only when good deeds are done in many births that the mind is drawn towards the Lord.')

The most trivial things bring tears to our eyes, but the Lord's Name does not move us to tears. What is to be done then? This *sadhana*, as the saints say, is easy in one sense, but difficult in another; it has become all the more difficult in the modern times.

4. Today, the scales of materialism have obscured our view. We begin by doubting God's existence. Nobody finds Him anywhere. Life is full of lust, passions and distortions and iniquities. The greatest among the philosophers of our time cannot think of anything higher than providing two square meals daily to all. They are not to be blamed for it; it is a fact that many do not get even that. How to provide food to all is the biggest problem today, and the best brains are busy in tackling it. Sayanacharya has defined Rudra as 'बुभुक्षमाण: रुद्ररूपेण अवतिष्ठते' – the hungry people are Rudra[1] incarnate. A number of ideologies, isms

---

[1] The dreadful form of the Lord, out to annihilate the world.

and programmes have arisen to solve the problem of hunger. We have no time to look beyond this problem and think of anything else. The most strenuous efforts are being made to find out how people could have a couple of morsels in peace without clashing with each other. In such a strange social order, it is no wonder that the simple idea of dedication to the Lord appears exceedingly difficult. What is the remedy? We shall see in the Tenth Chapter how to master the *yoga* of dedication to the Lord, how to make it easy to practise.

50. An easy way to learn to see God

5. The methods that we employ in teaching the children have been suggested in this Chapter to enable us to see the Lord everywhere. The children are taught the alphabet in two ways. One method is to teach the letters first by writing them in big size. When the children are conversant with them, they are acquainted with the letters in smaller sizes. The other method is to teach simple letters first and the complicated 'joint'[2] letters thereafter. In the same way, we should first learn to see God in His greater Divine manifastations. The Lord manifest in oceans or high mountains can be grasped at once. When we come to experience His presence therein, we shall realise subsequently that He is present even in a drop of water or a speck of dust. There is no difference between the capital 'A' and the small 'a'. This is one way. The other way is to see

---

[2] In Nagari script, alphabets are joined to form joint alphabets. Their form often changes in the process. Therefore, they are more difficult to learn.

Him first in His simpler manifestations, and then move on to His complicated manifestations. One can quickly comprehend His Divine manifestation. For example, one can easily discern God in Rama. Rama is like a simple letter. But what about Ravana? Ravana is like a 'joint' letter. In Ravana, His manifestation is difficult to discern because there is a mixture of good and evil in the person of Ravana. Ravana's penance and energy are indeed great, but they are mixed with cruelty. So, to begin with, learn to behold God manifest in Rama, who is full of love and compassion. It will take time to discern divinity in Ravana. But one has to reach that stage. One should first learn to discern God in a good person, but ultimately one should be able to discern Him in an evil person too. The Lord who is in an ocean is present in a drop of water too. The Lord who is in Rama is present in Ravana too. What is present in the gross is present in the subtle; what is present in the simple is present in the complex. Our vision should be informed with this outlook while reading the book of this world.

6. This vast creation is like the Lord's Book. When our eyes are covered with thick veils, we think that the Book is closed. Everywhere in this Book, the name of the Lord is written in beautiful letters. But we fail to read that. A major obstacle is that a man does not recognise the Lord in the ordinary and simple forms which are near him and His distant and dazzling manifestations are too difficult to grasp. If you tell him to see God in the mother, he will say, "Is God so simple?" But if the Lord appears before you with

His dazzling splendour, will you be able to stand the sight? Kunti[3] wished to see the sun-god face to face, but when he approached her, she could not stand the scorching heat. We cannot bear the Lord with all His power and glory. But we do not accept Him in milder and gentler forms. We cannot digest sweets made from milk and do not relish ordinary milk! These are the symptoms of our wretchedness and doom. Such a sick mind is a great obstacle that prevents us from seeing Him. We must discard this state of mind.

51. God in human form

7. The first and the foremost form of the Lord for us is our mother. The Veda says, 'मातृदेवो भव ।' ('Let your mother be your God.') Who but the mother does the new-born baby see first? The Lord Himself stands there as the embodiment of tenderness. We can move on from the worship of the mother to the worship of Mother India and still further to the worship of Mother Earth. But in the beginning the mother is the highest form in which the Lord appears before the child. It is quite possible to attain *moksha* through the worship of the mother. Worship of the mother means worship of the Lord as love incarnate; the mother is just the medium. The Lord endows her with His affection and impels her to toil for her child. The poor mother does not understand why she feels so much love and affection for the child. Does she do everything for the child with the calculation that it might be of use to her in her old age? Not at all.

---

[3] The mother of Pandavas and the aunt of Lord Krishna.

She undergoes labour pains while giving birth to the child. That pain makes her passionately attached to her child. That pain makes her love the child. She just cannot help loving it. The mother is the embodiment of boundless service. To worship her is the highest form of the worship of the Lord. It is as 'Mother' that we should address the Lord. Is there a word nobler and more exalted than this? Mother is the most prominent and the simplest manifestation of the Lord that we come across. Learn to see God in her; and then in the father and in the teacher. The teacher imparts knowledge to us, makes of us human beings in the true sense. How indebted are we to him! Thus, we should start with seeing God in the conspicuous forms of the mother, the father, the teacher and the saints, in this order. Where else can we see Him if not there?

8. Likewise, how nice would it be if we could see Him in children! Dhruva, Prahlad, Nachiketa, Sanak, Sanandan, Sanatkumar – all these were children, but Vyasa and other authors of the Puranas (the ancient mythological tales) are so fond of them that they are never tired of talking about them, of extolling them with love and admiration. Even as children Shuka, Shankaracharya, Jnanadeva were free from desires and attachment. Nowhere else did the Lord manifest Himself in a purer form. Jesus was greatly fond of children. Once his disciples asked him, "You talk so much about the Kingdom of God. Who can enter it?" Jesus lifted up in his arms a child standing nearby and said, "Only those who are like this child." What Jesus

said is indeed true. Saint Ramdas was once playing with children. Someone asked him with surprise, "What has happened to you today?" Ramdas said,

'वयें पोर ते थोर होऊन गेले ।
वयें थोर ते चोर होऊन ठेले'

('Children have attained greatness, while those advanced in age have proved to be scoundrels.')

As the age advances, innocence gets eroded. Then one hardly thinks of the Lord. The minds of children are pure and unsullied. We teach a child, "Do not tell lies." He asks, "What is a lie?" Then we explain that the statement must correspond to the facts. The child is nonplussed. How can one make a statement that does not correspond to the facts? It is like telling that a rectangle must be called a rectangle and not a circle. The child is surprised at this teaching. Children are the purest manifestations of God. Adults give them wrong ideas.

In short, if we cannot see the Lord in the mother, the father, the teacher, the saints and the children, we will not be able to see Him in any other form, as these are His best manifestations. One must first learn to recognise Him in His gentler manifestations, wherein divinity is inscribed in bold capital letters – where it is the most conspicuous.

52. God in creation

9. We must first learn to see Him in pure and gentle forms among human beings. Likewise we should also see Him first in His grand and beautiful forms in nature.

10. Look at the divine glow that precedes sunrise on the horizon at the dawn. Vedic sages looked upon it as a goddess and danced in ecstasy while singing her hymns : "O Usha! You are the messenger of the Lord. You are bathed in dew drops. You are the banner of immortality." So captivating and magnificent their descriptions are! The Vedic sage says, "If I do not comprehend Him even after seeing you, the divine messenger, what else can convince me of His presence?" Such is the splendour of Usha at the horizon. But we have no eyes for her.

11. Likewise, look at the sun. To see him is to see the Lord. He keeps on painting an endless variety of pictures on the canvas of the sky. Artists labour hard for months in trying to catch the beauty of the sunrise on the canvas. But rise early in the morning and just have a look at the Lord's art on the horizon. With what can we compare that divine art, that infinite beauty? But who bothers to look at that? The Lord is there with all His splendour; but man, the wretched creature, pulls the sheets over his eyes and continues to snore. The sun says, "You lazy man! I shall not let you sleep any more," and it wakes him up with his warm rays. 'सूर्य आत्मा जगतस्तस्थुषश्च' – the sun is

the soul of all that moves and all that is still. It is the support of everything animate and inanimate. The sages have called it 'Mitra' (the friend). 'मित्रो जनान् यातयति ब्रुवाण: मित्रो दाधार पृथिवीमुत द्याम्' – 'This friend calls out people and makes them work. He sustains the heaven and the earth.' The sun is indeed the support of life. See God in him.

12. And the holy river Ganga! When I was at Kashi (Benares), I used to go and sit alone on her banks in the silent hours of the night. How lovely and pleasing the Ganga is as she flows by! That serene and majestic expanse and the countless stars in the sky reflected therein would make me silent. This holy river has descended from the matted locks of Lord Shiva, that is, from the Himalayan forests. Many kings cast off their kingdoms, considering them no better than a bauble, and performed austerities and penance on its banks for Self-realisation. The sight of that holy river would give me an experience of sheer peace. How can I describe that peace? Words fail in describing it. I would then realise why a Hindu wishes that if he cannot take a bath in the Ganga during his life-time, at least his remains should be immersed in her after death. You may ridicule such sentiments; that does not matter. I find such sentiments sacred and worth cherishing. It is a custom to put a couple of drops of the Ganga-water in the mouth of a dying man. Those drops symbolize God's grace. The Ganga is a form of the Lord. In the form of the Ganga, it is His compassion that is flowing. Like a mother, Mother Ganga cleans us all over, washes off all the impurities

of our body and mind. If you do not find the Lord in the Ganga, where else could you find Him? The sun, the rivers, the majestic roaring ocean, all these are forms of the Lord.

13. And the winds! Whence they come and where they go, nobody knows. They are the messengers of the Lord. In India, winds blow from the unmoving Himalayas in the north as well as from the serene ocean in the south. These holy winds touch us and awaken us. They whisper melodies in our ears. But who cares to hear their message? If the jailor withholds an ordinary letter addressed to you, you feel dejected. Poor wretch! What is there so precious in that letter? The winds are bringing the Lord's loving messages every moment. Listen to them.

14. The Veda has prescribed fire-worship. Fire (Agni) too is a form of God. How bright and blazing it is! When you rub two wooden sticks against each other, it reveals itself. Who knows where it was hidden till then? It is so full of warmth and luminous! The very first hymn in the RigVeda, in fact, is about fire-worship –

‘अग्निमीळे पुरोहितं यज्ञस्य देवमृत्विजम् । होतारं रत्नधातमम् ।।’

Look at the fire, with whose worship the Veda begins. The flames of fire remind me of the quest of the human soul to reach up to the Lord. The flames may be from a kitchen stove or they may belong to a forest fire – they are always striving to go upwards. They are always agitated and restless. Scientists may say that their fluttering is due to ether or air-pressure. But I see in it their quest to reach the Supreme Spirit, to reach the sun-god who is the ocean of luminosity. It is a quest of the part to merge into the whole. The endless quest of the flames starts with their creation and ceases only on their extinction. That the sun is too distant never bothers them; all they know is to make the best possible effort. It appears that the bright and glowing heat of *vairagya* has assumed the form of the fire. The flame of *vairagya* also does not remain still wherever it is. That is why the Veda began with the word 'अग्निमीळे'.

53. God in the animals

15. And the cattle that serve us! How full of love, tenderness and affection the cow is! In the evening it rushes to its calf over hills and through forests. The Vedic sages are reminded of heavy-uddered cows rushing to their calves to feed them when they see rivers gushing through hilly ranges. The sage says to a river, "O Goddess, like cows, you bring milk-like holy and sweet water. Just as cows cannot stay back in the forest, you too cannot stay back in the hills. You rush to meet your thirsty children." 'वाश्रा इव धेनव: स्यंदमाना:' ('The waters rushed to the sea like the loving cows eager to meet their calves'). The Lord is there at your door in the form of the affectionate cow.

16. And the horse! How noble, how faithful, how loyal it is! How dearly the Arabs love their horses! Do you know the story of the Arab who was compelled

by financial difficulties to sell his horse? He went to the stable with the bagful of money received as its price. But the moment he glanced at the serene and loving eyes of the horse, he threw away the money and said, "Come what may. Let me die of hunger if I must. But I will not sell the horse. God will help me." How the horse snorts when we pat its back! How lovely its mane is! Indeed, the horse has many qualities. What is there in a bicycle? Look after a horse well, and it will be ready to die for you; it will become your friend. A friend of mine was learning to ride, but the horse would not let him mount it. When he complained about it, I told him, "You try to ride the horse, but do you ever care for it? When someone else looks after the horse and you want to ride it, how will it work? Rub it down, give it food and water, and then try." The friend did accordingly. He came to me after a few days and said, "Now the horse does not throw me off." The horse too is a form of the Lord. Will the Lord throw off His devotee? That horse yielded to my friend's devotion. A horse does see whether the rider is a devotee or not. Lord Krishna used to look after the horses Himself. Unlike a bicycle, a horse jumps over ditches and ascends the hills. The graceful and loving horse is verily a form of God.

17. In my childhood, I was at Baroda. There I used to hear a lion's resonant roar in the morning. That majestic sound would move my heart. It used to reverberate in the depth of my heart like the sound in the sanctum sanctorum of a temple. How gallant

and benign the lion looks! It has a regal gait and elegance. Its beautiful mane appears like a royal insignia. That lion in Baroda was caged. It would roam inside that cage. There was not a trace of cruelty in its eyes; they were rather full of pity. It appeared absorbed within itself, totally unconcerned with the world. One feels that such a lion must indeed be a manifestation of the Lord. In my childhood, I had read the story of Androcles and the lion. How fascinating it is! The famished lion remembered Androcles' kindness and, instead of devouring him, began to lick his feet lovingly. What does this mean? This means that Androcles had seen the Lord in the lion. Lord Shiva is always accompanied by a lion. The lion is a manifestation of the Lord.

18. And is the tiger less fascinating? Divine brilliance shines through it. It is not impossible to befriend it. Panini, the great grammarian, was teaching his students in the forest when a tiger came there. The students shouted in alarm, *'vyaghra, vyaghra'* (Tiger, Tiger)! But Panini calmly began explaining to them the etymology of the word *'vyaghra'* (tiger) : 'व्याजिघ्रतीति व्याघ्र:' – *vyaghra* is one having an acute sense of smell. The students had got frightened, but to Panini, *'vyaghra'* was just an innocent and interesting word. The tiger ate him up. But so what? What is striking is that Panini did not run away. He was a devotee of God in the form of words. For him, God was in everything, even in that tiger. That is why he is reverentially referred to as 'Lord Panini' in the commentaries, and his contribution is acknowledged with deep gratitude:

'अज्ञानान्धस्य लोकस्य ज्ञानाञ्जनशलाकया ।
चक्षुरुन्मीलितं येन तस्मै पाणिनये नमः:'

('We bow to Panini who opened the eyes of the people, blind with ignorance, by putting the collyrium of knowledge in them.')

Jnanadeva has said,

'घरा येवो पां स्वर्ग । कां वरिपडो व्याघ्र
परी आत्मबुद्धीसी भंग । कदा नोहे'

('Let heaven descend to his house, or a tiger attack him, he remains anchored in the Self.')

Panini had reached such a stage. He had realized that a tiger too was a manifestation of the Lord.

19. This is true of the snake too. People are very much afraid of it. But look, how scrupulously clean and beautiful it is! In its stern regard for cleanliness, it is comparable to an orthodox *Brahmin*. Dirty *Brahmins* are, however, in abundance; but has anybody ever seen a dirty snake? A snake is like a hermit living in solitude. It looks like a pure, bright and charming garland. Why should one be afraid of it? In fact, our ancestors have prescribed snake-worship.[4] You may call it an idiotic superstitious practice in Hinduism, but anyway it is there. In my childhood, on the *Nagpanchami* day, I would draw a snake with

---

[4] The snakes are worshipped on *Nagpanchami*, the fifth day in the month of *Shravana*.

sandalwood paste for my mother to worship. I would tell her, "Nice pictures of snakes are available in the market." But she would say, "They are no good. What is drawn by my child is the best for me." What does the snake-worship mean? Is it craziness? Let us think over it. In the month of *Shravana* (in the rainy season), the snake comes as a guest to our house, as its habitat is swamped by water. What can the poor creature do then? This sage-like, solitude-loving creature wants to give you the least possible trouble and therefore coils itself taking minimum space. But we go after its blood. Does it behove us to kill a guest in difficulty? It is said of Saint Francis that he would call the snakes in the forest and they would come and play and crawl all over his body. Do not disbelieve this. Love does have such a power. The snakes are said to be poisonous. But is man less so? A snake bites very rarely; it never bites without provocation. Nine out of ten snakes, at any rate, are non-poisonous. They protect your fields by killing pests that would otherwise destroy the crops. Such a helpful, clean and shining snake, the lover of solitude, is a form of the Lord. Snakes are associated with all our gods in some way or the other. Lord Ganapati wears a snake round His waist, Lord Shiva has it round His neck and Lord Vishnu reclines on a snake for a bed. Try to understand the secret of it. All this means that the Lord has manifested Himself in the snake too. Get acquainted with Him in that form.

20. How many such examples should I give? I am just illustrating a point. The essence of the Ramayana

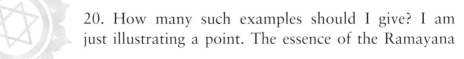

lies in such fascinating ideas. In the Ramayana, there is depiction of love between father and son, between mother and son, between brother and brother, between husband and wife. But it is dear to me not because of that, but because of Rama's friendship with the *vanaras* (monkeys). Now it is said that the *vanaras* were humans belonging to the Naga tribe. It is the job of the historians to dig up the past and make such discoveries. I do not intend to join issue with them. But why should it be impossible for Rama to befriend the monkeys? Rama's greatness and the charm of His personality lie precisely in this friendship. Similar is the relationship between Krishna and the cows. Worship of Krishna is based on that relationship. In every picture of Krishna we find Him surrounded by the cows. He is adored as Gopalkrishna (Krishna the cowherd.) Krishna without the company of cows and Rama without the company of *vanaras* are simply inconceivable. Rama saw God in the *vanaras* and made friends with them. This is the key to the Ramayana. Without it you would miss the charm in it. You would find the depiction of relationship between parents and children elsewhere too, but the beautiful relationship between *nara* and *vanara* – men and monkeys – is found only in the Ramayana. The Ramayana made us realize that there is God in the monkeys too. The sages admired the monkeys fondly. Those monkeys would travel from Ramtek to the Krishna river,[5] skipping from tree to tree, without ever touching the ground. Such dense forests and the monkeys playing therein

---

[5] Ramtek is over 800 kms. from the river Krishna. All that area was covered with dense forest in the time of the Ramayana.

with gay abandon would move the sages to write poetry. In an Upanishad, *Brahman* (God) is described as having eyes like a monkey. A monkey's eyes are restless; they are always watching everything around. *Brahman*'s eyes ought to be like them. God cannot sit still with closed eyes; we may. If God sits still, what will happen to the world? In the monkey's eyes the sages see the eyes of the *Brahman* watching all of us solicitously. Learn to see God in a monkey.

21. And what about the peacock! Peacocks are rare in Maharashtra, but Gujarat has them in plenty. I am habituated to walking ten to twelve miles daily. While in Gujarat, I used to see a lot of peacocks during my walks. When the clouds gather in the sky and the rain looks imminent, the peacock gives a call. To hear that cry emerging from the depths of its heart is a stirring experience. Our whole science of music is based on the note of that cry – the *shadja*. *Shadja* is the basic note of the Indian system of music. The peacock, with its eyes raised towards the rain-heavy clouds, gives a deep-throated cry and spreads its plumage the moment the clouds begin to thunder. It certainly is a bewitching sight. The beauty and elegance of that plumage is enough to humble man's pride. Kings may bedeck themselves with all the fineries, but they cannot excel a peacock. Its plumage with innumerable shades of colours is indeed a piece of marvellous artistry. Enjoy its beauty and also see God therein. The whole creation is bedecked in such a fascinating way. The Lord is there all around; but we, wretched creatures, fail to behold him. Tukaram has said, 'देव आहे सुकाळ

देशीं, अभाग्यासी दुर्भिक्ष ॥' – The Lord is everywhere, but to the wretched He is elusive. For the saints there is prosperity everywhere, while for us there is famine.

22. How can one forget the cuckoo? Whom does it call? In the summer, rivers and streams dry up, but tender green leaves sprout on trees. Does it ask, 'Who brought about this marvel? Where is its creator?' How intense and sweet is its voice! A religious observance named *kokilavrata* has been prescribed in Hinduism. Women observing this *vrata* take food only after hearing the cuckoo's voice. This observance teaches us to see the Lord in the cuckoo. The cuckoo seems to be chanting the Upanishads in its melodious voice. One hears its voice, but it remains hidden. The poet Wordsworth was so enchanted by the cuckoo that he would wander in the forest in search of it. The great poet of England is mad after a cuckoo; but in India, even ordinary housewives do not take food without hearing its voice. This *kokilavrata* has put ordinary Indian women at par with the great poet! To hear the cuckoo's sweet singing is the height of joy. The Lord has manifested Himself in the form of the cuckoo also.

23. A cuckoo is worthy of admiration; is a crow less so? I like it very much. Its call may be shrill; still it has its own sweetness. How nice a crow looks when it arrives flapping its wings! Little children are particularly attracted to it. A child does not like to take his food within the four walls of the house. You have to take him into the open yard and make him eat by turning his attention towards crows and

sparrows. Is this attraction of a child for a crow a sign of craziness? No. Rather, it is a sign of wisdom. A child instantly identifies itself with the Lord manifested in the crow. A mother may try in many ways to persuade him to eat; the child remains stubborn. But he gets absorbed in observing the crow flapping its wings, and eats unmindfully what the mother puts into his mouth. Aesop's fables are based on the child's curiosity about the creation. Aesop saw the Lord everywhere. If I prepare a list of the books I like, Aesop's Fables would be on the top of that list. Aesop's world does not have human beings only; it has also foxes, dogs, hares, wolves, crows, tortoises etc. The whole creation speaks to Aesop. He has a divine vision. The Ramayana too is based on that vision. Tulsidas, while describing Rama's childhood, has narrated a little incident. Rama, playing in the courtyard, tries to catch a crow nearby, but in vain. Then Rama hits upon an idea. He takes a piece of sweet in his hands and lures the crow. Tulsidas has written verse after verse describing such an ordinary incident. Why? Because the crow too is a form of the Lord. God that is in Rama is there in that crow too. The acquaintance between Rama and the crow is one between two manifestations of the Supreme Self.

54. Seeing God in the evil too

24. To sum up, God is everywhere in the universe. As holy rivers, high mountains, serene oceans, tender-hearted cows, noble horses, majestic lions, sweet-voiced cuckoos, beautiful peacocks, clean and solitude-loving snakes, crows flapping their wings, the upward-rising

flames, the still stars – He is pervading the whole creation in different forms. We should train our eyes to see Him everywhere, first in simple forms and then in the complex ones. We should first learn simple letters and then the complex 'joint' letters. Until we learn the 'joint' letters, there is no progress in reading. Unless we are able to see God manifest in crooked forms, our progress will be hampered. At every step, we shall come across the 'joint' letters. We shall come across crooked and evil forms every now and then. In the end, we must learn to see God in them too. God in Rama is readily acceptable, but we must also comprehend divinity in Ravana. God in Prahlad is readily acceptable, but we must also comprehend divinity in Hiranyakashipu.[6] The Veda has said, 'नमो नमः स्तेनानां पतये नमो नमः... नमः पुंजिष्ठेभ्यो ... नमो निषादेभ्यः:...' 'ब्रह्म दाशा ब्रह्म दासा, ब्रह्मैवेमे कितवाः:' – 'Salutation to the robber chieftain, salutations to the cruel and the violent. The robbers, the cruel, the swindlers, all are *Brahman*. Salutations to them all.'

What does this mean? This means that after mastering the small letters, we should master the capital letters; after mastering the simple, we should master the complex. Carlyle has written a book on hero-worship. Therein he has called Napoleon a hero. God in him is not in a pure form, there is a mixture; but we must discern Him there too. That is why Tulsidas has called Ravana 'Rama's devotee in opposition.' Ravana

---

[6] Hiranyakashipu, the demon king, was the father of Prahlad, a devote of Lord Vishnu. He tried to kill his own son for worshipping his arch-enemy, but failed in every attempt. Lord Vishnu finally killed him, assuming the form of Narasimha (the lion-man).

too is a devotee, albeit of a different type. Fire burns and causes swelling in the burnt part of the body, but the swelling subsides after fomentation, that is, after using a different form of the same element. Different forms of the same element thus do different things. Rama and Ravana are manifestations of one and the only God, although appearances differ.

Gross and subtle, simple and complex, small letters and capital letters – learn everything and realise in the end that there is no place where the Lord is not present. He is present in every atom. He pervades the whole universe. The Lord who cares equally for all, who is full of knowledge and wisdom, love, compassion, power, beauty and holiness, is everywhere all around us.

(24.4.32)

CHAPTER 11

Vision of the Cosmic form of God

55. Arjuna's eagerness to behold the cosmic form of God.

1. Brothers, last week we learnt how to recognise divine presence in the countless things in this universe and how to let that comprehension sink deep into us. We saw that one should discern divinity step by step, first in the simple and the gross and then in the complex and the subtle manifestations of the Lord. One should thus see God everywhere, realise Him and through constant practice, learn to see the whole creation as the Self.

Now we turn to the Eleventh Chapter. In this Chapter the Lord has showered His highest grace on Arjuna by showing him His divine cosmic form. Arjuna had expressed a desire to see the Lord in His fullness, in the form in which all His splendour and glory are fully manifest. What Arjuna sought was to behold the cosmic form of the Lord.

2. Our world is only a small part of the universe, and we do not have an adequate understanding of even this small part. In relation to the universe this world, which appears so vast to us, is quite insignificant. If we look up at the night sky, we see it dotted with innumerable points of light. Do you know the real nature of those festoons of light hung up in the sky, those lovely little flowers, those millions of twinkling stars? They are actually many times bigger and brighter than the sun. And they are countless. Even the naked eye can see thousands of them; a telescope would

reveal them in millions. With an advanced telescope, trillions could be visible. There seems to be no end to them. Our earth is but a tiny fragment of this boundless creation; still we find it so vast!

3. This vast creation is but one aspect of the Lord. Another aspect is that of time. If we consider the past, our knowledge of history goes back at most to ten thousand years. Of the future, we know nothing. The span of known history is ten thousand years, and our own lifespan is of hardly hundred years! Time is, in fact, without beginning and without end. It is impossible to count the time that has passed into the past. It is equally impossible to have any idea of the time that is yet to come. Just as our world is insignificant compared to the universe, the ten thousand years of known history are insignificant compared to the infinite time. The past is without a beginning and the future is without an end. As for the infinitesimal present, it is slipping into the past every moment. Even as we try to point out its presence, it has already passed into the past. This fleeting present is all that is with us. I am speaking now, but the moment I utter a word, it becomes a part of the past. The stream of time is flowing continuously. We know neither its beginning nor its end. What comes to our view is just a tiny portion of that stream in the middle.

4. Thus, when we look at the creation we find a vast expanse of space on one hand, and on the other there is flow of time that has neither beginning nor end. It

then becomes clear that howsoever much we stretch our imagination, we can never see the limits of it. In Arjuna's mind arises a desire to have a vision of the Lord in His omnipresent and all-pervading form, the form that fills all the three-dimensional space and all the three-dimensional time. He wants to see Him all at once, at the same moment. This Chapter has its genesis in that desire.

5. Arjuna was very dear to the Lord; so dear that, in the Tenth Chapter, while mentioning different manifestations in which He is to be contemplated, the Lord has said, "Among the Pandavas, contemplate Me in the form of Arjuna." Can love ever be more crazy? This is the height of madness in love. The Lord's love for Arjuna knew no bounds. The Eleventh Chapter is the blessed gift of that love. The Lord endowed Arjuna with the divine vision and fulfilled his desire to see His cosmic form.

56. Full vision even in a small image

6. This Chapter contains the beautiful and magnificent description of that Supreme divine form. However, I am not particularly enamoured of it. I am quite happy with the small and lovable form which I see. I have learnt to appreciate the beauty therein. The Lord is not made up of a number of parts. It does not appear to me that what I see is only a part and the rest of Him is somewhere else. The Lord who pervades this vast universe is present in His fullness in a small image; and even in a speck of dust. He is not a bit less there. An ocean of nectar and a drop

therein have the same sweetness. I am inclined to enjoy the sweetness in the little drop of nectar that I have got. I have purposely chosen the example of nectar and not that of milk or water. The sweetness that is in a cup of milk is certainly there in a jar of milk; but the nourishment they provide is not the same. But such is not the case with nectar. Even a drop of nectar will make you immortal.

In the same way, the divinity and sanctity that are present in the Lord's Supreme form are there even in a small image. If I cannot judge the quality of wheat from the sample of a handful of grains, how can I judge its quality from a sackful of it? If I fail to recognise Him in His small form that is before my eyes, how can I recognise Him in His cosmic form? Hence I am not eager to have the vision of His cosmic form; nor am I worthy, like Arjuna, to ask for it. Moreover, what I see is not a part of the cosmic form. We would not have an idea about the whole of a photograph from its fragment. But the Lord is not made up of parts. He has not been cut up and divided into fragments. He is fully there even in a small form. What is the difference between a small photograph and its enlarged copy? Everything that is there in the big photograph is there in the small photograph too. The latter is not a fragment of the big photograph. A word may be printed in big type or small type; this makes no difference as far as its meaning is concerned. Image-worship has its basis in this way of thinking.

7. Many people have assailed image-worship. Many thinkers from India and abroad have found fault with it. But the more I think of it, the more I realise its beauty. What does it signify? It is the art of learning to experience the whole universe in a small object. Is it not right to learn to see the whole universe in a small village? It is not mere fancy; it is a matter of experience. That which inheres in the cosmic form is there in a small image as well. The world is in a grain of sand. In a small theatre troupe, the same set of actors play a variety of roles. The Lord does likewise. Like a playwright who acts in a play written by him, the Lord writes innumerable plays and enacts innumerable roles in them. Recognising Him in one role is as good as recognising Him fully.

8. The basis of image-worship is the same as that of similes and metaphors in poetry. A circle or a sphere is nice to see, as there is order and symmetry in it, and these are divine attributes. The Lord's creation is beautiful in all respects. There is order and harmony in it. A sphere symbolises the shapeliness of the Lord. A twisted and disorderly tree in a forest is also His manifestation; therein you find the Lord's freedom. That tree knows no constraints; and it is true of the Lord as well. The unconstrained and self-willed Lord is there in that unshapely tree. A straight column shows His straightness. In a pillar with decorative engraving we see the Lord who decorates the sky with stars. We see His restraint in a well-laid out garden and in a primeval forest we see His freedom and grandeur. We experience joy in a forest as well as in

a well-maintained garden. Is it strange? No. It happens because divine attributes are visible in both of them. An image may be smooth or misshapen; nevertheless, the divinity therein is the same. I would not, therefore, mind if I could not get to see the cosmic form of the Lord apart from His presence in the creation.

9. It is because the Lord is present in different objects as different attributes that we find joy in them and feel a kind of relationship with them. The joy is not without a cause; it is there because we are somehow related to them. A child is a source of joy to his mother, as she knows the kinship. So, relate every object to the Lord. Realise that the Lord within you is there in that object too. As this realisation grows, your joy too will increase. There is no other source of real joy. Start establishing relationships of love and see the wonderful results. You will then see in every speck of dust the Lord who is immanent in the whole creation. Once one gains this realisation, what more would one ask for? But, for this purpose, the sense organs must be disciplined and trained. When the lust for sensual pleasures gives way to the pure spirit of love, you will find Him and Him only in each and every object. There is a beautiful description of the colour of the Self in an Upanishad. What could be its colour? The sage says lovingly, 'यथा अयं इंद्रगोप:' ('The Self is like an *indragop*').[1] The sight of an *indragop* fills us with immense joy. Why? Because that which

---

[1] *Indragop* is an extremely beautiful insect with bright red velvet-like skin. It appears at the beginning of the rainy season.

exists in me exists in the *indragop* too. Had there been no relation with it, I would not have felt such joy. The *indragop* too has the same beautiful soul that I have. That is why the simile of *indragop* is given. Why do we use similes? Why do we find joy in them? A simile pleases us as there is some similarity between the objects compared; otherwise it would not be pleasing. If somebody says that salt is like pepper, we would call him crazy; but if somebody says that the stars are like flowers, we see the likeness and appreciate the simile. We find nothing common between salt and pepper; but if someone's vision has become broad enough to see that the Lord who is present in salt is present in the pepper too, he would be delighted with the statement 'salt is like pepper.' What all this means is that everything in the world is filled with the Lord's presence. To realise this, one need not have the vision of the cosmic form.

57. Vision of the cosmic form is difficult to bear

10. Besides, how can I bear the vision of that cosmic form? That form may not perhaps give rise to the same feelings of love and tender intimacy that I have for a small, beautiful and *saguna* form. It happened with Arjuna too. He started trembling and beseeched the Lord to assume the familiar and lovable form again. Arjuna is thus cautioning us from his own experience that we should not have the desire to see the cosmic form. It is good for us that the Lord has pervaded the entire three-dimensional space and three-dimensional time. If He were to condense Himself and appear before us as a glowing and fiercely hot

ball of fire, what would our plight be? The distant stars appear tranquil. They seem to speak to us. But what would happen if a star that soothes the eye from afar were to approach us closely? It is a ball of fire which is sure to burn us down. Let all things in the cosmos remain where they are; what is the sense in bringing all of them in a single room? One feels strange in watching thousands of pigeons packed in a small aviary. What freedom do they have? It is good that the creation is spread all over the space.

11. What is true of space is true of time too. We do not remember the past and have no idea of the future; and that is good for us. The Holy Koran has mentioned five things which are exclusively under the control of God, and man can do nothing about them. Knowledge of the future is one of those things. We can at best make a guess; but a guess is not knowledge. It is indeed a happy situation that we do not have knowledge of the future and forget most of the past. Even if a bad man becomes good, we remember his past and do not respect him. We cannot forget his past sins, howsoever hard he may try to convince us about his transformation. It is only when the person dies and is reborn in a different form that the world will forget his sins.

Remembrance of the past distorts the mind. All our problems will be solved when all the memories and perceptions of the past are forgotten. There must be some way of forgetting both the sinful and meritorious deeds. Death is such a way. When we cannot endure the suffering in this birth, why rake up the muck of the past births? Is the muck in this birth not enough? We even forget most of our childhood years. It is good that we forget our past. For instance, the only means to achieve Hindu-Muslim unity is to forget the past. Yes, Aurangzeb did commit atrocities; but how long are we going to harp on them? There is a famous *garba* song by Ratanbai in Gujarati. It says at the end, "In this world, the good that the people achieve will be remembered; their sins will be forgotten." Time is sifting everybody's deeds. We should take only what is good from history and cast off what is evil. It would indeed be wonderful if one remembers the good only. But alas! It does not happen. Hence forgetting is extremely necessary. God has created death for this purpose.

12. In short, the world, as it is, is auspicious. There is no need to pack this vast world of time and space into a little spot. Excessive familiarity is not good. We should be intimate with some things and maintain a distance from some things. We respectfully keep a distance from the teacher, but would love to sit in the mother's lap. There is an appropriate way to behave with anybody and deal with anything. A flower may be taken in the hand, but fire should be kept away. The beauty of the stars can be admired from a distance only. It is true for all creation. It is not that something that gives delight from afar will give more delight when brought near. Let the things remain where they are. It is in our interest to let them be at a proper distance, appreciate them from a distance

and derive joy from them, rather than trying to bring them near in a clumsy and overbearing manner for the sake of excessive familiarity.

13. Thus, it is good that we do not live in Time in all its aspects – past, present and future. Knowledge of all of it is not necessarily pleasing or beneficial. Arjuna beseeched the Lord with love, and He fulfilled his desire by revealing to him His cosmic form. But for us, His small form is sufficient. It is not, after all, a part of the Lord; the whole of the Lord is present therein. Even if it is only a part, I would consider myself blessed if I could have a glimpse of even that part. This is what experience has taught me. When Jamnalalji Bajaj opened the Laxminarayan temple at Wardha to the untouchables, I was there. My gaze was fixed on the image for some fifteen or twenty minutes. I was as it were in a state of *samadhi*. Beholding the Lord's image from top to toe, my eyes finally rested at His feet. There was no thought in my mind except 'गोड तुझी चरण-सेवा' ('Sweet indeed is Your humble service!'). If the great Lord cannot be contained in a small form, it is enough to behold His feet. Arjuna pleaded for the vision of the cosmic form. He was worthy of asking for it. How intimate was his relationship with the Lord! What claims can I have? If I could see His feet, it is enough for me; I deserve nothing more.

58. The Quintessence of the Gita

14. I am not at all inclined to use my reason or intellect in analysing the description of that divine cosmic form; that would be a sacrilege. We should instead recite those holy verses again and again and purify ourselves. To analyse the cosmic form would be a monstrosity. It would be like following in the footsteps of the *aghorpanthis* who go to the cremation grounds and mutilate the corpses to gain occult powers. We should instead recite those holy verses that describe the Lord's grand and infinite form, which has also been described as 'विश्वतश्चक्षुरुत विश्वतोमुख: विश्वतोबाहुरुत विश्वतस्पात्'[2] ('The one whose eyes are everywhere, whose mouths are everywhere, whose hands are everywhere, whose legs are everywhere - -') and make our mind sinless and pure.

15. In this description, there is only one point at which the mind begins to think. The Lord has said to Arjuna, "All these warriors are going to die. Be only an occasion, an instrument. I have already slain them." These words keep ringing in the ears. When the idea that I should become His instrument arises in the mind, one begins to think. How to do it? How could I become the Lord's flute? To become His flute, I shall have to become hollow; then only He can produce sweet tunes through me. I shall have to be free from all passions, vices and evil propensities. If I am fully stuffed with them, how can He play

---

[2] RigVeda, Mandal 10.

melodious tunes through me? I am stuffed with ego.
I must purge myself of that and become hollow. But,
in fact, it is preposterous of me to aspire to become
His flute. Even if I wish to become the sandals on
His feet, it is not easy. The sandals should not pinch
or otherwise cause any pain to His feet. So I would
have to become soft to such an extent. I would have
to protect His feet from the thorns. I would have to
cure myself to be firm and strong, yet supple and soft.
It is not thus easy to become His sandals. If I want
to become His weapon, I must not just be a lump of
iron; I must sharpen myself through penance so that
I could become a sword in His hands. This thought
reverberates in my mind and I lose myself in it.

16. The Lord has Himself told us, in the last verse of
this Chapter, how to do it, how this can come about.
Shankaracharya has, in his commentary on the Gita,
called this verse 'the quintessence of the Gita' –

'मत्कर्मकृन्मत्परमो मद्भक्त: सङ्गवर्जित: ।
निर्वैर: सर्वभूतेषु य: स मामेति पाण्डव ।।'

He who is free from enmity to all creatures, who is
ever engrossed in serving the world impartially without
any expectations, who dedicates all his actions to the
Lord, who is full of devotion, who forgives all and is
detached and full of love, becomes an instrument of
the Lord. This is the essence of the Gita's teaching.

(1.5.32)

CHAPTER 12

Saguna and *Nirguna bhakti*

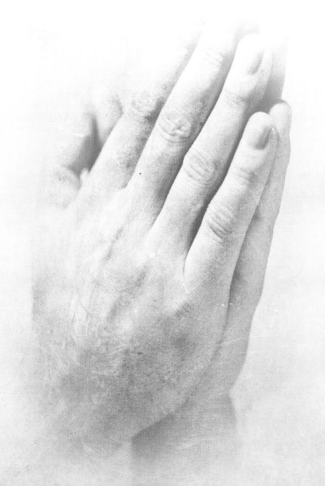

59. Chapters 6 to 11 : From one-pointedness to totality

1. Brothers, the waters of the river Ganga are holy everywhere, but some places on her banks like Haridwar, Kashi (Benares) and Prayag (Allahabad) are considered particularly holy. They have blessed the whole world. The Gita too is holy from the beginning to the end, still some of its Chapters have special holiness like the places of pilgrimage. The Chapter on which I am going to talk today is one such Chapter. The Lord Himself has described it as the nectar : 'ये तु धर्म्यामृतमिदं यथोक्तं पर्युपासते ।'. This is a small Chapter with only twenty verses; but it is as sweet and life-giving as a spring of nectar. The Lord has Himself eulogised here the greatness of *bhakti*.

2. In fact, the principle of *bhakti* has been introduced in the Sixth Chapter itself. The first five Chapters deal with the science of life. They deal with *karma* (in the form of performance of *swadharma*), *vikarma* (the mental *sadhana*, the inner complementary process which helps that *karma*) and the final state of *akarma* that results from their confluence and burns to ashes all the *karma*. With this, the exposition of the science of life is complete. In one sense, it is the principle of *bhakti* that has been discussed thereafter from the Sixth Chapter to the Eleventh. The Sixth Chapter tells us how to have one-pointedness of mind and discusses the means therefor and the need for it. The Eleventh Chapter presents the complete and holistic vision. Let us now see how we have made the long journey from one-pointedness to this vision.

Beginning was made with one-pointedness of mind. Once this is achieved, one becomes capable of pursuing any study. One-pointedness of mind can be utilized for the study of any subject with good results. But such a study is not the highest goal of the concentration of mind. The study of mathematics, for example, does not fully test the concentration of mind. Concentration of mind can surely help in achieving proficiency in mathematics or any other branch of knowledge, but this is not its true test. Hence it was recommended in the Seventh Chapter that we should concentrate our mind on the feet of the Lord. The Eighth Chapter exhorts us to try continuously, till the moment of death, to be at the feet of the Lord with all the sense organs devoted to Him and the whole being dedicated to His service. All our sense organs must be trained to serve this one purpose. 'पडिलें वळण इंद्रियां सकळां । भाव तो निराळा नाहीं दुजा ।।' ('All the senses have become used to devotion; there is nothing else in the mind.') – This is what should happen. All the senses should be madly in love of the Lord. Those around us may be wailing or singing hymns, they may be absorbed in weaving webs of desires and passions, or one may be in the company of saintly persons; whatever may be the condition, the senses should be trained by constant practice in such a way that the thought of the Lord would be in mind at the moment of death. This lesson of constancy has been given in the Eighth Chapter. To sum up, there is teaching of concentration of mind in the Sixth Chapter, that of *prapatti* or concentration directed to the Lord in the Seventh, of the *yoga* of ceaseless striving in the Eighth and that of dedication to the Lord in the Ninth Chapter. The Tenth Chapter tells us how to proceed step by step to grasp gradually that the Lord is pervading the entire creation right from an ant to the creator of all beings. The Eleventh Chapter presents the complete and holistic vision. I call this vision of the cosmic form the *yoga* of totality. This vision essentially means realising that the whole world is contained in a grain of sand. This is the complete and total vision. The element of *bhakti* has thus been examined from different angles from the Sixth to the Eleventh Chapter.

60. The saguna and the nirguna devotee

3. This discussion of *bhakti* is going to be completed in the Twelfth Chapter. Arjuna has asked a question here, which is similar to what he had asked in the Fifth Chapter, when the exposition of the science of life was concluded. He asks : "Some devotees worship you in *saguna* form while others worship you in *nirguna*[1] form. Whom do you like more?"

4. What answer could the Lord give? It is just like asking a mother having two sons, "Whom do you love more?" The younger son is a little child, deeply attached to his mother. He is happy only in her company and is restive if she is out of sight even for a moment. He cannot bear separation from her. Without her, the world is like a big void for him. The elder son too is full of love for the mother, but he is grown up and mature. He can stay away from her. He serves her and takes all the burden and responsibility upon himself. Being absorbed in work, he can endure

---

[1] Please refer footnote in Chapter 5.28.

separation from her. He is admired by the world and his reputation pleases his mother. If you tell this mother that she can have only one of these two sons and she will have to choose between them, what could she do? How can she make a choice? Try to understand her plight. She will be totally nonplussed and may mumble, "I can bear separation from the elder one if I cannot help it." It is more difficult for her to tear away the younger son from her bosom. His special attachment to her will weigh with her and she may reply accordingly. But it cannot be said to be the real answer to the question as to which of the two sons is dearer to her. She will reply, if she must; but it would not be proper to take her words literally.

5. The Lord has been put exactly in the same predicament. Arjuna asks the Lord, "O Lord! One of the two devotees loves You madly. His mind is riveted on You. His eyes long to see You, his ears are eager to hear Your praise, his hands yearn to serve and worship You. The other one is self-reliant, he has controlled his senses and is ever-absorbed in working for the well-being of all. Engaged in selfless service of the society day and night, he does not even seem to remember You. He has realised oneness with the entire creation. Out of these two, whom do You love more?" The Lord has replied exactly like that mother. He says, "I love the former – the *saguna bhakta* – and the latter too is Mine." The Lord is clearly on the horns of a dilemma. He has somehow given a reply just for the sake of replying.

6. In fact, there is absolutely no difference between these two types of devotees. Both have equal merit. To compare the two is to transgress the limit of propriety. The question that Arjuna had asked in the Fifth Chapter about *karma* has been asked here about *bhakti*. In the Fifth Chapter, it has been told that man attains the state of *akarma* with the help of *karma* and *vikarma* and that the state of *akarma* appears in two forms. The *yogi* works ceaselessly, but does nothing inwardly; while the *sannyasi* sets the world in motion without doing anything outwardly. How to compare these two states? How to compare the two halves of the same sphere? They are completely identical. For the two states of *akarma*, two different terms have been used – *yoga* and *sannyasa* – but they have the same meaning. The question of choice between them has finally been clinched on the ground of relative easiness.

7. The question of choice between *saguna* and *nirguna* is similar. The *saguna* devotee serves the Lord through his organs, whereas the *nirguna* devotee thinks of the good of the whole world. The former appears absorbed in outward service, but his mind is absorbed in the contemplation of the Lord. The latter does not appear to be rendering any concrete service, but he is certainly rendering a great service from within. Which one of these two devotees is superior? These two types of devotees may appear outwardly different, but they are intrinsically one and the same. Both of them are dear to the Lord. But *saguna bhakti* is easier. The answer given here is similar to the one given in the Fifth Chapter.

61. Saguna is easy and safe

8. In the *yoga* of *saguna bhakti* all the organs can be directly employed. They could be either a help or a hindrance or both. Whether they save or destroy depends on the way we look at them. Suppose a man's mother is on her deathbed and he wants to meet her. But there is a distance of fifteen miles between them. There is no motorable road; only a narrow trail passes through a jungle. Now, in this situation, is the trail a means or a hindrance? The man may curse the trail at every step and say, "But for this trail, I would be at my mother's side this moment." For him, the trail is an enemy. He would walk on, as he must, but he will stamp his feet all along with irritation. If he looks upon it as his enemy and sits down in despair, his supposed enemy will conquer him. But if he walks fast, he will overcome it. Another man may say, "The jungle separates me from my mother. But, thank God, at least this narrow trail is there. It will take me to my mother. Otherwise, how could I have crossed this wilderness?" He would consider the trail as a means and walk swiftly along it. He would regard it as a friend and would have gratitude for it. It does not matter what you think of the road; there is no alternative to walking on. It is your attitude and outlook which will decide whether the road is a means or a hindrance. This is true about all our organs.

9. For the *saguna* devotee, they are the means (to realise the Lord). They are like flowers that are to be offered to the Lord. With his eyes he beholds His

form; with his ears, he listens to His praise and His edifying stories; with his mouth, he chants His Name. He uses his legs for pilgrimage and hands to render service. In this way, he dedicates all the organs of perception and action to the Lord. For him, they are no longer the means for enjoyment. The flowers are there to be offered to the Lord; one should not put garlands around one's own neck. Likewise, the organs should be used in the service of the Lord. This is the outlook of the *saguna* devotee. But to a *nirguna* devotee they appear to be a hindrance. He restrains them, starves them, keeps a watch over them. The *saguna* devotee feels no need to do so. He surrenders them at the feet of the Lord. Both these are methods of controlling the organs. Whatever be the way, it is imperative to restrain them and prevent them from wallowing in the pleasures of the senses. But one way is easier while the other one is difficult.

10. *Nirguna* devotee is dedicated to the good of all. This is no ordinary thing; it is easier said than done. One who is absorbed in thinking about the good of the whole world can do nothing else. Hence *nirguna sadhana* is difficult. *Saguna* worship, on the other hand, can be done by anybody according to his capacity. To serve the small village we are born in or to look after our parents is a form of *saguna* worship. Such service should, of course, not go against the interests of the world. No matter how small your service is, it will have the character of *bhakti* if it does not go against the good of others. Otherwise it will be a sort of attachment. The *saguna* worship consists of serving

the parents, the friends, the distressed people and the saints, considering them as forms of the Lord, and is content therein. It is easy. Hence, although both *saguna* and *nirguna bhakti* are essentially the same, *saguna* is preferable on the ground of relative easiness.

11. Apart from the point of easiness, there is one more point. *Nirguna* worship is fraught with some risk. *Nirguna* is all knowledge (*Jnana*). But *saguna* is full of love and tenderness and the warmth of feelings. A devotee is more secure therein. There was a time when I relied much on knowledge, but experience has taught me that knowledge alone is not enough. It does burn down gross impurities in the mind, but is powerless to wash away subtler impurities. Self-reliance, enquiry (into the nature of the Self), discrimination (between the Self and the not-Self), *abhyasa* (constant practice), *vairagya* (detachment and dispassion) – all these means taken together are of little avail here. The subtle impurities can be washed away only by the waters of *bhakti*. Only *bhakti* has the efficacy to do it. You may call it dependence; but it is dependence on nobody else but the Lord. The mind cannot be completely cleansed without His help.

12. Some may say, "You are giving a narrow meaning to the word 'knowledge' (*Jnana*). To hold that knowledge cannot cleanse the mind completely is to undervalue it." This is certainly a valid objection. But my point is that it is hard to attain pure knowledge while encased in the mortal body. The knowledge that we can have while we are in this body is bound to

be somewhat imperfect and incomplete; its power is bound to be limited. Pure knowledge will undoubtedly burn to ashes all the impurities in the mind; and alongwith it, it will burn down the mind itself. But when associated with the weak flesh, its power proves to be inadequate. It cannot therefore wash away subtle impurities. One has to take recourse to *bhakti* for this purpose. A man is therefore more secure in *bhakti*. This is my personal assessment. *Saguna bhakti* is easier, as there is reliance on the Lord whereas in *nirguna bhakti* there is self-reliance. But, after all, what does 'self' in 'self-reliance' mean? It means reliance on the Lord that dwells within us. You cannot find anybody purified solely through reason. Through self-reliance, that is, through knowledge of the Self within, we shall have pure knowledge. Thus, even in the self-reliance of the *nirguna bhakti,* reliance is on the Self.

62. *Without nirguna, saguna is defective*

13. I mentioned easiness and security as two plus points of *saguna* worship. I can mention a few plus points of *nirguna* worship also. In *nirguna*, one remains within limits. To take an example, we establish institutions to undertake various kinds of service. Initially an individual establishes an institution. He is its main pillar. Everything revolves round him. But as the institution grows, it should not remain dependent on a single individual; it should then be guided by principles. Otherwise decline is bound to set in soon after the departure of that individual. To take my favourite illustration, one cannot continue spinning when the belt of the spinning wheel snaps

nor can then one wind up the yarn already spun. This is what happens to the institution when it loses the key person. It, as it were, becomes orphaned. This would not happen if the institution advances from devotedness to an individual, to devotion to principles.

14. *Saguna* needs help from *nirguna*. One must eventually learn to free oneself from attachment to and preoccupation with individuals and outer forms. The Ganga emerges from the Himalayas, from the locks of Lord Shiva, but she does not linger there; leaving that support behind, she flows through the hills and the forests to the plains, and thus benefits the people. In the same way, an institution should be ready to adopt principles as its mainstay in the eventuality of losing the support of the key individual. While constructing an arch, support is given to it; but the support has to be withdrawn later. If the arch remains firmly in place after the support is removed, the support can be said to have done its work. *Saguna* is indeed the source of inspiration, but the ultimate culmination must be in *nirguna,* in commitment to principles. Self-knowledge must ultimately emerge from the womb of devotion. The plant of *bhakti* must blossom into the flower of Self-knowledge.

15. Lord Buddha had realised this. He therefore prescribed three-fold surrender. Initially, one may be loyal to an individual, but that loyalty should, in due course, grow into commitment to principles. If this is not immediately possible, it should at least develop into a commitment to *sangha* (the community of like-minded persons). Respect for one individual should

be replaced by respect for a group of individuals. If there is no love and commitment for the *sangha*, there would be dissensions and conflicts within it. Loyalty to an individual should thus advance to commitment to the community of the like-minded and from that to commitment to the principles. 'बुद्धं शरणं गच्छामि । संघं शरणं गच्छामि । धर्मं शरणं गच्छामि ।' ('I take refuge in Buddha, I take refuge in *sangha*, I take refuge in *dharma*.') – This is the three-fold surrender prescribed in Buddhism. Love for an individual or for a group is shaky. There must eventually be commitment to principles. Then only the institution will be beneficial to the society. Even though the initial source of inspiration is *saguna*, the *saguna* must ultimately reach fruition in *nirguna*. *Saguna* becomes defective in the absence of *nirguna*. *Nirguna* keeps *saguna* balanced and within bounds; and the latter must be thankful for it.

16. There is image-worship, in some form or the other, in all the religions including Hinduism, Islam and Christianity. Although it is not considered the highest form of worship, it has been accepted and respected. As long as it remains within the bounds set by *nirguna*, it remains free from defects. As soon as it crosses these bounds, defects appear in it. This has happened in all the religions – *saguna* therein has degenerated in the absence of restraint from *nirguna*. Animal sacrifice was prevalent in *yajnas* and other rites in ancient times, and even today animals are sacrificed to Goddess Kali. It is a travesty of image-worship. It means that image-worship has crossed the bounds and has gone astray. This risk is averted if *saguna* is restrained by firm commitment to *nirguna*.

63. Complementarity between Saguna and nirguna : Examples from the Ramayana

17. *Saguna* is secure and easy, but it needs *nirguna*. *Saguna* should, in fact, grow and eventually blossom into *nirguna*, into devotion to principles. *Nirguna* and *saguna* are not opposed to each other; in fact, they are complementary. One must advance from *saguna* to *nirguna;* and *nirguna* also needs the warmth of *saguna* to remove subtle impurities from the mind. They thus enrich and gain lustre from each other.

18. Both these types of *bhakti* are beautifully depicted in the Ramayana. We find them first in the Ayodhyakand (the second Chapter) and they have been described extensively throughout the rest of the Ramayana. Bharat, Rama's brother, is an example of *nirguna* devotee and Lakshman, another brother, is an example of *saguna* devotee. The nature of *saguna bhakti* and that of *nirguna bhakti* will be clear from their examples.

19. When Rama set out for the forest, he was not ready to take Lakshman with him. He felt that there is no ground for taking him along. He told him, "I am going to the forest at the behest of our father. You should stay at home. If you accompany me, our parents would be more disconsolate. Serve them and the people. If you are with them, I shall be free from any worries. Be my representative here. Do not be worried about me. Going to the forest is not a matter of misfortune; in fact, I would thereby have

the opportunity to visit the *ashrams* of the sages."
Rama thus tried to dissuade Lakshman from his
resolve, but Lakshman cut short all the arguments in
one stroke. Tulsidas has pictured this incident vividly.
Lakshman says, "You are explaining to me the path
of duty prescribed by the scriptures. I should certainly
follow it. But I would not be able to bear the burden
of princely duties. I am not competent to be your
representative. I am just a child :

दीन्हि मोहि सिख नीकि गुसांई । लागि अगम अपनी कदराई ।
नरवर धीर धरमधुरधारी । निगम-नीतिके ते अधिकारी ।
मैं शिशु प्रभुसनेह प्रतिपाला । मंदर-मेरु कि लेहिं मराला ।।

Can a swan lift up the mountains? O, Rama! I have
been nourished on your love. Please tell about princely
duties to somebody else. I am only a child." Thus he
put a stop to the discussion.

20. Just as fish cannot live outside water, Lakshman
could not live without Rama. With his whole being
he lived for Rama. His joy lay in serving Rama; in
keeping vigil at night when Rama slept. If the eye
is attacked, the arm immediately rushes to receive
the blow. Lakshman was such a protective arm for
Rama. Tulsidas has given a striking simile. A flag
flutters proudly and is lustily cheered; but who cares
for the flag-staff? Lakshman was like the flag-staff; it
was because of his solid and unstinted support that
the flag of Rama's glory has been fluttering high in
the world. He never faltered; never bent. The world
sees the flag and adores it, but the value of the staff

is hardly reckoned. A spire attracts the attention of the people, but the foundation catches no eye. The banner of Rama's glory is still fluttering, but Lakshman remains unremembered and unsung. For fourteen years, he stood upright and strong. He stayed in the background and spread Rama's glory. Rama entrusted many difficult, delicate and unpleasant tasks to him. It was Lakshman who was asked to take Sita to the forest and leave her there. Poor Lakshman obeyed that command too. He had virtually become Rama's eyes, His hands, His mind. He had merged himself into Rama, just as a river merges into the sea. He had become Rama's shadow. Lakshman's *bhakti* was *saguna*.

21. Bharat, on the other hand, was a *nirguna* devotee. Tulsidas has beautifully sketched his character too. When Rama left for the forest, Bharat was out of Ayodhya. When he returned, Dashrath, their father, had already died. Bharat was asked by Vasishtha (preceptor of the royal family) to take up the reins of the kingdom. But Bharat insisted on meeting Rama at the earliest. He was impatient to see Rama, but busied himself in making necessary arrangements for the kingdom. He did not consider the throne as his own; and felt that the kingdom rightfully belonged to Rama and he must look after it as Rama's representative. Like Lakshman, he could not just abandon everything and follow Rama. For him, devotion to Rama meant doing his work; otherwise, what value could such devotion have? He first made necessary administrative arrangements and only thereafter proceeded to meet

Rama. He met Rama and said, "Dear brother, it is your kingdom, you should ---", but Rama did not let him complete the sentence and told him to go back and discharge the kingly duties. Bharat hesitated, but bowed before that command. Rama's word was law for him; he had left everything to Rama.

22. He went back. But, interestingly, he did not live in Ayodhya. He preferred to stay in a nearby forest doing penance and ruled from there. When Rama and Bharat met after fourteen years, it must have been difficult to make out who of them was the true ascetic doing penance in the forest. If somebody draws a picture of this meeting,[2] depicting Rama and Bharat looking alike, with just a little difference in age and having the same lustre of penance on their faces, it would indeed be a remarkable and elevating picture. Bharat was physically away from Rama, but his mind was never away from him even for a moment. Although he attended to the affairs of the kingdom, his mind was with Rama. *Nirguna bhakti* is thus filled to the brim with *saguna bhakti*. How can one then speak of separation? That is why Bharat did not feel any sense of separation. After all, he was doing the Lord's work.

23. Young people often say, "We cannot understand all this talk of *Ramanama*, Rama's *bhakti*, Rama's worship. But we are ready to do God's work." Bharat has shown how to do God's work. He overcame the

---

[2] Interestingly, a stone image depicting this meeting was found while digging at Vinoba's ashram at Pavnar, much later. He built a temple for it, now known as Bharat-Rama temple.

pangs of separation by immersing himself in that work. To keep doing God's work and so to have no time to feel the sense of separation from Him is one thing; but it is quite a different thing to have nothing to do with the Lord. To do the Lord's work and lead a life of self-control is rare indeed. Bharat's attitude was that of a *nirguna bhakta*, but *saguna* continued to support *nirguna*. Bharat bowed to Rama's command to bid farewell to him and go back to Ayodhya; but he immediately turned back and said, "Rama, my heart is still not reconciled to your decision. I feel that something is lacking." Rama understood the state of his mind and gave him his sandals. The respect for *saguna* thus remained intact. *Saguna* did soften and brought warmth to *nirguna* in the end. Lakshman would not have been content with Rama's sandals; he yearned for much more. Bharat's standpoint was different. Though he stayed away from Rama and worked from afar, his mind was full of Rama. To him, work was worship; still he did feel the need for the sandals. It would have been difficult for him to carry on without them. He ran the administration deriving his authority from those sandals. Both Lakshman and Bharat were Rama's devotees. Their standpoints were outwardly different. But although Bharat was committed to his duties and principles, that commitment too needed the reassuring warmth of a symbol.

64. Complementarity between saguna and nirguna : Examples from Krishna's life

24. Tenderness and warmth of devotion must be there. That is why the Lord told Arjuna, 'मय्यासक्तमनाः पार्थ' – 'O Arujna! Have attachment to Me"[3] – and repeated the advice again and again. The Gita otherwise detests the word 'attachment' and repeatedly exhorts us to work without attachment, love or hate, and expectations. Non-attachment is its constant refrain. Still it asks Arjuna to have attachment to the Lord. But, then, attachment to the Lord is a lofty ideal; it has nothing in common with attachment to worldly things.

Saguna and *nirguna* are closely intertwined with each other. *Saguna* cannot altogether dispense with *nirguna*'s support and *nirguna* does need *saguna's* warmth. Work is certainly worship, but it needs warmth of feelings. The Lord says, 'मामनुस्मर युध्य च ।' ('Remember Me and fight.') Work is worship in itself, but devotion has to be there in the heart. The mechanical action of offering flowers to the Lord's image is no worship; that action has to be saturated with devotion. Offering flowers to the Lord's image is one form of worship; doing good work is another way. In both of them there must be warmth of devotion. If this warmth is not there, offering flowers to an image will be no different from offering them to a stone. It is the inner feeling that matters. It is devotion that makes the difference. *Saguna* and *nirguna*, work and love, *jnana* and *bhakti* – all these are completely identical. They all lead to the same ultimate experience.

---

[3] Gita, 7.1.

25. Look at Uddhava and Arjuna. I am taking a jump from the Ramayana to the Mahabharata; but I do have a right to do so, as there is complete identity between Rama and Krishna. Uddhava and Arjuna are like Lakshman and Bharat respectively. Uddhava always used to be with Krishna, busy in serving him. He could not bear even a moment's separation from him. Without Krishna, life was dull and insipid for him. Arjuna too was Krishna's dear friend, but he used to live at Hastinapur, away from him, doing his work. Such was their relationship.

26. When it was time for Krishna to leave His body, he told Uddhava, "Uddhava, I am going now." Uddhava pleaded, "Why don't you take me along? Let us go together." But Krishna said, "No, I am not for that. When the sun sets, it endows fire with its essense – heat and light; likewise I am leaving my essence, my light with you." He then revealed Self-knowledge to Uddhava and sent him on a journey. During the journey, Uddhava came to know from sage Maitreya that Krishna had bidden farewell to this world. But the news made absolutely no impact on Uddhava's mind. His case was not like 'मरका गुरु रडका चेला, दोहींचा बोध वायां गेला ।' ('When the master died, the pupil cried. The teaching and the learning were both wasted.') He did not feel that there was any separation. All his life he had performed *saguna* worship. He had always lived in the company of Krishna. Now he had begun to experience the joy of *nirguna*. He had to reach finally the destination of *nirguna*. *Saguna* may come first, but it must be followed by *nirguna*; otherwise there is no perfection, no fulfilment.

27. Arjuna's case was just the opposite. Krishna had asked him to protect all the womenfolk after His departure from this world. Arjuna came to Dwarka, took them along and proceeded to Delhi. On the way, dacoits robbed them near Hissar in Punjab.[4] Arjuna was known as a man among men, as one of the greatest warriors of his time. He was known as Jaya (the victorious) as he knew no defeat. Once he had even challenged and humbled Lord Shiva. But such a fighter could not face a bunch of dacoits and had to flee for his life! Krishna's departure from this world had affected him so deeply that he had as it were lost all his vitality and strength; he had become a shadow of his former self. Thus separation from Krishna in the end overwhelmed Arjuna, the *nirguna* devotee. His *nirguna* ultimately gave way. All his activity came to a standstill. His *nirguna* experienced the value of *saguna* in the end. Thus *saguna* has to go in with *nirguna* and *nirguna* has to go in with *saguna*. They complement each other.

65. *Saguna and nirguna are one : My own experience*

28. Hence, words fail while attempting to describe the difference between the *saguna* devotee and the *nirguna* devotee. *Saguna* and *nirguna* come together in the end. Though the spring of *bhakti* may flow out of *saguna,* it reaches *nirguna* in the end. Long back, I

[4] The town is now in the state of Haryana in India.

had gone to Vaikom at the time of *satyagraha*[5] there. I knew that the birth-place of Shankaracharya was somewhere on the Malabar coast. While passing along the Malabar coast, it occurred to me that Kaladi, the birth-place of Shankaracharya must be somewhere nearby. On enquiry, my local companion told me that it was just 10-12 miles away and enquired whether I would like to go there. But I declined. The purpose of my visit was to observe the Vaikom *satyagraha*. I thought that it was not proper for me to go anywhere else. I still think that what I did was right. But every time I went to bed, the village of Kaladi and the image of Shankaracharya would stand before my eyes and I could not sleep. That experience is still fresh in my mind. Thoughts about Shankaracharya – the power of his wisdom, his divine certitude in the *advaita*[6] philosophy, his rare and fiery *vairagya* that considered the phenomenal world as trash, the serenity in his language, and the infinite debt that I owe him – crowded in my mind. Then I realised how *nirguna* is filled with *saguna*. Had I visited Kaladi, I perhaps would not have felt such surging emotions. Even in *nirguna, saguna* is at its zenith. I rarely write letters to friends making routine enquiries, but the thought of them is always there in my mind. *Saguna* thus lies hidden in *nirguna*. They are essentially one. Worship of an image or visible acts of service and

---

[5] The famous Vaikom *satyagraha* took place in 1924 for opening the roads round the temple to the untouchables. Vinoba had gone there as an observer at Gandhiji's instance.

[6] *Advaita* (Non-dualism) philosophy believes that there is no duality between the individual self and *Brahman*, the Supreme Self.

constant thinking about the world's welfare without any outward indication of worship – both these have the same worth and value.

66. Saguna and nirguna are only apparently different : To become a true devotee is what matters

29. Lastly, I want to say that it is not easy to clearly distinguish between *saguna* and *nirguna*. What appears *saguna* from one angle may appear *nirguna* from another. In s*aguna* worship a stone image is looked upon as a symbol of God. But it is in the mother and in the saints that divine consciousness is clearly manifest. Wisdom, love, tenderness of affection are palpable in them. Still they are not worshipped as the images of the Lord. Instead of serving the people full of consciousness, instead of seeing *saguna* God in them, God is seen in an inanimate stone! To see God in a stone is, in a sense, the height of *nirguna*. It is easier to see God in the saints, in the parents and in the neighbours who are seen to possess wisdom, love or altruism. It is far more difficult to see God in a stone. Still we worship the stone image. Is it not verily a form of *nirguna* worship?

30. On the other hand, one feels that if God is not to be imagined in a stone, where else can we see Him? A stone is the most appropriate thing to become God's symbol, as it is unruffled, unmoved, peaceful and undisturbed under any condition. Our parents, neighbours, the people in general, all these have their weaknesses. You are bound to find some weakness or fault in them. Hence, serving them is, in a sense, more difficult than worshipping a stone.

31. To sum up, *saguna* and *nirguna* are complementary to each other. *Saguna* is easier than *nirguna*. But in another sense, *nirguna* is easy and *saguna* is difficult. Both lead us to the same end. In the Fifth Chapter, it has been said that the *yogi* who does not get attached to *karma* though he is continually engaged in action and the *sannyasi*, who does all the *karma* while being apparently inactive, are one and the same. Similar is the case here. *Saguna* state of *karma* and *nirguna* state of *sannyasa* are one and the same. The Lord therefore faced the same predicament as when he was asked whether *yoga* was better or *sannyasa*. Finally, He replied on the basis of comparative easiness. Otherwise, there is no difference between *yoga* and *sannyasa* or between *saguna* and *nirguna*.

32. The Lord says in the end, "O, Arjuna! You may prefer *saguna* or *nirguna*, but be a *bhakta* (devotee); do not remain untouched by devotion." And then the Lord describes the characteristic attributes of *bhakta*. The nectar may be sweet, but we have never tasted it. The verses describing the *bhakta*'s attributes, however, have a rare sweetness that we can experience directly. There is no need for any imagination. Like the verses describing the attributes of *sthitaprajna*, these verses too should be read daily, reflected upon, ruminated over again and again. We should try to imbibe these attributes bit by bit and go on enriching our life; and thus lead it gradually towards the Lord.

(8.5.32)

CHAPTER 13

Distinction between the Self and the not-Self

67. Distinguishing between the body and the Self helps karmayoga

1. Vyasa has poured into the Gita the essence of his life. He has written many voluminous works. The Mahabharata alone contains more than a hundred thousand verses. In fact, the word 'Vyasa' has acquired the meaning of 'extensiveness' in Sanskrit. But in the Gita, he is not inclined towards elaboration. Here he has only tersely stated, like Euclidean geometry, the principles useful for life. There are no long discussions in the Gita; brevity is its distinctive characteristic. It is so mainly because everybody can test for himself the veracity of the Gita's teaching in his life; and it is meant to be so tested. The Gita tells only those things which are useful for life. That being the object, Vyasa has contented himself with stating the principles concisely. It shows his firm faith in the power of truth and the possibility of its being directly experienced. That which is true does not need special efforts to substantiate it.

2. Our main reason in studying the Gita is to get help and guidance in the life whenever we need it. Such help is always forthcoming. The Gita is a treatise that tells us how life is to be lived. That is why it lays stress on *swadharma*. Performance of *swadharma* is the foundation of human life. The whole edifice of life has to be erected over this foundation. Stronger the foundation, more enduring the edifice will be. It is the performance of *swadharma* that the Gita calls '*karma*'. Around this *karma*, the Gita has built its architectonics.

It has fortified it with many *vikarmas*. To make the performance of *swadharma* meaningful and fruitful, it should be given all the help and support that it needs. In this connection we have examined many things so far. Most of them belonged to the realm of *bhakti*. In the Thirteenth Chapter, we have to take a look at something extremely important to the performance of *swadharma*. That thing is discriminating reason.

3. One who performs *swadharma* should give up the fruit of actions : it is the main thing that is emphasised everywhere in the Gita. One must act, but one must also renounce the fruit; one must water a plant and tend it with care, but should not expect for himself any return therefrom in the form of its shade, fruit or flower. This is what *karmayoga* in the form of performance of *swadharma* means. *Karmayoga* does not just mean doing *karma*. *Karma* is, in fact, going on everywhere in the world; there is no need to tell anybody that it should be done. It may be easy to say or even understand, but difficult to put into practice, that one should perform *swadharma* properly – not just any sort of *karma* – and renounce the fruit, as desire for fruit is considered to be the incentive for action. Action without desire for the fruit for oneself is against the prevalent current; it is diametrically opposite to what normally goes on in the world. We often say that a man doing a lot of work is a *karmayogi*. But it is an inaccurate use of the word. This is not *karmayoga* as per the Gita's definition. You can hardly find a single *karmayogi* of the Gita's definition among the millions who work; he is rare

even among the millions who perform *swadharma*. In fact, judging by the true and subtle meaning of *karmayoga*, a perfect *karmayogi* can hardly be found. To work and then to renounce its fruit is something most unusual. The Gita has elucidated this particular point so far.

4. Another complementary point has been put forth in the Thirteenth Chapter. It is the distinction between the body and the Self. If we can make this distinction, it can help us in renouncing the fruit. We see something with the eyes and call it a form, a body or an image. But the eyes make us familiar with the outer form only; to get to know a thing fully we have to enter into its interior. We have to peel off the skin of a fruit to taste the pulp within. We have to break a coconut to get its soft kernel. A jackfruit too has a rough exterior but inside there is sweet and juicy pulp. We need to distinguish between the outer and the inner while looking at ourselves as well as at others. The outer cover is to be set aside. What does it mean? It means that we should make a distinction between the outwardly visible form of anything and its inner essence. Everything has an outer body and an inner soul; just as we have a physical body outside and the soul or the Self within. This is true about *karma* as well. The fruit of the *karma* is like its outer body which should be discarded, and the purification of mind that results from it is its soul which should be cherished. We should inculcate the habit of making this distinction; we should acquire this penetrating insight. We should train and discipline the eyes, the

mind and the reason through constant practice to achieve this purpose. Everywhere we should leave aside the body and adore the Self. The Thirteenth Chapter has explained this distinction for us to reflect on it.

68. The basic foundation of betterment

5. It is extremely important to have the habit of looking at the essence of things. How nice would it be if this habit could be inculcated right in the childhood itself! This is an outlook which is worth imbibing. Many feel that the science of spirituality has nothing to do with life. Some others feel that even if it has, it should have nothing to do with it. But it would indeed be a happy situation if the distinction between the body and the Self could be ingrained through education right since the childhood. Nowadays, bad education is imparting extremely evil *samskaras*. This education does not lift us out of our total identification with the body. We are doing everything to pamper the body. Yet the quality that the body should attain, the form that should be given to it, is found nowhere. The body is thus being vainly worshipped; there is no awareness of the bliss that lies in the experience of the Self. This condition has resulted from the present system of education. Day and night, indulgence of the body is being continually and insistently taught.

Education of cherishing the body begins right from the childhood. When a child stumbles while playing and gets a little hurt, he hardly pays any attention to it. He takes ordinary bruises and abrasions in his

stride. But it is not so with his parents. They draw the child near and fuss over it, saying, "Oh dear! Have you hurt yourself badly? How did it happen? Oh, it is bleeding!" All this fuss makes the child cry. What can one say about it? A child is told not to jump, not to play lest he should get bruised or hurt. He is thus trained solely to think of the body.

6. It is in relation to his body that we fondly admire a child, and it is in relation to his body that we scold him. If a child has a running nose, we call him dirty. How greatly it hurts the child! How false the accusation is! It may be true that the child's nose is dirty and it should be cleaned. But instead of cleaning the nose without making a fuss over it, we reproach the child. He cannot bear this. He feels miserable. When his heart and soul are full of purity and cleanliness, why this wrong accusation of dirtiness? The child is not really dirty; he is the Lord Himself in all His purity, beauty, love and holiness. He is a spark of the Divine. Yet we call him dirty! Is the outward dirtiness so important? The child does not even understand what this is all about. He feels hurt. His mind gets disturbed and agitated; and such a state of mind stands in the way of improvement. We should therefore explain things properly and keep the child clean and tidy.

7. Instead of this, we impress on the child's mind the idea that he is nothing but the body. It is an important pedagogical principle that the teacher should regard the pupil as faultless in every respect. If a pupil fails

to solve a mathematical problem, the teacher slaps him. Now, what is the connection between the slap and the pupil's failure to solve a problem? Likewise, the pupils are thrashed if they are late for school. Yes, the slap may cause blood to circulate faster, but how will it help in making them punctual? In fact, by such treatment, we only strengthen the animal in them. It hardens the pupil's notion that he is nothing but the body. We thereby build his life on the foundation of fear. Real improvement can never be brought about through coercion and by strengthening identification with the body. It is possible only when one realises that one is distinct from the body.

8. There is nothing wrong in being aware of the defects in the body and the mind. It helps in removing them. But one must understand clearly that one is not the body. My 'Self' is altogether distinct from the body. It is wholly beautiful, faultless, pure, sublime and holy. The man who examines himself to remove the defects in him, does so by making a distinction between the Self and the body. He does not, therefore, get angry when someone points out his defects. Instead, he himself tries to find out whether there are any defects in his body and mind and tries to remove them. He who does not make this distinction can never improve himself. How can a man improve himself if he identifies himself with the body, which is nothing but a lump of clay? There can be improvement only when it is realised that the body is but an instrument given to us. Do I get angry if someone points out that something is wrong with my spinning wheel? I rather

try to remove the fault, if there is any. The same is true about the body too. It is like an agricultural implement, an implement to cultivate the Lord's field. If it is impaired, it should be repaired. The body is here as a means. I should strive to purge myself of defects and faults by detaching myself from the body. I am distinct from the body, which is an instrument. I am the master, the owner of the body. I am the one who gets good work done by the body. Such a discerning attitude should be inculcated right from childhood.

9. Just as an impartial spectator can judge the game better, we can observe the merits and defects of the body, mind and intellect only when we detach ourselves from them. We hear some people say, "My memory is getting feeble. What should I do about it?" When one says so, it clearly means that one is distinct from one's memory; that the memory is an instrument or a tool that is not working properly. Somebody may lose a book or some other thing; he cannot lose himself. Even at the time of death, when the body has become totally worn-out and useless, the Self is as healthy and faultless as ever. This is a vital point to be clearly understood. If we could understand this, a lot of our problems will be solved.

69. Attachment to the body wastes life

10. Identification with the body is prevalent everywhere. As a result, man has thoughtlessly devised all sorts of ways and means to cater to the body. Even a glance at them is disquieting. Man is always striving

to somehow prolong the life of the body even after it has become old and decrepit. But how long can this body, this shell be sustained? At most until death; not a moment longer. All the vanity is reduced to naught when death stares one in the face. Still man continues to produce various things for this worthless body; he ceaselessly worries about it. Nowadays, some people find no harm in meat-eating to sustain the body. In their view, human body is so precious that one may eat flesh without compunction to sustain it; animals' bodies, on the other hand, have little value. But what, after all, is the ground for this opinion? The only ground could be that animals eat anything and think nothing beyond themselves while human beings take care of the creation around them. This very basis for considering human beings superior is undermined by meat-eating. Human beings are superior because they exercise self-control, because they care for other creatures. Man is superior because of this quality that is not found in the animals. That is why it is said to be a rare gift to be born as a human being. How can man be considered superior, if he undermines the very basis of his superiority? When man begins to eat flesh like other animals without any qualms, he undermines the foundation of his superiority. It is like cutting the branch of a tree on which one is sitting.

11. These days, medical science is performing all kinds of miracles. Germs are injected into the bodies of living animals, multiplied there and diseases produced there to watch their effects. Living animals are thus tortured and the knowledge gained is then used to prolong

the life of this worthless human body. All this goes on in the name of compassion and humanitarianism! Inoculation is only one among the many horrid things invented by medical science. But the body for whose sake all this is done is as fragile as glass. It can break any moment. What is the outcome of all these efforts to sustain the body? Even as we are trying to sustain this fragile body, we see that it is disintegrating. Yet we continue to pamper the body.

12. It never occurs to us to find out the kind of food that would make the mind and intellect *sattvik*. Man never considers what should be done and whose help should be sought to purify the mind and the intellect. All that he is anxious for is to make the body plump, to increase layers of flesh thereon. But these layers are bound to peel off in the course of time. Then what is the use of letting the fat accumulate in the body until it becomes a burden and an encumbrance? The body is an instrument at our disposal and we should certainly do whatever is necessary to keep it in order. We take work from a machine, but do we identify ourselves with it? Why cannot one have the same attitude towards the body-machine?

13. To sum up, the body is a means and not an end. Once this is deeply realised, man will not make much ado about nothing. Life will then appear markedly different. Man would not then revel in decorating the body. Indeed an ordinary cloth is sufficient to cover the body. But we want the cloth to be soft; we want various designs on it. For the sake of this,

we make a number of people labour. What is all this for? Does not God, the Creator, know His job? Had human body needed designs or colours on it, would He not have designed stripes on it, as He has done for the tiger? Would He not have given plumage to human beings like the peacock? Was it impossible for Him? But He has thought otherwise. Man, as he is, is beautiful. God does not want his body to be decorated. Is not there marvellous beauty in nature? Man should be content in beholding it. But he has been deluded by artificialities. We accuse Germany of driving natural Indian dyes out of the market. Dear friend, you first lost your real colour – your true nature – and got enamoured of artificial dyes. As a result, you became dependent on others. You have been lured by the superfluous idea of decorating the body and that has led you astray. You should be concerned about making the mind and the heart pure and beautiful, about developing the intellect; but all that has been lost sight of.

70. 'You are That'

14. Therefore, the idea that the Lord is putting forth in the Thirteenth Chapter is extremely valuable : 'You are not the body, you are the Self' (*Tat tvam asi*). This thought, this saying is most noble, sublime and holy. We find this idea everywhere in the Sanskrit literature : 'You are not the outer cover; you are the pure, indestructible kernel within.' The moment a man realises that he is That – the Supreme Self – and not the body, a new kind of joy that has never been experienced before will surge up in the mind.

Nothing in the world can destroy, nothing is capable of destroying the Self. This subtle thought is implied in this saying.

15. I am the Self – the imperishable, unsullied element transcending the body. I have been given this body for the sake of the Self. Whenever there is likelihood of that divine element getting sullied, I shall discard the body to prevent that happening. I shall ever be ready to keep the divine flame glowing. I have not come into the world riding this body to demean and humiliate myself. I must have control over the body. I shall use it for the well-being of all. 'आनंदें भरीन तिन्ही लोक ।' ('I shall fill the entire universe with bliss.') I shall sacrifice the body at the altar of a great principle and acclaim the glory of the Lord. A rich man throws away clothes the moment they are soiled and puts on new ones. I shall treat the body in the same way. The body is needed for work. When it becomes useless for the purpose, I would not hesitate to throw it away.

16. This is what we are learning from *satyagraha*. The body and the Self are separate entities. The day a man realises this truth and its significance, his true education and true development begin. It is only then that he will be able to offer *satyagraha* successfully. Therefore each one of us should imbibe this spirit in our hearts. The body just happens to be a means; it is only an instrument given to us by the Lord. It is to be discarded the moment it ceases to be of any use. We put away our winter wear in the summer; we put away the quilts used during the night when

the day breaks. That is what should be done with the body. It is to be preserved as long as it is useful and flung aside when its utility is over. The Lord is showing us this way for spiritual development.

71. An end to the power of the tyrants

17. As long as we do not realise that we are distinct from the body, tyrants will continue to torment and enslave and torture us. It is fear that makes tyranny possible. There is a story of a demon who had captured a man. He would make him work round the clock. If he paused a little, the demon would threaten him, 'I shall kill and devour you.' The frightened man would then submit meekly. But when the man could stand it no longer, he said, "All right, if you want to kill and eat me up, do so by all means." But was the demon going to eat him up? What he wanted was a submissive servant. Who would do the work if the man were killed? The demon used to threaten the man with death; but the moment the man said, "Well, you may eat me up", tyranny stopped. Tyrants know that people have intense attachment to their bodies; so if you inflict pain on their bodies, they will submit and become your slaves. Give up that attachment and you will be the master of all. You will be free. You will be all-powerful. Nobody will then be able to exercise authority over you. The very basis of tyranny will break down. The power of the tyrants hinges on your identification with the body. They threaten and intimidate you because they think that if they inflict pain on your bodies, you would submit.

18. When I feel that 'I am the body', others are induced to persecute and torment me. But look at Cranmer, the British martyr. When he was going to be burnt at the stakes, he said, "If you would burn me, by all means, do so. Here, burn this right hand first, for this hand hath offended." In the same vein, Latimer said, "We shall this day light such a candle by God's grace in England as (I trust) shall never be put out." Their task was to burn the candle of the body to spread the light of truth. The body, in any case, being perishable, would perish one day.

19. When Socrates was sentenced to death by poison, he said, "I am old. This body would anyway have disintegrated soon. What is so great in putting to death that which is mortal? I fail to understand what is so great in killing that which is anyway mortal." The night before he was to drink hemlock, he was explaining to his pupils the immortality of the soul. He was merrily describing the pain he would feel with the spread of poison in the body. When the discussion on the immortality of the soul was over, a pupil asked, "Sir, how should we bury you after your death?" Socrates exclaimed, "How clever you are! Is it that they will kill me and you will bury me? Is it that the killers are my enemies and you are a friend? They will kill me in their wisdom and you will bury me in your wisdom! Who are you, after all, to bury me? I shall be there even when all of you are dead and buried in your graves. Nobody can kill me, nobody can bury me. What, after all, have I been explaining all along? The Self is immortal. Who can kill it or

bury it?" And the great Socrates has indeed outlived all of them; he is remembered even after more than two thousand years.

72. *Faith in the power of the Supreme Self*

20. To sum up, as long as there is attachment to the body, as long as there is fear, a sense of insecurity would continue to haunt you. Would not a snake bite me in bed, would not a thief come and attack me? – Fears like these would not let you sleep even if you shut your eyes. You may sleep with a staff near the bed to use it against the thieves if they come. But can a thief not use the same staff to hit you? You are making the staff readily available to him, in case he has forgotten to bring one with him! After all, on whom do you rely when you sleep? You are then totally dependent on others for protection. It is only when you are awake that the question of your protecting yourself arises. Who protects you when you are asleep?

21. We go to sleep trusting some power; the same power which all the animals trust when they sleep. Even a tiger goes to sleep. The lion, which has enmity with the whole world and which, therefore, looks back again and again with suspicion and apprehension while walking, also goes to sleep. Had there been no faith in that power, the lions would have had to evolve an arrangement of having a few of them keeping vigil while others sleep! We too go to sleep in the lap of that all-pervading power, relying on which savage tigers, lions and wolves also sleep. A child

sleeps in his mother's lap happily and confidently. At that time the child is, as it were, the master of the world. We too must learn to sleep in the lap of the Lord, the all-sustaining Mother, with love and trust and the knowledge that we are safe there. We should make ourselves more and more familiar with the power which sustains the whole of our life. We should feel the presence of that power more and more. The more we are convinced of its presence, the more shall we be secure. The more we feel the presence of that power, the more shall we grow. The Thirteenth Chapter gives some indication of the steps needed to be taken in this direction.

73. Progressive realisation of the Supreme Self

22. Man is absorbed in ordinary worldly activities as long as there is no thought of the Self within the body. He knows little else than eating when hungry, drinking when thirsty, sleeping when drowsy. To be able to do all these things he will fight. He will crave for them. He is engrossed only in bodily activities. True development is yet to commence. The Self only watches all this. It stands silently like a mother keeping a watchful eye on her child crawling towards the well. It just looks at all the activities silently. This state has been described as that of a Witness.

23. The Self watches, but does not give its assent to what is being done. The *jiva* (individual soul), which has till now been acting under the impression that it is nothing but the body, then wakes up. The realization dawns that it has been living like an animal. When the

jiva comes to this point, the realm of ethics begins. Then the question whether something is right or wrong, moral or immoral crops up at every step. At this stage, man starts exercising rational discrimination. His analytical mind starts working. Impulsive actions cease. Self-restraint takes the place of self-indulgence.

24. When the *jiva* ascends to this moral plane, the Self no longer remains a silent spectator. It gives its approval from within. A voice is heard from within : 'Well done!' The Self now no longer remains a mere witness. It gives its assent; it upholds the *jiva*'s actions and expresses appreciation.

Suppose a hungry man comes to your door when you have just sat down to eat and you give your plate of food to him. When you remember this good act in the night, you will experience a different kind of joy. The Self will say softly, "You have indeed acted well!" When a mother pats her child on the back and says, "Well done, my boy!", he feels that he has got the highest possible reward. Likewise, such words from the Lord within encourage us and provide us impetus to do better. The *jiva* at this stage stands on the moral plane, leaving the life of self-indulgence behind.

25. Then comes the next stage. Man tries to cleanse his mind in the course of doing duties while living a moral life. He strives hard, but gets exhausted at some point. The *jiva* then prays to the Lord, "Oh Lord! I have come to the end of my tether. Give me more strength." Until a man realises that he cannot

succeed by his own efforts, however hard, the true significance of prayer does not dawn on him. One should first exhaust all his strength and when it is found insufficient, cry earnestly for the Lord's help, as Draupadi did.[1] The eternal spring of the Lord's grace and compassion is ever-flowing. Whosoever is thirsty can come to it and quench his or her thirst as a matter of right. Whosoever lacks anything can ask for it. Such is the relationship in this third stage. The Lord has now come closer. He not only expresses His approval by words, but also rushes to help.

26. At first, the Lord was standing at a distance. The teacher asks the pupil to solve a problem and then watches from a distance. Likewise, the Lord lets the *jiva* grapple with the problems when it is immersed in the life of self-indulgence. The *jiva* thereafter ascends to the moral plane. Now the Lord can no longer remain neutral. Finding the *jiva* doing good deeds, He approves them and compliments the *jiva*. When the good deeds cleanse the mind of gross impurities and the time comes for the removal of subtle impurities, human efforts prove to be inadequate. Then we beseech the Lord and He responds. He rushes to help us. Whenever the *bhakta* begins to lose heart, He is there ready to help. The sun-god is ever waiting at your door. But he would not forcibly open the door and barge into the room; he would not even knock the door. His job is to serve and he behaves

---

[1] Draupadi cried for Lord Krishna's help when Dushshasan tried to disrobe her in the Kaurava court. The Lord thereupon supplied her innumerable garments.

accordingly. But the moment you open the door, he will come in with all his rays and dispel darkness. The Lord acts likewise. The moment you call Him for help, He will rush to you with outstretched arms. Tukaram has said, 'उभारोनि बाहे । विठो पालवीत आहे ।' ('With outstretched hands, the Lord Pandurang is calling you.') If the nostrils are open, air is bound to come in. If the door is open, light is bound to come in. But I find even these examples unsatisfactory. The Lord is nearer to us, He is more eager to come in. So He does not remain content in being a Witness or a Permitter, He becomes a Supporter – one who helps and supports wholeheartedly. When we find ourselves unable to purify the mind completely, we make impassioned pleas, we cry helplessly, 'मारी नाड तमारे हाथे प्रभु संभाळजो रे' ('I am wholly in your hands; O Lord, take care of me.'), we pray, 'तू ही एक मेरा मददगार है, तेरा आसरा मुझको दरकार है' ('You are the only one to help me. I need Your support'). Will the Lord, who is all compassion, then stand aloof? He will rush to help His devotees, to provide whatever they lack. That is how He helped Rohidas in tanning leather, Sajan the butcher in selling meat, Kabir in weaving cloth, Janabai in grinding corn.

27. The next stage is to dedicate to the Lord the fruit of actions which we have received by His grace, instead of taking it ourselves. The *jiva* then says to the Lord, "This fruit belongs to you; take it." Namdeva insistently urged the Lord to drink the milk that he had offered. This is an extremely adorable sentiment. Namdeva is offering to the Lord the fruit of his actions

in the form of the milk. Whatever you have achieved and acquired is because of His grace and is, therefore, to be dedicated to Him. When Dharmaraj was about to set foot in the heaven, the dog accompanying him was stopped at the gate. Dharmaraj then instantly renounced the privilege of entering the heaven that he had become entitled to as a result of the merits acquired in life. A *bhakta* also offers to the Lord the fruit of his actions readily and instantaneously. The Lord who appeared as the Witness, the Permitter and the Supporter, now becomes the Experiencer. The *jiva* now ascends to a stage wherein the Supreme Lord Himself, present within the body, becomes the enjoyer of the fruit.

28. Hereafter, making resolves (*sankalp*) should also be given up. There are three stages in any work. First, we make a resolve, then we act and finally we receive the fruit of the actions. We have acted with His help and have dedicated the fruit to Him. It was the Lord who acted and who enjoyed the fruit thereof. Now let Him be the one to make resolve. Let Him be there in the work throughout all its stages. Jnanadeva has said,

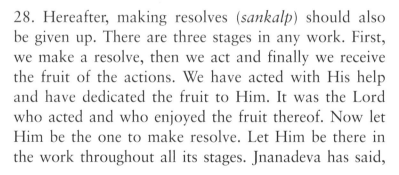

'माळियें जेउतें नेलें । तेउतें निवांत चि गेलें
तया पाणिया ऐसें केलें । होआवें गा'

('The water flows without demur, as directed by the gardener. One should become like that.' – That is, one should let one's life be guided by the Lord.) The water nourishes the plants and the trees of the gardener's liking. In the same way, let the Lord decide what actions should take place through me. Let me entrust to Him all the responsibility for all the resolves of my mind. When I am riding a horse, making it carry all my weight, what is the point in carrying the baggage on my head? Let that burden also be placed on horseback as, anyway, the horse is going to bear all the weight even if I keep the load on my head. Thus the Lord eventually becomes one who moves my life and makes it blossom. My life is then completely in His hands and He does with it what He likes. He thus becomes 'Maheshwar' (the Supreme Lord) who holds the reins of my life. Progressing in this way, the whole life becomes saturated with His presence. Only the curtain of the body then separates me from Him. When that is removed, *jiva* and *Shiva* (God), *atman* and *paramatman* (Self and the Supreme Self) become one.

29. Thus we have to realise God progressively as the Witness, the Permitter, the Supporter, the Experiencer, and finally as the Supreme Lord – 'उपद्रष्टाऽनुमन्ता च भर्ता भोक्ता महेश्वर:'. To recapitulate, the Lord is at first a silent spectator. He encourages us when we ascend to the moral plane and start doing good deeds. When our efforts are found inadequate to remove subtle impurities in our minds and we pray to Him, He rushes to help us. We should then dedicate the fruit of our actions to Him and let Him be the enjoyer thereof. And finally, we should surrender to Him the right to make resolves, and let our whole life be suffused with Him. This is man's ultimate goal. A seeker is to reach this goal soaring on the two wings of *karmayoga* and *bhaktiyoga*.

74. Basic means for knowledge : freedom from pride, deceit etc.

30. To achieve all this, the firm foundation of moral *sadhana* is a *sine qua non*. We should discern between truth and untruth and follow truth. We should discern between the essential and the non-essential and stick to the essential. We should throw away the shell and keep the pearl. This is how we should begin our quest. We should procced further through our own efforts as well as God's grace. If we have learnt to make the distinction between body and soul, it will be immensely useful. In this context, I am reminded of Jesus' crucifixion. While he was being crucified, words came to his lips, 'O God! Why are they tormenting me?' But he immediately collected himself and said, "Thy will be done, Lord. Forgive them, for they know not what they do." This example of Jesus has a profound significance. It shows the extent to which the Self should be dissociated from the body. Jesus' life shows how far we should and could progress. Here, a point has been reached where the body has dropped like a rind. Whenever I think of disengaging the soul from the body, Jesus' life stands before my eyes as a perfect example. It shows how there could be complete dissociation from the body, how the link with the body could be almost severed.

31. Without the power to discern between truth and untruth, we cannot distinguish between the body and the Self. This discrimination, this knowledge should become a part of our being. We associate *jnana*

(knowledge) with knowing, but knowing through reason only does not lead to true knowledge. Eating does not just mean stuffing the mouth with food. Food should be properly chewed and it should get digested and converted into blood which would then run through the veins. Only then the action of eating is complete in the true sense. Likewise, intellectual understanding is not enough; knowledge should be fully assimilated; it should become a part of our being and should get reflected through every action of ours. We should reach the state when all the organs of action and perception work with full consciousness. The Lord has therefore given a beautiful definition of knowledge (*Jnana*) in this Chapter. The attributes of knowledge are similar to those of *sthitaprajna*. The Lord has enumerated twenty attributes including humility, non-deceitfulness, non-violence, uprightness and forgiveness. The Lord has not only declared that these attributes constitute knowledge; He has also said that whatever is opposite of these constitutes ignorance. Knowledge is nothing but the *sadhana* done in its pursuit. Socrates used to say, 'Virtue is knowledge.' The end and the means are identical.

32. Although the Gita mentions twenty attributes (which are also means) Jnanadeva has reduced them to eighteen. He has written on them with a rare earnestness. The Gita contains only five verses listing these attributes, but Jnanadeva has elaborated them in seven hundred verses. He is eager to see that these attributes permeate the society and the glory of the Lord as Truth shines throughout the society. He has

put in all his (spiritual) experience for the elucidation of these attributes. Marathi-speaking people will always be indebted to Jnanadeva for this. He was a personification of these attributes. His empathy with all the creatures was so great that when a buffalo was whipped, marks of the lashes were seen on Jnanadeva's back. Jnaneshwari, his commentary on the Gita, emerged out of such a compassionate heart. Jnanadeva's elucidation of these attributes should be read, reflected upon and assimilated. I consider myself fortunate for having got an opportunity to read Jnanadeva's beautiful writing in the original. I would consider myself blessed even if I get another birth, as I could then again have his sweet words on my lips. The essence of this is that all of us should go on rising higher and higher, dissociating body from the Self and trying to make the life divine, to fill our being with God.

(15.5.32)

CHAPTER 14

The *gunas*: developing them and going beyond them

75. *Analysis of prakriti*[1]

1. Brothers, the Fourteenth Chapter, in a way, complements the last Chapter. The Self has really nothing to achieve. It is complete and perfect in itself. The natural movement of the Self is upwards. But just as any object is dragged down by a heavy weight tied to it, the Self is pulled down by the body. We saw in the last talk that progress is possible if, by some means, the body and the Self could be separated. This is certainly difficult, but the reward that we shall have will also be great. If we could break the fetters – the body – that bind the Self, we shall experience great joy. Then the suffering of the body would not make us miserable. We would then be free. Who can rule over a man who has conquered his body? One who rules himself is the master of the universe. Therefore, end the domination of the body over the Self. The pleasures and pains of the body are all alien; they have absolutely no connection with the Self.

2. I had given the example of Jesus Christ to give an idea of the extent to which one should disassociate oneself from the pleasures and pains of the body. Jesus shows how peaceful and cheerful one should be even when the body is succumbing to death. But, separating body from the Self needs discernment on one hand and restraint on the other. Tukaram has spoken of 'विवेकासहित वैराग्याचें बळ' (Strength of non-attachment in association with discernment). Discernment and

---

[1] Please see footnote in Chapter 2.13

non-attachment (*vairagya*), both are necessary. Non-attachment means, in a sense, self-restraint and endurance. The Fourteenth Chapter shows how we could proceed towards self-restraint. The oars propel the boat, but the rudder sets the direction. The oars and rudder, both are necessary. In the same way discernment and self-restraint, both are needed to separate the Self from the bodily pleasures and pains.

3. Just as a doctor examines the health of a patient and prescribes treatment, the Lord has examined the entire *prakriti,* analysed it and diagnosed the diseases. *Prakriti* has been neatly classified here. There is a principle in diplomacy that if we could create dissensions and divisions in the enemy's camp, the enemy can soon be vanquished. The Lord has done the same here.

Prakriti of everything and every being consists of three constituents. Just as in *ayurved* (the Indian system of medicine), nature is divided in three categories – *kapha* (phlegm), *pitta* (bile) and *vata* (wind) – , *prakriti* has three *gunas* (modes) – *sattva*, *rajas* and *tamas*. All things comprise of these three qualities; the difference being only in their proportion. Only when we separate the Self from all of them, could we succeed in separating it from the body. To examine these *gunas* and to conquer them is the way to separate the Self from the body. With restraint and firmness, we have to go on subduing and conquering them one by one and reach the final destination.

76. Bodily labour: cure for tamas

4. Let us take *tamas* first. We are observing its terrible consequences in the present social situation. Its main consequence is laziness which, in turn, gives rise to sleep and blunders. Only if we overcome all the three things, we may take it that we have conquered *tamas*. Among them, laziness is extremely dreadful. It ruins the best among men. It is an enemy which destroys the peace and happiness in the society. It spoils everyone, from a child to an old man. It spares no one. It always lies in wait to pounce on us, and strikes at the slightest opportunity. A little more food induces us to lie down and a little more sleep makes us dull. Everything is in vain until this laziness is overcome. But, strangely, we look forward to idleness. We want to earn as much as possible in as little time as possible, so that we could relax later. The idea is to earn a lot to provide for idleness later! We believe that we must get rest in old age. But this is an erroneous idea. If we lead our life in a right way, we shall be able to work even in old age. In fact, we could be of greater service in old age because of our experience. And still we seek rest at that time!

5. We should be alert lest indolence should get the better of us. King Nala was a great man, but once he did not wash his feet properly and it is said that Kali (the evil spirit) entered into his body through the dry spot on the foot. Although Nala was pure and clean in all respects, a little neglect, a little laziness gave Kali an opportunity to enter into him. But our

negligence is so total that indolence can gain an entry into us at any time, from anywhere. When the body becomes indolent, the mind and the intellect follow suit. The present-day structure of the society rests on laziness. This has given rise to innumerable miseries. If laziness could be removed, we would be able to eliminate a substantial number, if not all, of those miseries.

6. At present, everywhere, there is talk of social reform. People are discussing about the minimum comforts that common man should have, the structure of society necessary for it, and such other questions. At one end, there are excessive luxuries and at the other, there is extreme privation. At one end, there is excessive wealth and at the other, there is total destitution. How to remove these social disparities? How could everybody have minimum happiness? There is only one natural way for everyone to get the necessaries of life; and it is that all should shake off laziness and be ready to work hard. Laziness is the cause of our main woe, and this woe would be no more if all resolve to do physical labour.

But what do we observe in our society? On one side, there are men getting rusty and useless. The rich do not use their organs, which get rusted due to disuse. On the other side, some people are required to toil so hard that their bodies get worn out through overwork. There is a tendency in the whole of the society to evade bodily labour. Those who have to toil till the point of breakdown do not do so willingly and cheerfully, but

because there is no other alternative. Clever people devise all sorts of excuses to avoid physical labour. Some say, "Why waste time in bodily labour?" But no one ever says, "Why should one sleep? Why waste time in eating?" They eat when they are hungry and sleep when they feel sleepy; but when the question of doing bodily labour arises, they say, "Why waste time in bodily labour? Why should we do such work? Why should we toil? We are already doing mental work." To them I would say, "My dear friend, you talk of mental work; then why don't you take mental food and mental sleep?"

7. Thus, there are two sections in the society : some work to the point of breakdown while others do no work at all. A friend once said, "In society, some are intelligent while others are stupid. Some have only heads while some have only trunks." The brains think and the trunks work. Society has been divided in this manner. But, had there actually been separate trunks and separate brains, some arrangement for cooperation between them could have been evolved. The lame can lead the blind and the blind can carry the lame. But in reality, everybody has a brain as well as a trunk. This combination of head and trunk is found in each and everyone. What should then be done? Everybody must, therefore, shake off laziness.

8. To shake off laziness one must do physical labour. It is the only way to conquer laziness. If we fail to do this, nature will make us pay for this lapse. The price may be in the form of diseases or in some other

form. As we have been given a body, it is imperative for us to use it for labour. The time spent in physical labour is not wasted. We get its reward in the form of sound health and pure, sharp and bright intellect. Physical discomforts like headaches are often found reflected in the thinking of many thinkers. If they work in the open, in contact with nature, their ideas would certainly be brilliant and healthy. It is a matter of experience that just as diseases of the body have adverse effect on the mind, good health of the body has a positive effect on the mind. What is the point in going to health resorts after contracting diseases? Why not instead work in the open, do gardening, digging or wood-cutting to keep healthy?

77. Another cure for tamas : to conquer sleep

9. Overcoming laziness is one thing; another is to overcome sleep. Sleep is, in fact, something sacred. When saintly persons put in selfless service till they get tired and then go to sleep, that sleep is a kind of *yoga*. Only the blessed ones can have such a sound and peaceful sleep. The sleep must be deep; its duration is immaterial. It does not depend on the kind of bed or the duration of its use. The deeper the well, the purer and sweeter the water. Likewise, deep sleep is more rewarding even if it is short. Half an hour's study with full concentration is more fruitful than three hours' study done with a wandering mind. Similar is the case with sleep. It is not that a long sleep is always beneficial. Patients lie in the bed for twenty four hours a day, but sleep eludes them. True sleep is essentially sound and dreamless. Whatever one

may have to suffer in hell, one does not know; but when sleep eludes and nightmares haunt, the torment is indeed hell-like. Troubled by such a situation, the Vedic sage says, 'परा दुःस्वप्न्यं सुव' – 'Let me not have such a cruel sleep full of nightmares.' The sleep is meant to give rest, but if all kinds of dreams and thoughts assail therein too, where is the question of rest?

10. How can we have deep and sound sleep? The cure for laziness is applicable here too. The body should be continuously used; then one will sleep like a log the moment one retires to bed. Sleep is like death on a small scale. One must prepare thoroughly throughout the day to have such a nice sleep. The body must get completely exhausted. Shakespeare has said, 'Uneasy lies the head that wears a crown.' A king cannot sleep. One of the reasons is that he does not do any bodily labour. One who is sleepy during the day is bound to be awake when it is time for sleep. Keeping the body and the intellect idle during the day is nothing but sleep. Then the mind wanders at the time of sleep and the body too does not get real rest. Then one just keeps lying in the bed. Life is given to us to attain its highest ends, to fulfil its mission. If half of it is eaten up by sleep, how can anything worthwhile be achieved in life?

11. When a lot of time is consumed in sleep, the third manifestation of *tamas* – blunders – occurs naturally. A sleepy man's mind is not alert. That results in inattentiveness. Too much sleep gives rise to laziness

which results in forgetfulness; and this forgetfulness is detrimental to spiritual progress. It is, in fact, harmful even in worldly affairs. But it has become a normal phenomenon in our society. Nobody feels that it is a grave fault. We fix up an appointment with somebody and miss it, and then say casually that we forgot about it. We have no sense of having erred and do not feel bad about it; and the one to whom this answer is given is also satisfied with this explanation. It looks as though people think that there is no remedy for forgetfulness. But such negligence is harmful both in worldly and spiritual matters. Forgetfulness is a serious disease. It corrodes the intellect and saps the vitality of life.

12. Lethargy of the mind is the cause of forgetfulness. If the mind is awake, it will not forget things. Inattentive mind is bound to contract the disease of forgetfulness. Hence Lord Buddha had said, 'पमादो मच्चुनो पदं'. Forgetfulness is death itself.

To overcome it, one must conquer laziness and sleep, do physical work and be ever alert. Whatever you do, do it after due deliberation. Nothing should be done casually and impulsively. Thinking should precede as well as follow action; the Lord in the form of reason should be present in all the stages of an action. If such a habit is ingrained, the disease of inattention will be cured. The whole of the time at our disposal should be carefully planned. One should keep an account of every moment. Laziness will not then get any opportunity to penetrate one's life. Efforts should thus be made to conquer *tamas* in all its forms.

78. Cure for rajas: Living within the bounds of swadharma

13. Thereafter, we should turn to *rajas*. *Rajas* too is a terrible foe. It is the other side of *tamas*. In fact, '*rajas*' and '*tamas*' should be considered interchangeable terms. After resting for long, the body feels like doing something and after too much activity, it seeks rest. Thus *rajas* follows *tamas*, and vice versa. Wherever one of them is there, the other is invariably present. Like bread in the oven with the flames below and the embers above, man is caught between *rajas* and *tamas*. They toss him towards each other and together ruin him. His life is spent in getting kicked around by *rajas* and *tamas*, like a football.

14. The main characteristic of *rajas* is the itch and ambition to engage in all sorts of activities. There is an intense desire to do daring deeds. *Rajas* gives rise to limitless hunger for and attachment to actions. Then it becomes impossible to withstand the onslaught of desires and passions. Man wants to do something or the other. He feels an urge to move mountains, to fill up lakes and create new ones in the deserts. He wants to dig a Suez canal here and a Panama canal there. He is completely seized with such wild ideas. There is no thought except that of doing this or that thing. A child takes a piece of cloth, cuts it up and tries to make something out of its pieces. Activities impelled by *rajas* are of the same kind. Man is then never satisfied with what exists and wants to interfere with everything. He sees a bird, wants to fly and

makes aeroplanes; he sees a fish, wants to live like it in water and makes submarines. Thus, in spite of being a human being, he feels a sense of achievement in emulating the birds and the fish! Although residing in a human body, he yearns to enter into the bodies of other beings to have different experiences. Some even want to go to Mars. The mind is thus never at rest; it wanders all the time. A multitude of desires possesses man like an evil spirit. He wants change, activity, excitement. He is not satisfied letting things alone. He feels that if the things remain in their places in spite of him, it is an affront to him! A wrestler cannot contain the energy within him and bangs anything which comes in his way, without rhyme or reason. *Rajas* is always gushing forth driving man to do this or that. It makes man dig the earth and bring out stones which he then calls diamonds; it makes him dive deep into the sea and bring out rubbish which he then calls pearls. He then pierces holes through them, and through his own nose and ears as well, so that those could be worn there! Why does a man do all this? All this is under the influence of *rajas*.

15. Another effect of the *rajas* is the loss of stability and patience. *Rajas* wants immediate results. A slight obstruction therefore makes man give up the activity. Under the influence of *rajas* man starts new projects endlessly, leaving earlier projects incomplete. He is thus always vacillating between different activities. As a result nothing concrete is achieved. 'राजसं चलमध्रुवम्'. A *rajasic* activity is invariably marked with fickleness, wavering and lack of firmness. A man with *rajas* is

like a child who sows a seed and impatiently digs after a few minutes to find out whether it has sprouted. He is impatient to have everything quickly and lacks restraint. He does not know how to plant his feet firmly on the ground. Having done some work at a place and earned some recognition, he wants to go to other places seeking recognition there. Rather than doing concrete work steadily at one place, he prefers hopping from place to place in the pursuit of name and fame. His mind is fixed on that only. This lands him in a terrible condition.

16. Under the influence of *rajas*, man intrudes into all sorts of activities. He forgets his *swadharma*. In fact, performance of *swadharma* implies giving up all the other activities. *Karmayoga* as enjoined by the Gita is the cure for *rajas*. Everything in *rajas* is unsteady and fickle. If the water falling on the mountain-top runs down in different directions, all of it disappears eventually; but if it flows down in a single stream, it becomes a river, gathers strength and benefits all. Similarly, if a man concentrates all his energy and applies it to a single task in an orderly manner instead of frittering it away in a variety of activities, it will prove fruitful. That is why pursuit of *swadharma* is important.

One should, therefore, always reflect upon one's *swadharma* and devote all the energies to it. The mind should never be drawn to anything else. This is the test for *swadharma*. *Karmayoga* does not mean excessive or stupendous work. *Karmayoga* is not about how much you work. *Karmayoga* of the Gita is something quite different. The distinctive feature of *karmayoga* is the performance of *swadharma,* which is in tune with our nature and which comes to us naturally and inescapably, without any attention to the fruit, and progressive purification of the mind thereby. Otherwise, activities are continually going on in the world. *Karmayoga* means doing everything with a particular frame of mind. Sowing seeds in the field is not the same thing as throwing them here and there. There is a world of difference between these two actions. We know what we gain by sowing seeds and what we lose by throwing them. *Karma* that the Gita prescribes is like sowing the seeds. There is tremendous potency in performing one's *swadharma* which is one's duty. Here no effort is too great. There is, therefore, no scope for running around helter-skelter.

79. *How to determine one's swadharma?*

17. How to determine one's *swadharma*? The only reply to this question is that it is natural. It comes naturally to everyone. The very idea of going in search of it is strange. When a man is born, his *swadharma* too takes birth. *Swadharma*, like one's mother, is not to be searched for; it is already there when one is born. The world existed before we were born and it will be there after our departure. We are a part of the stream of existence. Service of our parents and our neighbours is our naturally accruing duty. We also have the experience of our inborn natural urges; they are common to all. We feel hunger and thirst; it is therefore our natural *dharma* to feed the hungry and

give water to the thirsty. Serving others, doing good to others, is thus our *dharma* which we do not have to go in search for. In fact, if we find that there is a search on for *swadharma,* it is a sure sign that there is something wrong, something is being done which is neither rightful nor righteous.

A man devoted to service does not have to search for the type and form of service; he finds his work laid out before him. But it has to be borne in mind that what appears to have come unsought is not necessarily a righteous duty. Suppose a farmer comes to me at night and says, "Let us shift the fence of my farm by a few feet so that the area of my farm will be larger. We can do it unnoticed." Although this work has certainly come unsought before me, it is clearly not my duty, as it is unethical.

18. The *chaturvarnya*[2] system appeals to me essentially because there are naturalness and *dharma* (duties) in it. Nothing can be gained by evading one's *swadharma.* My birth gives me my parents. Can I say that I do not like them? Whatever I might feel, they will continue

---

[2] Please refer footnote in Chap. 1.8. The system of *chaturvarnya* has been under fire from diferent quarters for being iniquitous. Vinoba too held that as it has been distorted because of hierarchical stratification, it has become irrelevant. However, he looked to it as a social arrangement which avoids unnecessary competition and is, therefore, conducive to peace and order in the society. He held that all the *varnas* or occupations should have equal social and spiritual status and should earn equal remuneration. He also believed that all should have the good qualities irrespective of their *varna* or occupation. It must also be pointed out that although Vinoba spoke of *chaturvarnya* in appreciative terms at times, referring to the basic idea underlying that system, he was against the caste system. He believed that it has nothing to do with the *chaturvarnya* and called it a blot on Hinduism.

to be my parents. The parent's calling comes naturally to the children. It is a distinguishing characteristic of *chaturvarnya* that the people should continue to follow their ancestral callings, provided they are not unethical. This system has now decayed and adherence to it has become difficult. But it would be nice if it could be properly reformed and revived. Nowadays the first 25-30 years of life are spent in learning a new vocation and thereafter people try to get a job or start a business. Thus, one spends the first 25 years of his life without doing anything else and this education has absolutely no connection with life. This period is taken as the time for preparation for the life ahead, which perhaps means that it is not part of life; life is to come later! It is as if one has to get education first and live thereafter. Learning and living have thus been divorced from each other. But anything unrelated to living is akin to death. The average expectation of life in India is 23 years[3] and people spend 25 years in learning a vocation! The best and the most precious period in life, which should be used in fulfilling oneself through energetic and enthusiastic service to the society, is thus wasted. But life is not child's play. It is indeed tragic that a valuable part of life is wasted in finding a calling. To avoid this, Hinduism has devised the concept of *varnadharma*.

19. But, even if the concept of *chaturvarnya* is set aside, everybody in all the nations of the world has his *swadharma* accrued to him even where there is no such system. All of us are born in a stream, in a

---

[3] This was the expectation of life at the time of these talks. Now it is well over 50. However, this does not affect the essence of the argument.

continuum, in a particular situation, and that defines our duties. It is, therefore, imperative that one is not attracted to duties which are out of context from the situation that one is placed in, even though they appear good and attractive. In fact, they should not be called duties at all. Often, a distant thing looks attractive and man is taken in by it. A man surrounded by fog feels that the fog is denser at a distance, although it is equally dense everywhere. Thus, things that are closer often go unnoticed and man feels attracted to what is distant. But this is a delusion that must be shunned. *Swadharma* may appear to be commonplace, imperfect and uninteresting; still that alone is good and beneficial. When a man is drowning in the sea it is the log floating near him, however rough and misshapen, that will save him. There may be a number of beautiful pieces of polished and carved wood in a carpenter's workshop; they are of no use to the man who is struggling for life in the sea. It is in his interest to catch hold of the log at hand. Likewise, the calling that has come to me as *swadharma* is beneficial to me even if it appears unattractive and commonplace. I should follow it and be immersed in it. Therein lies my redemption. If I set out to search for another sphere of service, I may end up losing both of them; and also the very urge for service. One must, therefore, be ever-absorbed in the performance of *swadharma*.

20. When one is absorbed in *swadharma*, *rajas* loses its force because the mind gets concentrated; it then never swerves from *swadharma*. Fickle *rajas* then becomes

powerless. If a river is deep, it can contain within its banks the onrush of any quantity of water without getting unduly disturbed. The river of *swadharma* can likewise hold all the force and power of man. Energy spent in the performance of *swadharma* is never too much. Pour all your energy into it and then the restlessness, which is a distinctive characteristic of *rajas*, will disappear. The sting of fickleness will be broken. This is the way to conquer *rajas*.

80. How to deal with sattva?

21. What now remains is *sattva*. One must be very careful in dealing with it. How can one detach the Self from *sattva*? It is a matter for subtle thinking. *Sattva* is not to be completely destroyed. *Rajas* and *tamas* are to be completely rooted out; but the matter is different with *sattva*. If a big mob is gathered at a place and it is to be dispersed, the police are ordered to shoot below the waist, so the people are not killed, but they do get wounded. *Sattva* is also to be wounded; it is not to be killed. After the disappearance of *rajas* and *tamas*, pure *sattva* remains. So long as the body is there, one must be in some mode or the other. What then does detachment from *sattva* mean?

When we have *sattva*, we become proud of it. This drags down the Self from its true nature. If we want bright light from a lantern, the soot deposit inside its chimney has to be wiped off; but this is not sufficient. The dust on the outer surface of the chimney has also to be removed. In the same way, the soot of *tamas* has to be wiped off and then the dust of *rajas*

should also be removed, so that the light of the Self could spread. Only the clean glass of pure *sattva* then remains between the light and us. Should the chimney be broken now? No. The lantern will then become useless. It needs the chimney. Therefore, instead of breaking the glass, one should fix a piece of paper on it in such a way that we can have the light but avoid its glare. Conquering *sattva* means elimination of pride about and attachment to *sattva*. We should make use of *sattva*, but that has to be done with care and skill. *Sattva* should be freed from pride.

22. How to overcome the pride that 'I have *sattva* in me'? Constant practice is a way, which will make it our second nature. Continuous performance of *sattvic* actions withers the pride about it. Through such actions, *sattva* becomes an integral part of our being. It should not remain a guest; it should rather become a member of the family. We feel proud of things that we do once in a while. We sleep daily, but do not consider it something special and do not talk about it. But if a patient has no sleep for days, and then has sleep for a while, he would tell everybody about it. An even better example is that of our breathing. We breathe for twenty four hours a day, but never talk about it or brag about it. A piece of straw may be carried along the stream of a river for miles; it will not brag about it. But swimming a few feet against the current will make one extremely proud of it. In short, one does not feel proud of something when it is natural.

23. We feel proud when some good action gets done through our hands. Why? Because it has not happened in the routine course. When a child does something good, the mother pats it on the back; otherwise the child is familiar with the mother's scolding only! When in the thick darkness of night there is only one firefly, look how proudly it shows itself off! It does not display its light steadily all the time. It twinkles and stops and twinkles again. That intermittent light fascinates us. A steady light does not attract us to that extent. Unbroken continuity makes a thing appear natural. One does not feel that there is anything special about it. Likewise, if all of our actions become *sattvic*, *sattva* will become part of our nature. A lion is not proud of its prowess; it is not even conscious of it. *Sattvic* attitude should thus become so natural that one is no longer conscious of it. Giving light is natural to the sun. It takes no pride in it. In fact, for it, to exist means to give light. A *sattvic* man should attain the same state. *Sattva* should be deeply ingrained in him; it should pervade every pore of his being. Then he would not feel proud of it. This is one stratagem for subduing and overcoming *sattva*.

24. Another is to give up attachment even to *sattva*. Pride and attachment are two distinct things. This is a subtle idea which can be understood more readily by means of illustrations. The pride of *sattva* may disappear, but attachment to it may still remain. Take, for example, breathing. One does not feel proud about it, but attachment to it is very much there. We cannot stop breathing even for a few minutes. It goes on though there is no sense of achievement.

Socrates was snub-nosed and people used to make fun of it. But the witty Socrates would say, "In fact, it is my nose which is beautiful as wide nostrils take in more air." The point is that one feels attachment to *sattva*. Take, for example, compassion for all creatures. It is a good quality, but we should be able to keep away from attachment to it. We should have compassion, but no attachment to it.

The saints can guide others because they possess *sattva*. Their compassion attracts people to them so much so that the whole world showers love on them. As love has reached its zenith in them, they receive love from the whole universe. They give up attachment to their bodies, but the whole world gets attached to them. It cares for them. But the saints should give up this attachment too; they should get free from this bondage also. They should separate the Self from this love and adoration, which is their great reward. They must not feel that they are somewhat special or exceptional. *Sattva* should be assimilated in this way.

25. Thus, first pride about *sattva* should be conquered and then attachment to it. Pride can be conquered through constant practice of *sattvic* actions. To conquer attachment, one should work without desire for fruit and dedicate to the Lord the fruit that is received because of *sattva*. When *sattva* is fully assimilated in life, the fruit of *sattvic* actions appears before us in the form of supernatural powers or fame. But that should also be regarded as worthless. A tree never eats its own fruit, howsoever attractive and delicious it may be. Renunciation is sweeter than enjoyment.

26. Dharmaraj rejected the ultimate fruit of all the merits acquired in life : the enjoyment of pleasures in heaven. That was the crowning finale to his sacrifices. He was entitled to enjoy that sweet fruit. But had he enjoyed it, the merit would have got exhausted. 'क्षीणें पुण्यें मृत्यु-लोकास येती ।' ('Enjoyment of the heavenly pleasures consumes the merits and one has then to take birth again on the earth.') He would have again got caught in the cycle of births and deaths. How great was Dharmaraj's sacrifice! It always stands before my eyes. Thus, pride about *Sattva* is to be vanquished by ceaseless performance of *sattvic* actions and then attachment to it should be conquered by remaining detached from the fruit of actions and dedicating it to the Lord.

81. The concluding point : Self-realisation and refuge in bhakti

27. Now, to conclude, one last point. Even if you imbibe *sattva*, vanquish your ego and give up attachment to the fruit of actions, you shall continue to be vulnerable to the onslaught of *rajas* and *tamas* from time to time, so long as you are saddled with the body. You may for a while think that you have conquered *rajas* and *tamas*, but they will return again and again with a vengeance. You must, therefore, be ever alert. As the sea rushes in to encroach the land, the waves of *rajas* and *tamas* dash against the mind and make inroads into it. They should never be allowed to do so. Vigilance should not slacken even for a moment. And it must also be borne in mind that danger continues to lurk in the background

despite all the vigilance so long as there is no Self-knowledge, no Self-realisation. It must, therefore, be attained at any cost.

28. Mere vigilance is not sufficient for this purpose. Then how could Self-knowledge be attained? Will constant practice be sufficient? No. There is only one way, and that is *bhakti* with all the earnestness and love. You may conquer *rajas* and *tamas*, become steadfast in *sattva* and make renunciation of the fruit a habit, but still this is not enough to attain Self-knowledge; and there is no redemption without Self-knowledge. The grace of the Lord is essential for this purpose. Through loving devotion, we should make ourselves worthy of it. I see no other way. Arjuna asks the same question at the end of this Chapter and the Lord answers, "Be devoted to Me with mind absolutely one-pointed and without any desire for reward. Serve Me. He who serves Me thus can cross the *maya*. Otherwise this mysterious *maya* is hard to cross." This is the easy way of *bhakti*. This is the only way.

(22.5.32)

CHAPTER 15

The Integral Yoga:
Seeing the Lord everywhere

82. The way of bhakti is not different from the way of efforts

1. Brothers, in a way we have today reached the end of the Gita. In the Fifteenth Chapter, all the ideas put forward in the Gita reach their consummation. Chapters 16 and 17 are in the nature of appendices, and there is the summing-up in the Chapter 18. Hence the Lord has termed this Fifteenth Chapter 'a *shastra*' (science) – 'अत्यंत गूढ हें शास्त्र निर्मळा तुज बोलिलों' ('O blameless one, I have told you this most secret *shastra*.'), says the Lord at the end of this Chapter. The Lord says so not because this is the concluding Chapter, but because the elaboration of the principles of life and the revelation of the spiritual wisdom is complete here. The essence of the Vedas is in this Chapter. The very function of the Vedas is to make man aware of the realm of spirituality. This has been done in this Chapter and it has therefore earned the title, 'the essence of the Vedas.'

In the Thirteenth Chapter we saw that the Self should be separated from the body. In the Fourteenth Chapter we saw how efforts could be made in this regard. *Rajas* and *tamas* should be resolutely forsaken, *sattva* should be developed and attachment to it should be overcome. The fruit received because of it should be renounced. Efforts should be continued in this way. In the end, we were told that Self-realisation is indispensable for those efforts to be wholly successful. And Self-realisation is possible only through *bhakti*.

2. But the way of *bhakti* is not something different from the way of making efforts. To suggest this, the *samsara* has been compared, at the beginning of the Fifteenth Chapter, to a great tree. This tree has enormous branches that are nourished by the three *gunas*. It is said right at the beginning that this tree should be cut down with the axe of detachment and dispassion. It is clear that the ways and means described in the last Chapter have been mentioned here again. *Rajas* and *tamas* are to be destroyed and *sattva* nourished and developed. One is the destructive aspect and the other is the constructive one, but both of them belong to the same work, just as removing weeds and sowing seeds are two parts of the same job.

3. There are three brothers in the Ramayana : Ravana, Kumbhakarna and Vibhishana. Kumbhakarna is the embodiment of *tamas*, Ravana that of *rajas* and Vibhishana that of *sattva*. The drama of the Ramayana with these three characters is being continuously enacted inside our body. In this drama, Ravana and Kumbhakarna ought to be killed. Only the Vibhishana-principle, provided it takes refuge at the feet of the Lord, may be nurtured, as it can help our progress. We saw this in the Fourteenth Chapter. This has been repeated at the beginning of the Fifteenth Chapter : Cut down the *samsara* tree full of *sattva-rajas-tamas* by the axe of detachment. The Gita is here placing before us the ideal of the lotus flower.

4. In the Indian culture, the best and the noblest things in life are described using the simile of the

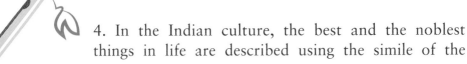

lotus. The lotus is the symbol of Indian culture. It expresses the most elevated thoughts. It is clean and pure and remains unsoiled by the mud around. Sanctity and detachment are its distinguishing characteristics. Different organs of the Lord are, therefore, described employing the simile of the lotus : He has lotus-eyes, lotus-feet, lotus-heart and so on. It is meant to show and impress on us that everywhere there is beauty, holiness and detachment.

5. This Chapter is intended to take the *sadhana* described in the last Chapter to its fulfilment. This fulfilment takes place when *bhakti* and Self-knowledge are combined with the effort. *Bhakti* is also a part of the effort. *Bhakti* and Self-realisation are parts of the same spiritual discipline. The Vedic sage says,

'यो जागार तं ऋच: कामयन्ते यो जागार तमु सामानि यन्ति'

– 'Vedas love him who is awake; they come to meet him.' It means that *jnana* and *bhakti* come to him who is awake. *Bhakti* and *jnana* are not different from the effort. They, in fact, make the effort interesting and add flavour to it. This is what this Chapter intends to show. The nature of *jnana* and *bhakti* that is revealed here must be grasped with full concentration .

83. Bhakti makes the effort easier

6. I cannot cut up the life. I just cannot conceive that *karma*, *jnana* and *bhakti* are disconnected from each other; it is just not true. Let us take the example of cooking in this jail. Some of us do this job. If a

man does not know cooking, he would make a mess of it; food will either be undercooked or burnt. But even if a man knows cooking, he would still not be fit for the job if he has no love or devotion for the work; if he does not feel, "This food is meant for my brothers, that is, for the Lord Himself. I should prepare it as best as I can. This is service to the Lord Himself." Thus, cooking needs knowledge as well as love. Food would not be tasty unless there is *bhakti* in the heart while cooking. That is why nobody can cook better than the mother. Who else can do it with the same love and care? Cooking needs hard work or penance as well. It is thus clear that love, knowledge and effort, all three are needed for any job. All the activities in life are supported by this tripod. If one of the legs of the tripod is broken, it cannot stand. All the three legs are necessary. The very term 'tripod' conveys this meaning. The same is true of life. *Jnana, bhakti* and *karma* – that is, ceaseless effort – are the three legs of the tripod of life. Life should be built on these three pillars. Logically, you may take *jnana, bhakti* and *karma* as different things, but they cannot be separated from each other in practice. The three together make one great entity.

7. Even though this is true, it does not mean that *bhakti* has no special merit of its own. If *bhakti* enters into any work, that work appears easy. Not that it ceases to involve toil, but that the toil does not then appear to be toil; it becomes a labour of love. To say that the way of *bhakti* is easy means that work does not appear burdensome because of *bhakti*. Work loses

its strenuousness. No matter how much work we do, we feel as if we have done nothing. Jesus has said that when you fast, your face should appear cheerful : "But thou, when thou fasteth, anoint thine head and wash thy face : that thou appear not unto men to fast." In short, we should be so full of *bhakti* that we do not feel any hardship. We talk of patriots walking smilingly to the gallows. Sudhanwa was smiling in the cauldron of boiling oil, chanting God's Name. It means that to such persons even the most terrible tribulations did not appear to be so because of *bhakti*. It is not difficult to row a boat in a river, but how difficult it would be to drag it over rocky land! The boat of our life should also have the water of *bhakti* beneath it, so that we could sail happily. If there is rocky and uneven terrain, then it would be extremely difficult to drag the boat of life. *Bhakti*, like water, makes easy the voyage of our life.

Bhakti makes *sadhana* easy. But without Self-knowledge, there is no hope of going beyond the three *gunas* permanently. How could then one have Self-knowledge? The only means is the way of *bhakti* which involves doing *sattvic* actions continuously, assimilating *sattva* thereby, and overcoming pride for it and attachment to its fruit. Only by continuous unremitting efforts on these lines one can reach the goal of Self-realisation. Till then, efforts should never be given up. This is a matter for the greatest endeavour. It is not child's play. It is not something that can be taken casually. Spiritual quest demands that one does not allow despair to creep in and slacken the efforts even for a single moment. There is no other alternative. The seeker does sometimes get exhausted and exclaims wearily, 'तुमकारन तप संयम किरिया, कहो कहां लौं कीजे!' ('O God! How long should I continue to be engaged in penance and self-control for you!') But such utterances should not be given much importance. Penance and self-restraint should become so ingrained that they become our very nature. It is unbecoming in the path of *bhakti* to ask, "How long am I to continue *sadhana*?" *Bhakti* will never allow impatience and despair to arise. This Chapter has put forth an extremely noble thought in order that one does not get tired and experiences ever-increasing joy and enthusiasm in *bhakti*.

84. The triad of service

8. We see countless objects in the world. They are to be divided into three categories. When a *bhakta* gets up in the morning, he has only three things in mind. First, he remembers the Lord. Then he makes preparations for His worship. The *bhakta* is the servant, while the Lord is the one who should be served. The rest of the creation is the means of worship. It exists to provide flowers, incense and sandalwood paste for the worship. This is the triad of service. This is the teaching in this Chapter. But normally a devotee worshipping an image does not look upon everything in the world as the means of worship. He picks and chooses a few things. He goes to a garden and fetches a few flowers, brings a few incense sticks, prepares some food-offerings. This is not in keeping with the teaching in this Chapter. All the means of doing penance, the

means of doing *karma* constitute the means for the Lord's service. The idea is to make all the actions the articles of worship in this way. Nothing exists in the world except these three : the worshipper, the Lord and the means of worship. The Gita is infusing the spiritual discipline of non-attachment (*vairagya*), which it wants to impress on us, with *bhakti*. Thereby it is removing the arduousness in *karma*, the 'action-ness' in action and rendering it easy.

9. When someone in the ashram has to do more work, he never thinks, 'Why should I work more?' There is great significance in this. If a devotee gets an opportunity to worship for four hours instead of two, would he complain about it? In fact, he would be more delighted. This is what we experience in the ashram. We should have this experience everywhere in life. Life should be fully devoted to service. There is the *Purushottam* (the Supreme Person) to whom service is to be rendered, and there is the *akshar purusha* (the imperishable person),[1] the eternal servant, who knows no weariness and who has been serving since the dawn of creation. He is like Hanuman, who is ever standing before Rama with folded hands.

---

[1] We have already referred to the concept of *Purusha* in the footnote in Chap.7.2. 'There are two persons in the world – the perishable and the Imperishable', says the Gita (15.16). 'All the contingent beings are perishable and the unchanging is called the Imperishable.' It also speaks of the third *Purusha* – the *Purushottam* – that is, the Supreme Lord. The Gita's speaking of three *Purushas* or rather the triple status of the *Purusha* differs from the standpoint of traditional *Sankhya*.

Hanuman knows no weariness. The servant, who is deathless like Hanuman, is also ever-ready for service.

Akshar purusha is such a lifelong servant. He says, "The Lord is ever there and I, the servant, too exist for ever. If He is deathless, so am I, the servant. Let us see whether He gets tired of my service or I get tired of serving Him! I shall follow Him in all His incarnations. If He comes in the form of Rama, I shall be Hanuman. If He comes in the form of Krishna, I shall be Uddhava. Every time He comes into being, I too shall be there." Let that be the spirit. *Akshar purusha*, the imperishable person, serves the Lord in this way age after age. It should always be borne in mind that He is *Purushottam*, the Master and the *bhakta* is His obedient servant; and the whole creation, which changes every moment and presents itself in innumerable forms, should be made the means of worship, the means of service. Every act should become the worship of the Lord.

10. The Lord who is to be served is *Purushottam* and *jiva*, the servant, is the *akshar purusha*. Both are imperishable, but the creation around us, which provides the means for service is perishable. And its perishability has profound significance. It is not a defect; it is its glory. It is because of this that the creation is ever new. Yesterday's flowers will not do for today's worship; everyday you can have fresh flowers. That the creation is perishable is a great blessing. It adds to the glory and splendour of service. 'Just as I use fresh flowers daily for worship, I shall also

put on new bodies and serve the Lord. I shall go on giving new forms to my means of worship.' – That is what the *bhakta* aspires for. Beauty is because of perishability.

11. Today's moon is not the same as yesterday's; tomorrow's moon will also be different. It exudes a different kind of charm every day. What a joy it is to behold the two days old waxing moon! It is the second day's moon that shines on the forehead of Lord Shiva. The beauty of the eighth day moon is quite different. Only a few stars are seen in the sky that night. On the full-moon night, stars are almost invisible. In the full moon we can see the Lord's face. The beauty of the new-moon night is truly serene. There is calmness everywhere. Innumerable stars twinkle freely in the absence of the overpowering brightness of the moon. The new-moon night celebrates freedom in its fullness. The moon on that night merges into the Lord – into the Sun from whom it receives its luminosity. Then it seems to show to the *jiva* how it should surrender itself to the Lord without causing any trouble to the world. The form of the moon is ever-changing; but that is, in fact, a source of ever-new delight.

It is its mutability that makes the creation perennial. The nature of the creation is like a gently flowing stream. If a stream stops flowing, it would become a stagnant pool. The water of the river flows in an unbroken stream. It is forever changing. One finds joy in something if there is newness, freshness in it. Traditional rituals have laid down that the Lord should be worshipped with different leaves and flowers and fruits in different seasons. This lends newness and freshness to the worship and makes it interesting. The children initially find the learning of the alphabet quite boring. Mastering the writing of the alphabet involves repetitive practice and the children try to wriggle out of it. But subsequently they become familiar with different words and sentences and start reading books. Then they develop a taste for literature, get acquainted with various classics and experience boundless joy. This happens in the realm of service as well. If the means of service are ever new, the enthusiasm for service grows and the spirit of service gets developed.

12. It is because of the perishability of the creation that we have fresh flowers every day. The cremation ground adds to the beauty of the town. Everyday, old people die and new children are born. That makes life interesting. Had there been no death, and therefore no cremation ground, life would have become a veritable hell. You would have got tired of seeing the same people day after day. In the hot summer, the earth is parched. But do not be troubled; summer days will pass. The heat of the summer is necessary to have later the joy of the rainy season. If summer is not hot enough, rains will make the earth slushy. We would not then have plentiful crops. Once I was wandering about on a hot summer day. My head felt the heat and it made me happy. A friend warned me that I could fall ill. I told him, "The earth below is getting heated. Let this head, a lump of clay, too get heated like it." How joyful is the experience of receiving the

shower on the heated head! But if a man is not in the habit of being out in the scorching summer heat, he would not feel like coming out in the open when it is raining; he would remain within the four walls of the house and bury his head in books; he would not dance under the grand and sacred shower. He would miss the divine joy. But the sage Manu was a great lover of nature. He writes in his *Smriti*, "When it starts raining, holiday should be declared." Should the pupils sit in the *ashram* roting something when it is raining outside? That is the time for singing and dancing, for becoming one with the nature, watching ecstatically the meeting of the earth and the sky. Nature is itself a great teacher.

In short, the perishability of creation implies newness in the means of worship. Thus we have creation endowed with energy to create endlessly new means, the eternal and ever-ready servant and the Lord. Let their game go on now. '*Purushottam*, the Supreme Person, is giving me different means of worship and taking loving service from me. He is engaging me in various activities by putting in my hands newer and newer means. I am nothing but His instrument.' – How joyful will the life be if this feeling, this spirit informs the life!

85. Bhakti means service without any sense of 'I'

13. The Gita wants every action to be imbued with *bhakti*. It is good to worship the Lord for half an hour. It is worthwhile to steady the mind and meditate on the Absolute, forgetting the ordinary worldly affairs

for a while, at the time of sunrise and sunset when the splendour of sunshine is particularly appealing. Such good habits must, of course, not be given up. But the Gita is not satisfied with this much only. It wants that all the activities that we do throughout the day should be done in the spirit of worship. While doing everything – be it bathing, dining, sweeping – we should have the Lord in mind. For instance, while sweeping we should feel that we are sweeping the Lord's courtyard. All our actions should thus become acts of worship. Let this spirit be ingrained in you, and then you would see how your behaviour changes. When we collect flowers for worship, we choose them carefully, put them delicately in the basket, see that they are not crumpled and remain fresh, and do not even smell them. Let all the activities in life be informed with this spirit. While sweeping the village roads, I should feel that I am serving the Lord in the form of my neighbours. The Gita wishes to imprint this attitude on us. It wants all the actions to become acts of worship. Worshipping for half an hour or so does not satisfy it. The holy text yearns to see the whole life charged with the Lord's presence, with the spirit of worship.

14. By teaching *Purushottamyoga*, the Gita is bringing the life of action to fulfilment. The Lord (*Purushottam*) is the Master, I am His servant, and this creation is the means for worship. Once this is realised, what else is needed? Tukaram says, 'झालिया दर्शन करीन मी सेवा, आणीक ही देवा न लगे दुजें ।' ('When I meet you face to face, I shall devote myself to your service; I do not need anything more.')

Then there will be never-ending service. Nothing like 'I' will exist. The sense of 'I and mine' will be completely erased. Everything will be for the Lord. There would be nothing else except wearing ourselves away for the good of others. The Gita is exhorting us repeatedly to remove the sense of 'I' and live a life devoted to the Lord, imbue the life with *bhakti*. The Lord is the Master, I am the servant and the creation is the means for service; there is then no question of getting encumbered with anything else. Life will then be free of any worries.

86. The mark of jnana : Seeing the Purusha everywhere

15. Till now, we have seen that *bhakti* should be combined with *karma*. But it is also necessary to have *jnana* (Self-knowledge) fused with them. The Gita is not otherwise satisfied. This does not mean that these three things are distinct from each other. We use different terms for them for the sake of convenience only. *Karma* and *bhakti* are one and the same; there is thus no question of combining *bhakti* with *karma*. The same is true about *jnana*. How can we have *jnana*? The Gita says, "You will have it when you see the *Purusha* everywhere." The eternal servant is *Purusha*; the Lord, the recipient of service, the *Purushottam*, is also *Purusha* and the creation which flows continuously, takes different forms and provides different things for worship, is also *Purusha* – all are different forms of *Purusha* only.

16. What does this outlook imply? It implies an attitude of perfect and flawless service to all. If your sandals squeak, oil them. Keep them in good condition. The Lord is present in them too. The spinning wheel is a means of service. Lubricate it regularly. Otherwise it will refuse to let you spin. It too is *Purusha*. It should be kept neat and clean and in working order. The whole creation should be seen as full of consciousness; do not look upon it as inert. Nothing is inert, nothing is devoid of His presence. The spinning wheel that hums melodiously is not inert; it is the Lord's image. On the *Pola*[2] day we worship the bullocks, shedding our pride. This is not an ordinary thing. In fact, we should always have the *Pola* spirit in mind while taking due work from them; it should not be restricted to a single day. A bullock too is a form of the Lord. We should also take due care of the plough and the agricultural implements. All the means of service are sacred. How grand this vision is! Worship does not mean offering flowers etc. to the image of the Lord; keeping anything neat and clean and tidy is its worship – be it a lamp, a scythe or a door hinge. The means of worship should be spotless and faultless. Divine consciousness pervades everything. When we have this vision, *jnana* will enter into our *karma*.

17. First, *bhakti* was infused with *karma*, and now *jnana* too is poured into it, forming the divine elixir of life. The Gita has finally brought us to the path of

---

[2] A festival in rural Maharashtra, celebrated by the farmers.

service that is full of *advaita* (non-duality). There are three forms of *Purusha* in the whole of the creation, and it is the *Purushottam* who takes all these forms. These three together constitute one single *Purusha*. Nowhere is there any duality, any distinctions. This is the pinnacle of spirituality where the Gita has brought us. Here, *karma*, *bhakti* and *jnana* fuse together and become one. *Jiva* (the lower self), *Shiva* (the Absolute, or the Supreme Self) and the creation become one. There is then no conflict, no contradiction between *karma*, *bhakti* and *jnana*.

18. Jnanadeva has given in his 'Amritanubhava' an illustration that is dear to Maharashtra,

'देव देऊळ परिवारु । कीजे कोरूनि डोंगरु
तैसा भक्तीचा वेव्हारु । कां न होआवा ।'

('The temple, the image and the devotee are all carved out of a single rock. Why cannot *bhakti* be like that?')

The temple, the image of the Lord and that of the devotee and the flowers for worship are all carved in the same rock. A single rock takes different forms[3]. Why should not the same thing happen in the realm of *bhakti*? Why cannot there be unity between the *bhakta* and God even when the relationship of master and servant remains? Why cannot the creation, the means of worship, verily become the Self even though

---

[3] Ellora caves in central Maharashtra are famous for these sculptures.

they are distinct? All the three *Purushas* are after all one. *Jnana, karma* and *bhakti* should combine to form the spring of life. This is the perfect *Purushottamyoga*. The sport of loving devotion should then go on even though the servant, the master and the means of service are one and the same.

19. A true devotee is one who has fully assimilated this *Purushottamyoga*.

'सर्वज्ञ तो सर्वभावें सर्वरूपी भजे मज'

('He who knows Me, the *Purushottam*, knows all; and he worships Me in all the forms with all his being.')

Such a man is a *jnani* and still is a perfect *bhakta*. One who has attained *jnana* is invariably full of love. Knowing the Lord and loving Him are not two different things. If we know that something is bitter, we do not develop any love for it. Exceptions apart, bitter taste arouses dislike. But sugar immediately arouses liking. Likewise, knowing the Lord and loving Him are one and the same thing. But should one compare the Lord with so ordinary a thing as sugar? Knowing and loving Him being one and the same thing, there is no point in debating over the place of *bhakti* in *advaita* (non-duality). As Jnanadeva says, 'हें चि भक्ति हें चि ज्ञान । एक विठ्ठल चि जाण ।।' ('Know the Lord; that itself is devotion as well as knowledge.') *Bhakti* and *jnana* are two names for the same thing.

20. When supreme *bhakti* is infused into life, the *karma* that follows is not different from *bhakti* and *jnana*. *Karma*, *bhakti* and *jnana* together make a single beautiful form. And wonderful service, saturated with love and knowledge, springs from it naturally. If I love my mother, my love should express itself in my actions. True love always toils for the loved ones. It expresses itself in service. Service is the outer, visible form of love. Love adorns itself with innumerable acts of service. Where there is love, knowledge inevitably follows it. When I am to serve somebody, I must know what kind of service would please him; otherwise, the service could prove to be disservice. Love must therefore have knowledge of those whom it serves. Knowledge is needed to spread the grandeur of love through actions. But love has to be there primarily. Without it, knowledge would be of little use. An action done out of love is quite different from an ordinary action. When the son comes home tired from the field, the old mother looks at him with affection and concern and speaks a few comforting words, "My child, you really are tired; aren't you?" These few words have tremendous effect. Pour knowledge and devotion into all the actions in life. This is what *Purushottamyoga* means.

87. The essence of all the Vedas is in the palm of my hands

21. This is the essence of all the Vedas. The Vedas are many; but *Purushottamyoga* is their simple and sweet essence. Where are these Vedas? Their ways are strange indeed! The very first verse of this Chapter

refers to the tree having the Vedas in its leaves – 'ज्याच्या पानांमधें वेद'. The Vedas (the spiritual wisdom) are not, after all, hidden in a book; they are there in the whole universe for everybody to see. Shakespeare has spoken of 'books in the running brooks, sermons in stones.' The Veda is not made up of words, it is not in some book; it is in the creation around us. Devote yourself to service and it will be revealed to you.

22. 'प्रभाते करदर्शनम्' – One should behold one's palms in the morning. The Veda is there in those palms. They ask you to serve. See whether your hands have toiled yesterday, whether they are ready to toil today, whether your palms carry marks of labour. 'प्रभाते करदर्शनम्' implies that when your hands work tirelessly, that which has been ordained for you by Providence will become clear; you will know what you are destined to and are supposed to do.

23. What is the point in asking, "Where is the Veda?" The Veda is not somewhere else; all of us have received it when we are born. We are the living embodiment of the Veda. We are the consummation of a long tradition. We are the fruit of the tree that has sprouted from the Veda-seed. Within this fruit, there are seeds of innumerable Vedas. The Vedas have grown many times within us.

24. In short, the essence of the Vedas is in our hands; it is for us to realise it. It means that life has to be built on the foundation of service, love and knowledge. We can interpret the Vedas in the way we

like. The saints, who were embodiments of service, claim, 'वेदाचा तो अर्थ आम्हांसीच ठावा' ('We alone know the meaning of the Vedas'). The Lord is saying here, 'The Vedas know Me only; I am the *Purushottam*, the essence of all the Vedas.' Would it not be wonderful if we could assimilate this *Purushottamyoga* in our lives! The Gita is suggesting here that the Vedas express themselves in every action of the person who assimilates *Purushottamyoga*. This Chapter contains the essence of the Gita. The Gita's teaching is fully revealed here. Everybody should strive to follow this ceaselessly. What else can one say?

(29.5.32)

CHAPTER 16

Conflict between the Divine and the demoniacal tendencies

88. Divine qualities : The harbinger of Purushottamyoga

1. Brothers, in the first five Chapters of the Gita, we saw how life should be lived and its purpose fulfilled. From the Sixth Chapter to the Eleventh one, *bhakti* was viewed from various angles. In the Eleventh Chapter, we had the grand vision of *bhakti*. In the Twelfth Chapter, we compared *saguna* and *nirguna bhakti* and had a look at the noble attributes of the *bhakta*. *Karma* and *bhakti* were thus dealt with upto the Twelfth Chapter. *Jnana* was then discussed in the Chapters 13, 14 and 15. We learnt therein that the Self should be separated from the body, the three *gunas* should be conquered for that purpose and in the end, we should see the Lord everywhere. In the Fifteenth Chapter, the whole science of life was seen at a glance. Life reaches its consummation in *Purushottamyoga*. Nothing remains to be said thereafter.

2. I cannot bear to see *karma, jnana* and *bhakti* as separate entities. Some seekers are so inclined that they can think of nothing but *karma*, while some imagine *bhakti* as a distinct path and put exclusive emphasis on it. Some have disposition towards *jnana* only. But I am not an exclusivist; I do not believe that life means only *karma* or *bhakti* or *jnana*. I do not also subscribe to the doctrine that life is the combination of these three; nor do I subscribe to the utility-oriented view that life should have *karma, bhakti* as well as *jnana* in some measure. That *karma, bhakti* and *jnana* are the successive stages in *sadhana*, is also not acceptable to

me. I do not also think that there should be harmony between *karma*, *bhakti* and *jnana* in the life. I wish to experience complete identity of *karma*, *bhakti* and *jnana*. To understand what I mean, let us take the example of a piece of a sweet. Every piece of a sweet has sweetness, every piece has some volume and some weight. The sweetness, volume and weight are not distinct and separable things. When I put a piece of a sweet into my mouth, I taste its sweetness, devour its volume and digest its weight. It is not that some pieces have sweetness only, some have only volume and some have only weight. Every action in life should likewise be full of service, love and knowledge. *Karma*, *bhakti* and *jnana*, all should permeate the whole of life. Every action should be spiritual. This is what *Purushottamyoga* means. Infusing the whole of life with spirituality is, of course, easier said than done. When we go deep into its implications, we realise that for pure and selfless service *bhakti* and *jnana* must be there within the heart. *Karma*, *bhakti* and *jnana* are thus completely and absolutely one and the same. *Purushottamyoga* is the highest state in which this is attained. This is the pinnacle of life.

3. Now, what does this Sixteenth Chapter tell us? Just as the glow on the horizon proclaims that the sun is about to rise, the rise of *Purushottamyoga* in life is preceded by the glow of virtues. This Chapter describes this glow, and also the darkness which this glow dispels. We seek concrete proof to get convinced about anything. How are we to know that service, *bhakti* and *jnana* have become part of our life? We

must have some test. We toil in the field and measure the result in terms of the yield of the grains. Similarly, the progress in our spiritual quest should also be measured. We should assess our experience, see how far good tendencies have become part of our nature and how many virtues have been imbibed, how far life has been infused with the spirit of service. This is what this Chapter tells us. In this context, the Gita uses the term *'daivic sampatti'* (divine qualities) and calls the qualities opposed to them *'asuric'* (demoniacal). The Sixteenth Chapter describes the battle between these two sets of qualities.

89. The forces of light and darkness

4. Just as in the First Chapter Kauravas and Pandavas are found pitted against each other, here the armies of the divine and the demoniacal qualities have been pitted against each other. It has been the tradition to use allegories while describing the struggle between the good and the evil that has been raging since time immemorial in the human mind. There is fight between Indra and Vritra in the Vedas, between gods and demons in the Puranas, between Rama and Ravana in the Ramayana, between Ahura Mazda and Ahriman in the scripture of the Parsis, between God and Satan in Christianity, between Allah and Eblis in Islam. In all the religions, this fight has been described. In poetry, the gross is described by the subtle whereas in the religious texts subtle feelings are described in terms of gross images. I am not suggesting that the description of the battle at the beginning of the Gita is merely imaginary; it may have been a historical event. But

the poet has used it for his own purpose. Giving the allegory of a battle, he tells us what to do when there is conflict of duties. The Sixteenth Chapter depicts the battle between the good and the evil. Allegorical description of the battle is also there in the Gita.

5. Kurukshetra, the battleground of the Mahabharata war, is inside us as well. If you observe carefully, you will realise that it is the battle raging within the mind which we see in the world outside in the concrete form. The one whom I see as my enemy confronting me in the outside world is, in fact, the evil in my mind that has taken concrete shape. Just as a mirror gives my true image, the good and the evil thoughts in my mind have their images in the outside world as friends and enemies. I see in the dreams what I experience or think while I am awake. Similarly, that which is in my mind is seen by me in the outside world. There is absolutely no difference between the battle within and the battle without. In fact, the real battle is that which is waged within ourselves.

6. Virtues and vices are pitted against each other within our mind. Both the armies are in neat formations. Every army needs a commander. The virtues too have nominated a commander. He is 'abhaya' (fearlessness, or freedom from fear). Fearlessness has been given the first place in this Chapter. This has not happened accidentally; it must have been deliberate. No virtue can develop without fearlessness. Virtues have no value without truthfulness, and fearlessness is essential for commitment to truth. Virtues cannot develop in an

atmosphere charged with fear; in such an atmosphere they, in fact, prove to be vices. In such an atmosphere, even good tendencies get weakened. Fearlessness is the leader of all the virtues. An army has to be alert about attacks both from the front and the rear. It can be surreptitiously attacked from the rear as well. Therefore, while fearlessness is in front, humility should guard the rear. It is indeed an excellent strategy. In all, twenty-six virtues have been listed here. You may imbibe twenty-five of them excluding humility, but if your ego gets inflated thereby, an attack from the rear will make you lose whatever you have gained. That is why humility has been placed at the rear. In the absence of humility, there is no knowing when victory will turn into defeat. Virtues can be developed only by keeping fearlessness in front and humility in rear. Most of the twenty-four virtues in between them can be said to be synonyms of non-violence. Compassion for all creatures, gentleness, forgiveness, serenity, freedom from anger and malice – all these are different terms for non-violence. In fact, all the virtues are contained in truth and non-violence; truth and non-violence are the essence of all of them. But fearlessness and humility are in a different category. Fearlessness makes advancement possible and humility ensures safety. With truth and non-violence in our armoury, we should march ahead fearlessly. We ought to move freely over the whole expanse of the vast and extensive life. There must, of course, be humility to prevent us from slipping. We can then fearlessly move ahead, carrying out experiments in truth and non-violence. In short, truth and non-violence develop because of fearlessness and humility.

7. Against this army of virtues, the army of vices is pitted. About hypocrisy, ignorance etc., the less said the better. We know them well. Hypocrisy is as it were ingrained in us. The whole edifice of life as it were stands on that foundation. And of ignorance, it can be said that it has become an innocent excuse for us to cover our lapses. We seem to think that it is not, after all, a serious crime. But the Lord says that ignorance is a sin. Socrates had said just the opposite thing. In the course of his trial he said, "What you think as sin is only ignorance, and ignorance is excusable. How can there be any sin without ignorance, and how can you punish ignorance?" But the Lord is saying that ignorance too is a sin. We know that ignorance of law is no excuse in a court of law. Ignorance of the Divine Law too is a crime. In fact, both the Lord and Socrates mean the same thing. The Lord is telling us how to look at our ignorance while Socrates is telling us how to look at others' sins. The sins of others should be forgiven, but it is a sin to forgive ignorance in ourselves. We should not allow the least vestige of ignorance to remain in ourselves.

90. Four stages in the development of non-violence

8. Thus the divine and the demoniacal qualities are arrayed against each other. We should stick to the divine qualities and shun the demoniacal ones. Development of the divine qualities like truth and non-violence has been going on since time immemorial, but still there is much to be done. There is unlimited scope for their development in social life. Even if an individual develops himself to perfection, scope

for development in the social, national and global spheres remains. Individuals have to use their own development to stimulate development in others just as manure stimulates growth of the crops. We can take in this context the example of the development of non-violence which has been going on for ages.

9. It is worth studying how non-violence has developed progressively. That will show how spirituality has progressively developed in life and how it can develop further. The problem of protection from violent attacks had always been there before the non-violent man. At first he devised the idea of having a special class of fighters – the *Kshatriyas* – for the protection of the society. But later that class itself turned against the people. The non-violent *Brahmins* then had to tackle the problem of protection from the haughty and insolent *Kshatriyas*. Parshuram, although non-violent, took to violence and started exterminating *Kshatriyas*. He resorted to violence to make the *Kshatriyas* abandon violence. It was certainly an experiment in non-violence, but it could not succeed. Parshuram is said to have exterminated the *Kshatriyas* twenty-one times; still they survived, as the attempt was basically flawed. How can *Kshatriyas* be rooted out when you yourself become a violent *Kshatriya*? The seed of violence survived. One may go on cutting trees; but new trees will continue to come up so long as the seeds are not destroyed. Parshuram's intention was good, but his experiment was strange. He was trying to exterminate the *Kshatriyas* by becoming a *Kshatriya* himself. In fact, he should have begun by

chopping off his own head! I am pointing out the flawed nature of Parshuram's experiment, not because I am wiser; I am a child before him. But I am standing on his shoulders and can therefore see much farther; and it appears to me that the basis of his experiment was wrong. Resorting to violence to counter violence results only in increasing the number of the violent. But this was not realised at that time. Good-natured and well-intentioned people of that time, men of non-violence, experimented according to their lights. Parshuram was a firm believer in non-violence and he resorted to violence, not for the sake of it, but to establish non-violence.

10. That experiment failed. Then came the age of Rama. *Brahmins* again began to think about the matter. They had already given up violence and had resolved never to commit it. But then how to repel attacks from the demons? They thought that the *Kshatriyas* have anyway taken to violence; so it is better to make them fight the demons. Vishwamitra, therefore, brought Rama and Lakshman to protect his *yajna* (sacrificial worship) from the demons and got the demons destroyed through them. Today we think that non-violence should be able to take care of itself; it should not be dependent on others. But sages like Vasishtha and Vishwamitra did not consider it *infra dig* to utilize the services of *Kshatriyas* for their protection. But what would have happened, had Vishwamitra not found Rama? He would then have preferred to die rather than take up arms.

The experiment of fighting violence by violence had been a thing of the past, and the resolve to remain personally non-violent was now firm. The non-violent men were now ready to die if they could not get *Kshatriyas* to protect them. In the Ramayana, there is an incident wherein Rama enquires about the heaps of bones he had seen and the sages tell him that those were the bones of the non-violent *Brahmins* who, on being attacked by the demons, embraced death without putting up any resistance. This type of non-violence had the element of sacrifice in it, but there was also an expectation of protection from others. Such weakness cannot lead to perfect non-violence.

11. The saints of the mediaeval times carried out the third experiment. They resolved, "Now we will never seek protection from others and rely on non-violence itself to protect us. That alone can be the true protection." This experiment was on an individual plane; and on that plane, it was carried to perfection. But it did not have a social dimension. Had people asked the saints what should be done in the face of a violent attack, they would perhaps have failed to give an unequivocal answer; they would perhaps have admitted their inability to give unambiguous guidance to the people in such an eventuality. Again, it is childish impertinence on my part to blame the saints. But I am telling you what I can see standing on their shoulders. The saints should forgive me for my comments; and I am sure that they would, as they are large-hearted. The thought of collective experiments in non-violence might have crossed their minds, but they

must have thought that the situation was not ripe for such experiments. They made different experiments on the individual level only; but, a science, after all, develops through the synthesis of experiences gained thereby.

12. Now we are in the midst of the fourth experiment, in which the whole society is engaged in resisting violence through non-violent means.

These are the four experiments in non-violence. All of the earlier experiments were imperfect, and our present experiment too is imperfect. This is but inevitable in the course of evolution. But in the context of their times, the experiments of the past were the best possible ones. After thousands of years, our present non-violent war too would appear to have a large measure of violence in it. There will be many more experiments in non-violence in future. Not only *jnana*, *karma* and *bhakti*, but also all the virtues have been continually developing. Only the Lord, the Supreme Self, is perfect; none else is. *Purushottamyoga* in the Gita is perfect; but it is yet to be fully developed in individual and social life.

The sayings too go on acquiring newer and higher meanings and connotations. The sages are considered 'seers' of the *mantras* (Vedic verses), not their authors, as they 'saw' their meanings through a vision. But those are not the exclusive meanings of the *mantras*. More developed meanings can be seen by us. This is so, not because there is something special in us; it is on the basis of their experiments and experiences that we go ahead.

I have chosen non-violence as an example and reviewed its development, as it is the essence of all the virtues, and also because we are engaged in a non-violent struggle[1].

91. A great experiment in non-violence : Giving up flesh-eating

13. So far, we saw how non-violent men devised ways for protection from violent attacks. This is one aspect of non-violence. We saw how non-violence has been developing in human relationships characterised by conflicts and clashes. But there is conflict between the men and the beasts too. Men have still not been able to solve the conflicts among themselves and they are also unable to live without eating the flesh of animals of lower and weaker species. Human beings have been around for thousands of years and still they have not thought about how to live in a way befitting the human beings. They are still unable to live like human beings. But change is taking place in this respect as well. In all probability, men in prehistoric times ate roots and fruits only. But it appears that, in the course of time, perverse thinking led most of the mankind to take to flesh-eating. Good and wise men, however, did not like this and laid down a restriction that if anybody wants to eat meat, he should eat the meat

---

[1] Vinoba was addressing the political prisoners jailed during the *satyagraha* campaign in 1932.

of animals sacrificed in *yajnas* only. Their intention was to minimise violence. In the course of time, some people completely abjured meat and others, who could not do so, were permitted to eat it after offering the same to the Lord and undergoing some sacrifice and penance in a *yajna*. Permission for meat-eating only in *yajna* was thus for limiting violence, but this was later misused on a large scale; performance of *yajnas* just to have an opportunity to eat flesh became quite common. Lord Buddha then came forward and said, "Eat flesh if you like; but at least do not do so in the name of the Lord." This too was to limit violence and develop self-restraint. Thus, both through *yajnas* and through their rejection, we learnt to abjure meat. In this way, we gradually gave up flesh-eating.

14. This great experiment in the history of the world took place only in India. Millions of people became vegetarians. If we are vegetarians today, we can claim no credit for that. We have got used to it because of the merit of our ancestors. We are now surprised and shocked when we hear or read that the sages of yore used to eat flesh. We cannot imagine it. It is creditable that they abjured flesh through great efforts in spite of being used to it. We have inherited their virtues without any efforts on our part. The fact that they were not vegetarians and we are so does not mean that we are better; we have been benefited by their experience and vegetarianism has become natural to us. We should now proceed further. We should try the experiment of giving up milk also as it also is an animal product. It is unbecoming of man to take

the milk of animals. Perhaps our descendants in the distant future would be shocked to learn that their ancestors used to drink milk. They may consider us barbarians. Some of us take a vow not to take milk. Our descendants may fail to understand why a vow was necessary at all!

In short, we should go on experimenting with fearlessness and humility. There is ample scope for development; no virtue has yet been developed to perfection.

92. The three asuric ambitions : Power, Culture and Wealth

15. The Lord has described the demoniacal qualities too, so that we could keep away from them and concentrate on the development of divine qualities. The essence of the demoniacal way of life is in three things : power, culture and wealth. Those with this nature want to impose their culture on the whole world, believing it to be the best. And why is it the best? Because it is theirs! Individuals with this nature, and empires built up by such individuals, are after these three things only.

16. The *Brahmins* believe that their culture is the best, that all the knowledge is contained in their Vedas. They want hegemony of the Vedic culture established over the whole world. 'अग्रतश्चतुरो वेदान् पृष्ठतः सशरं धनुः' ('The four Vedas should be in front, and the arms should follow them') is what they want. But when arms are to follow the Vedas, the poor Vedas are as good as finished!

Muslims also believe that whatever is written in the Koran alone is true. Christians too believe that truth is contained in the Bible only. They believe that nobody, howsoever noble and virtuous he may be, can ever be redeemed if he does not believe in Jesus Christ. They have provided only one door to the house of the Lord – the door of Jesus! People provide a number of doors and windows to their houses, but how strange it is that they provide only one door to the God's house!

17. 'कुलीन मी चि संपन्न, माझी जोडी कुठें असे' ('I am of noble lineage. I have all the riches. None can equal me.') – This is what everybody thinks. We want to be known as descendants of some or the other great sage or king. This is the case in the West too. There too, people boast of being the descendants of Norman nobles etc. We have the *guru-shishya* (master-pupil) tradition also, wherein people relate themselves to great sages. This too is an attempt to claim greatness for themselves and their culture. But, if your culture is really great, let it be reflected in your actions, in your conduct. The people are, however, not bothered about that. To aspire to spread the culture that we do not have in our own life is a demoniacal (*asuric*) way of thinking.

18. In the same way, some people think, 'I am the only one fit to posses all the wealth in the world. I want all that wealth and I shall have it.' They claim that they want wealth to distribute it equally among all. Akbar used to feel sincerely that the Rajput kingdoms should be incorporated in his empire, so that there

would be reign of peace. Modern demons want to concentrate all the wealth in their hands ostensibly to redistribute it.

19. For this, they seek power. They want concentration in their hands. They want that their word must prevail. Everybody must follow their dictates. Freedom means obedience to them! – That is what they think. Thus the demoniacal nature lays stress on culture, power and wealth.

20. There was a time when the *Brahmins* were dominant in the society. They made laws and laid down codes of conduct. Kings bowed before them. That era passed, and was followed by the age of the *Kshatriyas*. The *Kshatriyas* waged wars of conquest and fought for political supremacy. The *Kshatriya* culture too passed on in course of time. The *Brahmins* believed that only they were fit to be teachers; others should learn from them. They were proud of their culture. The *Kshatriya*s revelled in killing others. Then came the age of the *Vaishyas*. They are concerned solely with making money. They are not bothered if they have to face humiliations provided their purse is intact. All they want is to acquire more and more money. Do not the British tell us, 'If you want Independence, have it by all means; but give us facilities and concessions for trading our manufactured goods. Then you may study your culture as much as you want. Remain poor and care for your culture; we are least bothered about that.' These days, wars are fought basically for economic gains. This age too will pass on; it is indeed on its way out.

93. Self-restraint : The scientific way to get rid of desire, anger and greed

21. We should try to get rid of the *asuric* tendencies. Desire, anger and greed represent the essence of the demoniacal character. These demoniacal passions have the world dancing to their tune. This dance must stop. We must shake them off. Anger and greed spring from desire. Greed follows desire when circumstances are opportune for the gratification of desire; and anger follows when desire is thwarted. The Gita has enjoined us repeatedly to keep away from these three enemies. The same has been said at the end of the Sixteenth Chapter. These are the three broad gateways to hell. Roads leading to hell are quite wide and there is a lot of traffic through them! One can find many companions on the way. But the path of truth is narrow.

22. How are we to guard ourselves from desire and anger? By accepting the scientific way of self-restraint. Experiences and experiments of the saints lead to the evolution of the science of life. Self-restraint is a cardinal principle of that science. Therefore, hold fast to it. Do not indulge in arguments like 'What will happen to the world in the absence of desire and anger? Is it not necessary to have them, at least in a small measure?' Desire and anger are already there in too large a measure – much more than needed. Why create unnecessary confusion? Do not worry that human race will come to an end if desire (for sensual pleasure) disappears. No matter how many

children you produce, a day is bound to come when the human race will disappear from the earth. This is what the scientists are telling. The earth is slowly getting colder. At one time the earth was extremely hot. There were no living creatures on it. A time will come when the earth will become excessively cold and all life on it will come to an end. It may take millions of years, but this is bound to happen. You may go on procreating; the final dissolution of the world cannot be averted. The Lord descends on the earth for the protection of *dharma* (righteousness), not for the protection of numbers. As long as there is one man devoted to *dharma*, one man who shuns sin and is committed to truth, there is no cause for worry. The Lord will take care of him. People without *dharma* are as good as dead.

23. Taking all this into consideration, live in the world with self-restraint and avoid excesses. Do not follow your whims; and the whims of others as well. *Loksamgraha* does not mean going by what the people want. Organising men in large numbers or accumulating wealth are not the indications of progress. Development does not depend on numbers. If population grows unchecked, men will kill one another. Firstly, they will kill birds and beasts and lose balance and will then kill and devour their own children. If desire, lust and anger are considered useful, there can be no doubt that men will end up devouring each other. *Loksamgraha* means showing the people the path of pure morality. If by freeing itself from lust and anger the human race disappears from the earth,

it may reappear on Mars. One need not have worry on that count. God is unmanifest, but immanent. He would take care of all. Therefore, emancipate yourself, redeem yourself first. Do not look too far into the future. Do not worry about the whole of creation and the human race. Increase your moral strength, eschew desire, lust and anger from your mind. 'आपुला तूं गळा घेई उगवूनि' ('Free your own neck from the noose.'). Even if you could do this much, it is sufficient.

24. It is a pleasure to watch the sea of *samsara* from a distance. How can a drowning man enjoy the beauty of the sea? The saints stand on the shore and enjoy the sight of the sea of *samsara*. There can be no joy without imbibing this attitude of remaining detached like the saints. Be detached like a lotus-leaf. Buddha has said that the saints stand on the hill-top and look down at *samsara*, which then appears trivial to them. Try to do likewise, and you too would find it trivial; you would lose interest in worldly affairs.

In short, the Lord has exhorted us in this Chapter to shun the demoniacal qualities and acquire the divine ones. Let us make efforts in this direction.

(5.6.32)

CHAPTER 17

Programme for the seeker

94. Disciplined life relaxes and frees the mind

1. Dear brothers, now we are gradually approaching the end of the Gita. In the Fifteenth Chapter, we viewed the complete philosophy of life. The Sixteenth Chapter was a sort of annexure to it. In the human mind, and in the society which is its image, a struggle between two types of tendencies, two ways of living or two types of human nature is continually going on. The Sixteenth Chapter teaches us to nurture and develop the divine nature. The Seventeenth Chapter is the second annexure. It can be said to contain *karyakramyoga* (the *yoga* of daily programme). In this Chapter, the Gita has suggested a daily routine. This Chapter deals with the programme for the seeker.

2. If we want our mind to feel relaxed and happy, we should have discipline in life. Our daily living should follow a well-thought out design. It is only when the life proceeds within particular pre-set bounds in a disciplined way that the mind can be free. A river flows freely, but its flow is bounded by the banks. If it were not so bounded, the water would run in different directions and go waste. Let us keep the example of the *jnani* before our eyes. The Sun is the preceptor of the *jnanis*. The Lord has said in the Gita that he taught *karmayoga* first to the Sun and Manu – the thinking man – learnt it from the Sun. The Sun is free and independent. The secret of its freedom lies in its regularity. It is our everyday experience that if we regularly take a particular route, we are able to think while walking, without paying any attention to

the road. But if we walk on different roads everyday, our attention would be focused on the road and the mind would not be able to think. Thus, we should have discipline in the life to have a free and joyful, and not burdensome, life.

3. For this purpose, the Lord has suggested a programme in this Chapter. We are born with three institutions or orders. The Gita is suggesting here a programme whereby they can operate in an efficient manner to make the life happy. The first of these is the body that wraps us. The vast world, the whole creation around us, of which we are a part, is the second one. The third one is the society into which we are born. It includes our parents, brothers and sisters and neighbours. Everyday we use these three and wear them out. The Gita wants us to endeavour continually to replenish what is lost through us, and thereby make our life fruitful. We should selflessly discharge our inborn duties towards these three orders.

These duties are to be discharged. But how? Through *yajna* (sacrifice), *dana* (charity) and *tapas* (penance and austerities) – these three together comprise the scheme for the purpose. We are familiar with these terms, but we do not comprehend them clearly. If we could comprehend them and bring them into our lives, the body, the creation and the society – all would fulfil their purpose and our lives will also be free and happy.

95. Triple endeavour for this purpose

4. Let us first see what *yajna* means. Everyday we make use of the nature. If a hundred of us crowd together in one spot for a day, that will spoil the place, pollute the atmosphere, and thus harm the nature. We should do something to recoup nature, to restore its balance. It is for this purpose that the institution of *yajna* was created. *Yajna* is intended to reimburse, to put back what we have taken from nature. We have been farming for thousands of years and eroding the fertility of the soil thereby. *Yajna* says, "Return to the soil its fertility. Plough it. Let it absorb heat from the sun. Manure it." To make good the loss is one purpose of the *yajna*. Another purpose is to purify the things we use. We use a well and make the place all around it dirty and slushy. The harm thus caused should be undone; so we should clean its surroundings. Production of something new is the third aspect of *yajna*. We wear clothes; so we should spin regularly to produce them. Growing cotton or foodgrains, spinning – all these are forms of *yajna*. Whatever we do as *yajna* should not have any selfish motive behind it; it should rather be done with a sense of duty to compensate the loss we have caused. There is no altruism in it; it is the repayment of what we already owe. In fact, we are born with a debt. What we produce for repayment of that debt is a form of service; we are not obliging anybody thereby. We use so many things in the world around us. *Yajna* should be done for their replenishment and purification as well as for the new production.

5. Human society is the second institution. Our parents, teachers, friends – all of them toil for us. *Dana* has been prescribed to discharge our debt to the society. *Dana* too is no altruism. We are already highly obliged to society. We were totally defenceless and weak when we were born. It is the society that looked after us and brought us up. We should therefore serve it. When we serve others without taking anything in return, that is altruism; but we have already taken much from the society. The service that is rendered to repay that debt is *dana*. *Dana* means contributing to the progress of mankind. While *yajna* means working for the replenishment of nature's loss, repayment of the debt to society through exerting oneself physically or through money or some other means is *dana*.

6. The third institution is the body. It too gets worn out daily by our use. We daily use our mind, intellect and organs. *Tapas* has been prescribed to remove the defects and distortions that arise in the body and to purify it.

7. Thus it is our duty to act in such a way that these three institutions – nature, society and the body – function smoothly and efficiently. We create a number of good or bad institutions, but these three have not been created by us. They had been given to us. They are natural, not man-made. It is our natural duty to replenish through *yajna*, *dana* and *tapas* the wear and tear in these three orders. If we follow this, our whole energy will be harnessed for this purpose. No strength will be left for anything else. All our strength would

be consumed for the sake of these three institutions. If we could say like Kabir, "O Lord! I am returning this shawl given by you without soiling it!", that would be a matter of fulfilment for us.[1] But for this, the triple programme of *yajna-dana-tapas* must be followed.

Here we have regarded *yajna, dana* and *tapas* as if they were different entities; but in fact, they are not so. Nature, society and the body are not completely distinct entities. Society is not something outside nature, nor is the body outside it. Therefore, productive labour (*yajna*), *dana, tapas* – all these can be called *yajna* in a broad sense. It is in this spirit that the Gita has referred to *dravyayajna* (sacrifice with material gifts) and *tapoyajna* (sacrifice with austerities) in the Fourth Chapter. The Gita has broadened the meaning of *yajna*.

Whatever service we render to these three institutions is bound to be a form of *yajna*. This should of course be without any desire or expectation for reward. In fact, there can be no room whatever for expecting any fruit of our actions, as we have already received much from these institutions. We are already burdened with debt. What we have to do is to return what we have already taken. Nature attains a state of harmony and equilibrium through *yajna*, society attains such a state

---

[1] Here, reference is to the famous poem of saint Kabir (who was a weaver by occupation) wherein he tells the Lord that the shawl (i.e. the body) given by the Lord is normally soiled by the people, but he has used it with meticulous care and is returning it to Him (while bidding farewell to the world) in the same spotless (i.e. sinless) condition.

through *dana* and *tapas* maintains equilibrium in the body. *Yajna-dana-tapas* is thus the triple programme for preserving balance and order in these three institutions. It will lead to purification and elimination of pollution.

8. To enable us to serve in this manner, we have to consume something. That too is a part of *yajna*. The Gita calls it *aahaara* (food). Just as an engine needs fuel, the body needs food. The food is not *yajna* in itself, but it is necessary for it. That is why we say before starting the meals, 'उदरभरण नोहे जाणिजे यज्ञकर्म' ('This is not for filling the belly; understand that it is an act of *yajna*.') Just as offering flowers to the Lord is worship, toiling in the garden to produce the flowers is also worship. Anything done for the performance of *yajna* is a form of worship. The body can be useful to us only when it is given food. Whatever is done for the sake of *yajna* is a kind of *yajna* itself. The Gita calls such actions 'sacrificial acts' (actions for the sake of *yajna*). Whatever is offered to the body to enable it to be ever-ready for service is a kind of sacrificial offering; it is a form of *yajna*. The food taken for the sake of service is indeed sacred.

9. Again, all these actions should have faith at their foundation. One should always have in mind the idea that all the service is to be ultimately dedicated to God. This is extremely important. Life cannot be full of service if such a spirit is not there. Dedication to the Lord is the key that must never be overlooked.

96. Making sadhana sattvic

10. But, when could we dedicate our actions to the Lord? Only when they become *sattvic*. *Yajna-dana-tapas* – all must be *sattvic*. In the Fourteenth Chapter, we saw the principle of making our actions *sattvic*. In this Chapter, the Gita tells us how that principle is to be applied.

11. The Gita is doing this with a dual purpose. The service that is being outwardly rendered to the world in the form of *yajna-dana-tapas* should itself become the inward spiritual *sadhana*. Service to the world and spiritual *sadhana* should not need two different courses of action. They, in fact, are not two different things. For both, the efforts made, the actions performed are the same. And such actions are to be dedicated to the Lord in the end. The *yoga* that combines service, spiritual discipline and dedication to the Lord should be realised by a single activity.

12. Two things are necessary to make the *yajna sattvic*. There should not be any desire for the fruit, but the actions must result in some fruit. If there is desire for the fruit, the *yajna* will be *rajasic*; if it is fruitless, it will be *tamasic*.

Spinning is a *yajna*. But if you have not poured your soul into it, if there is no concentration of the mind, it will be a lifeless and mechanical work. If there is no cooperation from the mind, the work will not be methodical and scientific. Unscientific work becomes lifeless. *Tamas* creeps into such work. Such work cannot create something excellent. It cannot yield any fruit. *Yajna* should be desireless, but it must yield the best possible fruit. If the mind is not in the work, if you have not poured your heart and soul in it, it becomes a burden. How can it then yield the best fruit? If the outward work gets spoilt, it is a sure indication of the lack of cooperation from the mind. Therefore, take to the work from the bottom of your heart, and have cooperation from your mind. We must work for the best possible returns to repay the debt due to the creation. Cooperation from the mind is the systematic way to ensure that the work does yield some fruit.

13. In this way, when desirelessness gets ingrained in the mind and systematic and fruitful actions begin to take place, only then the purification of mind will ensue. What is the test for the purification of mind? We should examine our outward actions for this purpose. If they are not pure and well-done, we may take it that the mind too is impure. When does the work become beautiful? When we work with pure heart and devote all our energy to it, the Lord, pleased with it, puts His seal of appreciation and approval on it. That makes the work beautiful. Beauty is the divine grace showered on pure and sacred efforts. A sculptor, absorbed in carving, feels that the beautiful image that is taking shape is not his creation; beauty somehow manifests itself in the image at the last moment. Can divine art manifest itself unless there is purity in the mind? We pour the beauty and purity

in our hearts into the Lord's image, and that makes the image holy. That image is but an image of our mind in the concrete form. All our actions are images of our mind. If the mind is pure, the actions too will turn out to be beautiful. We should judge the purity of outward actions by the purity of mind and the purity of mind by the purity of outward actions.

14. In this connection, one more important point is not to be missed. It is that all the actions should be charged with *mantra* – with the spirit, with the understanding of their true purport. Actions without *mantra* are meaningless. While spinning, one should always have the feeling of establishing a bond with the poor. If we spin for hours on end, but without this *mantra* in our heart, it is all wasted. It would not then purify the heart. Look at the action of spinning as the revelation of the Lord hidden in the sliver; then that action will become *sattvic* and beautiful. It will become a kind of worship; a sort of sacrificial service. Then that thin yarn will link you to the society, to the people, to the Lord. Yashoda saw the whole universe in the mouth of child Krishna.[2] You too will see the universe in the thin yarn when it is charged with the *mantra*.

---

[2] Yashoda, the foster-mother of Krishna, once suspected that he had stealthily eaten butter and asked him to open his mouth. When Krishna did so, she saw the whole universe in it and realised that the child was not an ordinary one, but was the Lord Himself.

97. Purity in food

15. To enable us to render such service, we must be vigilant about the purity of our diet. The state of our mind depends on the diet. We should take food in regulated and measured quantity. How much we eat is more important than what we eat. It does matter what food we choose to eat, but it matters even more that it is in the right measure.

16. Whatever we eat is bound to have its effect. Why do we eat? To enable us to render the best possible service. Eating too is a part of the *yajna*. We should eat because it is necessary to make the *yajna* of service yield fruit. Look at the food with this feeling. The food should be clean and pure. There is no limit to an individual's efforts for making his diet pure and *sattvic*. Our society too has made strenuous efforts for the same. Indian society made extensive experiments in this regard for thousands of years. It is difficult to imagine the hardships and austerities involved in those experiments. India is the only country in the world where a large number of communities have completely abjured flesh-eating. Even non-vegetarian communities do not have it as the main and regular item in their diet. Non-vegetarians too feel that it is unbecoming to eat flesh; they too have renounced it mentally. *Yajna* was introduced to discourage meat-eating and it was to fulfil this very purpose that it was later abandoned. Lord Krishna changed the very meaning of the word '*yajna*'. He impressed upon the people the value and importance of milk. Krishna did a lot of extraordinary

things, but in which form do the Indian people adore Him most? It is Gopalkrishna – Krishna the cowherd. Gopalkrishna, with a cow by His side and flute on His lips, is the most familiar image for Indians. The great benefit of learning to cherish the cow was that people gave up meat-eating. Cow's milk came to be greatly valued and the prevalence of meat-eating was reduced.

17. Still it cannot be said that perfect purity in food has been attained. We need to advance further. Bengalis eat fish and many people are surprised at this. But it is not right to condemn them on that account. They have nothing but rice in their diet. It does not provide enough nutrition to the body. We shall have to make experiments to find out vegetable substitutes for fish, which are equally nutritious. Individuals will certainly come forward for such experiments and make extraordinary sacrifices. Society progresses because of such individuals. The sun keeps burning brightly and that enables us to have the normal body temperature of 98°F. necessary to remain alive. Only when individuals whose *vairagya* (non-attachment) burns brightly like the sun are born in the society, when they free themselves from the shackles of circumstances and vigorously pursue their ideal, the ordinary beings like us can have a little detachment necessary in worldly affairs. In this context, I often think of the penance and the sacrifices of the sages, some of whom must have even laid down their lives to end the practice of flesh-eating prevalent at that time.

18. We have collectively achieved this much; we have reached this point in making our diet pure and *sattvic*. We should not lose what our ancestors attained through untold sacrifices. We should not let go this achievement of Indian culture. It is not enough that we somehow manage to exist. That is easy; even animals live likewise. Are we like them? No, there is a difference. Cultural development lies in increasing this difference. Our country carried out the great experiment of giving up flesh-eating. Let us continue it. At least we should not slip below what has already been achieved.

Such exhortation has become necessary as some of us have now begun to think that meat-eating is desirable. Today, the cultures of the East and the West are influencing each other. I am confident that good will come out of it in the end. Our superstitious beliefs are crumbling under the impact of Western culture. There is no harm in it. What is good will endure, what is bad will disappear. But superstitious beliefs should not be replaced by an unbelief which is held equally blindly and uncritically. Just as we should not believe in anything blindly, we should not disbelieve in something blindly. It is not that only belief can be blind; unbelief too can be blind.

People have begun to think again about meat-eating. Whatever may be the reason, appearance of a new idea delights me. It is an indication of the people's wakefulness, and it is reassuring. But if we begin to walk without being fully awake, we are likely to

stumble and fall. We must not, therefore, hasten to change our habits in a hurry. We may go on thinking furiously from all the possible angles. Do subject *dharma* to the test of reason. If it does not stand the test, it is good for nothing. Whatever part of *dharma* fails to stand the test of reason is useless and fit to be discarded. The *dharma* which is so robust that the tools of reason themselves break down while dealing with it is the true *dharma*. *Dharma* is not afraid of reason. One must never restrain thought; but one must not rush into action. Nothing should be done impatiently and impulsively until one is fully convinced of its rightness. One must have patience and restraint while acting. We should not give up the gains which are hard won.

98. The Gita's scheme for harmonious living

19. Purity of food keeps the mind pure. It also strengthens the body. One can then serve the society properly. Both the individual and the society will then be contented. There will be no conflicts in the sociey wherein *yajna-dana-tapas* are going on in the right manner and in the true spirit. Just as mirrors facing each other reflect the images in each other, contentment in the individual and in his society are reflected in each other. In fact, my contentment and contentment in the society are identical, as can be verified. One will then experience oneness (non-duality) everywhere. Duality and opposition will disappear. The Gita is suggesting a scheme to have harmony and orderliness in society. How nice it would be if we could organise our daily life in accordance with the Gita's plan!

20. But today, there is a conflict between the individual life and the social life. How to resolve this conflict? This question is being discussed everywhere. What are the proper spheres and limits for the individual and the society? Where is the boundary to be drawn? Who should have priority between the two? Who is superior? Protagonists of individualism regard the society as an inert entity. A military commander would speak gently to an ordinary sepoy while dealing with him as an individual, but he will order a battalion at his sweet will, as if it were inert, like a wooden block which can be moved at will. Even here, while I am addressing a couple of hundred persons, I am saying whatever occurs to me, irrespective of whether you like it or not, as if you all are an inert mass. But when I deal with an individual, I have to listen to him patiently and give an answer after thoughtful consideration.

Thus there are some who expound that the society is inert and only the individual is a conscious entity, while some others attach importance to the society. I may lose my hair, my hand may be amputated, I may lose eyesight, even one of my lungs may cease to function, still I continue to live. Each organ, looked at separately, has no life of its own. If any one of the organs perishes, the whole does not perish. The body is a collective entity; it continues to live. This is the standpoint of the collectivists. These are the two approaches opposed to each other. Your inference will depend on how you look at it. What you see is coloured by the colour of your eyeglasses.

21. Some give importance to the individual and some to the society. This is because the concept of 'struggle for existence' has come to have a hold on our minds. But is life meant for struggle? If it is so, why not prefer death? Discord and strife is a recipe for death. It is because of this concept that we distinguish between self-interest and the supreme interest, that is, the good of all. What could we say of the man who invented the idea that self-interest and the supreme good have nothing to do with each other? He could create the illusion of a difference where none existed! It is indeed surprising that this non-existent distinction is being widely accepted. It is like erecting a wall like the Great Wall of China, setting bounds to the horizon and then imagining that nothing exists beyond those bounds! All this is due to the absence of *yajna* in the life. Therein lies the genesis of the dichotomy between the individual and the society.

Such dichotomy is unreal. Suppose a curtain hung in a room divides it in two compartments. As the wind blows, sizes of these compartments vary. They are not fixed; they depend on the wind. The Gita has nothing to do with such imaginary divisions. It exhorts us to follow the dictates of the law of inner purification. Then no contradiction between the interests of the individual and those of the society would arise. Their respective interests would not then be opposed to each other. It is in ensuring this, in securing the interests of all that the Gita's ingenuity lies. A single individual following the Gita's law could make a nation rise. A nation is made up of the individuals comprising it. How can a nation be called a nation if it does not have individuals having wisdom and character? What gives India its distinctive character? India means Rabindranath (Tagore), India means Gandhi, and a few such names. People know India as the land of these individuals. Take a few individuals in the ancient times, a few in the mediaeval period, a few in the recent period, add to them the Himalayas and the Ganga, and that makes India as it is. This is the definition of India. You may have elaborate commentaries on this definition; commentaries only expand the definition. Just as the quality of milk is judged by the fat content in it, the quality of a society is judged by the individuals in it. There is no confict between the interests of individuals and that of the society. How can there be a conflict? In fact, there should be no conflict between different individuals as well. What does it matter if some are better off than others? Nobody should be a destitute and the wealth of the rich should be utilized for the society – that is enough. I may have the money in my left pocket or in the right one; it is mine all the same. Individual and social life can be organised skilfully in such a way that whenever any individual prospers, everybody prospers, and the nation also prospers.

Still we create divisions. But if the head is separated from the body, both the head and the trunk will be lifeless. So do not imagine any division between the individual and the society. The Gita is teaching how an action can be done in a way that is neither against the doer's self-interest nor against the supreme good. There is no opposition between the air in my room and the air outside. If I imagine any opposition between them and shut the doors and windows of my room, I am bound to die of suffocation. If I do not assume such opposition between them and open the doors and the windows, the boundless air outside the room flows into it. The moment I imagine opposition between my interests and the society's interests and cling to 'my' house, 'my' land etc., I deprive myself of the infinite wealth that lies beyond 'my and mine'. If this small house of mine is gutted by fire or collapses, I cry as if everything is lost. But why should I cry? What is the point in making petty and narrow assumptions first and then crying? When I say that a few rupees are mine, I deprive myself of the immeasurable wealth in the world. When I call a couple of individuals 'my' brothers, I deprive myself of having brotherly relations with countless other individuals. But we are totally oblivious of this. How petty a man becomes! In fact, self-interest of a man and the good of all should be identical. The Gita is showing a simple and beautiful way to have perfect cooperation between the individual and the society.

22. Take the matter of food. Is there any opposition between the mouth and the stomach, the two organs involved in eating? Mouth should provide to the stomach only as much food as it really needs. It should stop the moment the stomach signals it to do so. Both the stomach and the mouth are our organs. We are the master of both of them. There is perfect unity between their interests. Why do you create any

wretched opposition? The organs in the body are not opposed to each other; there is cooperation between them. This is true for the society as well. To promote cooperation within the society, the Gita is prescribing *yajna-dana-tapas*, to be performed with pure heart. Such *karma* will lead to the welfare of both the individual and the society.

A man whose life is full of the spirit of *yajna* belongs to all. Just as every child feels that the mother loves him, everyone feels that such a person belongs to him. The whole world cherishes such a person. Saint Ramdas has said, 'ऐसा पुरुष तो पहावा । जनांस वाटे हा असावा' ('Everybody wants such a man in their midst.') The Gita teaches us how to live such a life.

99. *The mantra of dedication*

23. The Gita further says that after infusing the life with the spirit of *yajna*, it should be totally dedicated to the Lord. It may be asked, 'What is the necessity of dedicating it to the Lord when it is already full of service?' The point is that it is easy to say that life should be imbued with service, but it is far more difficult to achieve this. It can at best be achieved partially; and that too after many births. Moreover, the actions may be full of the spirit of service, and still they can lack the spirit of worship. Hence the actions should be dedicated to the Lord with the *mantra* ॐ तत् सत् (*Om tat sat*).

It is difficult for the acts of service to be fully saturated with the true spirit of service. When we seek well-

being of others, we satisfy our own interest too. There is no action which is purely in the interests of others. It is impossible to do anything that is free from even a trace of self-interest. We should, therefore, wish that our service should become more and more selfless and desireless. If there is a wish to do increasingly purer service, then you must dedicate all the actions to the Lord. Jnanadeva has said, 'नामामृत-गोडी वैष्णवां लाधली। योगियां साधली जीवन-कळा।' ('*Vaishnavas*, i.e. *bhaktas* taste the nectar-like sweetness of the Name of the Lord, and the *yogis* have mastered the art of living.') Sweetness of the Name and the art of living are not two different things. Chanting the Name from within and mastering the art of living – these are in tune with each other. The *bhakta* and the *yogi* are one and the same. When actions are dedicated to the Lord, self-interest, altruism and the supreme interest (i.e. the supreme good) will become one. 'I' and 'you' are now apart; they should first be united to form 'we', which should then be united with 'Him', i.e. with the Lord. Firstly, we should achieve harmony with the world and then with the Lord – that is what the *mantra* ॐ तत् सत् (*Om tat sat*) suggests.

24. The Lord has countless Names. Vyasa compiled a thousand of them in the *Vishnusahasranam* (Thousand Names of Lord Vishnu). In fact, any Name that we can think of is His. Whatever Name appeals to us, we should take it to be one of His Names and should see the corresponding attribute present in the whole of creation and shape our life in accordance with it. To meditate on a Name, to see the corresponding attribute

present in the whole of creation and to imbibe that attribute – I call it *tripada Gayatri* (three-step sacred *mantra* of deliverance). For example, if we take the Name *'dayamaya' or 'Rahim'* (one full of mercy and compassion), that is, look upon the Lord as merciful and compassionate, we should envision the merciful and compassionate Lord pervading the entire creation. We should realise that He has given a mother to every child, He has given air for all to breathe. Thus, we should see that in the scheme of the merciful and compassionate Lord there are mercy and compassion, and then we should infuse mercy and compassion into our own lives. The Gita suggested the Name that was most prevalent in that age : ॐ तत् सत् (*Om tat sat*).

25. ॐ (*om*) means 'yes'. Yes, God does exist. He exists even in this twentieth century! 'स एव अद्य स उ श्वः' – He exists today, He existed yesterday and He shall exist tomorrow. He is always there. The creation too is always there, and we too are ever-ready to continue our spiritual quest in all earnestness. We are the seekers and the worshippers, He is the Lord, and everything in the creation is a means for worship. When our whole being gets charged with this feeling, we may be said to have digested the meaning of ॐ (*om*). The spirit of ॐ (*om*) should permeate our being and find expression in our *sadhana*. See the sun at any time. It is always there with its rays; never without them. In the same way, our *sadhana* should be clearly visible in our life to all at all the times. Only then it can be said that we have assimilated the spirit of ॐ (om).

Then comes सत् (*sat*). The Lord is *sat*; that is, He is good and auspicious. Look at the creation with this feeling and you will find His goodness and auspiciousness in it. When you take out a pitcherful of water from a river, a pit is not formed there; surrounding water rushes in immediately to fill the depression. What an expression of love and benignity! A river abhors depressions. 'नदी वेगेन शुद्ध्यति ।' ('The water of a river is clean and pure because it is flowing continuously and speedily.') The river of creation is also getting purified continuously and speedily. That is why it is good and auspicious. Let our actions too be likewise. To understand the Lord as सत् (*sat*), all our actions should be full of purity and devotion. All our actions, our entire *sadhana* should be continually examined and progressively purified.

Then comes तत् (*tat*). '*Tat*' means 'that', something different, something unattached to the creation. The Lord is distinct from the creation and is unattached to it. As the sun rises, the lotuses bloom, the birds leave their nests, darkness disappears. But the sun is somewhere far off, quite aloof from all these outcomes. When our actions become detached and disinterested, it can be said that we have digested '*tat*'.

26. In this way, the Gita teaches us to dedicate all the actions to the Lord, using the Vedic Name ॐ तत् सत् (*om tat sat*). The idea of dedicating all the actions to the Lord has already been introduced in

the Ninth Chapter. The verse 'यत्करोषि यदश्नासि'[3] tells the same thing. The same idea has been elaborated further in the Seventeenth chapter. This Chapter has particularly pointed out that the actions to be dedicated to the Lord must be *sattvic*, for only then they will be worthy of being offered to Him.

100. The Name of the Lord effaces sins

27. All this is very well. Still a question remains. A virtuous man may be able to digest the Name ॐ तत् सत्, but what about a sinner? Is there any Name that a sinner too could take? Yes, a sinner too can chant ॐ तत् सत्. All Names of the Lord can lead us from untruth to Truth, from sin to innocence. You must purify your life gradually. The Lord will then certainly help you. He will support you in your moments of weakness.

28. If I am asked to choose between virtuous, but egotistic life on the one hand and sinful, but humble life on the other, I may falter in giving an unequivocal answer, but my heart would certainly exclaim, 'Let me rather have the sin which turns me towards the Lord!' If a virtuous life is going to make me forget Him, then let me rather have a sinful life that makes me think of Him. It is not that I am justifying a sinful life. But vanity about the purity of life is a greater sin. Tukaram has said, 'बहु भितों जाणपणा । आड न यो नारायणा ।' ('Oh Lord! I am afraid of being learned;

---

[3] 'Whatever you do, whatever you eat, whatever you offer as sacrifice or gift, whatever austerities you practise, dedicate all to Me.' – Gita 9.27.

let it not separate me from You.') Let us not have such greatness. It is better to be a sinner and grieve. 'जाणतें लेकरूं । माता लागें दूर धरूं ।' ('A mother separates from herself a grown-up child.') But she would hold to her bosom her innocent child. I do not want to be virtuous and independent; rather let me be a sinner dependent on the Lord. His holiness is more than enough to wash away my sins. We should try to avoid sins; if we fail in our efforts, our heart will cry out for His help. He is always there, watching fondly. Tell Him, 'I am a sinner and that is why I have come to your door.' A virtuous man has the right to think of the Lord and seek refuge in Him because he is virtuous; a sinner has the right to do so because he is a sinner.

(12.6.32)

CHAPTER 18

Conclusion:
Renunciation of the
fruit of actions leads to the
grace of the Lord

101. Arjuna's last question

1. Dear brothers, by the grace of the Lord, we have now reached the last Chapter. In this world of chance and change, fulfilment of any resolve depends on the will of the Lord. Jail life, in particular, is marked by uncertainty at every step. It is difficult to expect that any work started here would be completed here itself. It was also not expected that these discourses on the Gita would be completed here; but the Lord willed so, and hence we have been able to reach the end of the Gita.

2. In the Fourteenth Chapter, life or *karma* was divided into three categories : *sattvic*, *rajasic* and *tamasic*. We learnt that what is *rajasic* or *tamasic* should be given up and what is *sattvic* should be cultivated. The Seventeenth Chapter taught the same thing in a different way. The essence of life is *yajna-dana-tapas*; or to use a single word, *yajna*. Actions like eating which are necessary for the performance of *yajna* should also be made *sattvic* and turned into a kind of *yajna*. Only such actions should be done; all others should be given up. This was hinted at in the Seventeenth Chapter. We also saw why we should constantly have in the mind the *mantra* ॐ तत् सत् (*om tat sat*). ॐ denotes constancy, *tat* denotes detachment and *sat* denotes purity. Our *sadhana* should have these three things : constancy, detachment and purity. Only then can it be dedicated to the Lord. All this indicates that only some and not all of the actions are to be renounced.

If we look at the whole message of the Gita, we find it advocating at several places that actions are not to be renounced. What it asks us to renounce is the fruit of actions. Everywhere in the Gita it is taught that we should act ceaselessly and renounce the fruit of our actions. But this is one side of it. The other side appears to be that certain actions should be renounced while certain other actions should be done. That is why Arjuna asks, at the beginning of the Eighteenth Chapter, "On the one hand, it is said that whatever action we do, it should be followed by renunciation of its fruit (*fala tyaga*) and on the other hand, it also appears that some actions must be strictly abjured while some actions should be done. How to reconcile these two positions?" This question has been asked to understand clearly the direction in which life should proceed and to have an insight into the true meaning of the renunciation of the fruit of actions. Actions in themselves are to be renounced in what the scriptures call *sannyasa*, while in the *fala tyaga* there is renunciation of the fruit of actions. Does renunciation of the fruit of actions as enjoined by the Gita need renunciation of the actions themselves? This is the crux of the matter. With reference to the criterion of the renunciation of the fruit, is there any role for *sannyasa*? What are the limits of *sannyasa* and *falatyaga*? This is what Arjuna asks.

102. *Renunciation of fruit : The universal test*

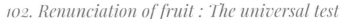

3. The Lord has made one thing absolutely clear while answering this question : Renunciation of the fruit is the universal test. It can be applied everywhere.

There is no contradiction between renunciation of the fruit of all the actions and the renunciation of *rajasic* and *tamasic* actions. The nature of some actions is such that they automatically fall off when the test of renunciation of the fruit is applied. When it is said that renunciation of the fruit should be associated with the performance of actions, it invariably implies that some actions will have to be given up. When we act in conjunction with renunciation of the fruit of actions, it naturally involves abjuration of certain actions.

4. Let us think over it in depth. When we say that whatever actions we do, we should renounce their fruit, actions prompted by desire for the fruit, actions prompted by selfish motives cease immediately. Such actions, as well as actions which are forbidden, being immoral and unrighteous, are ruled out when it is said that the fruit of actions is to be renounced. To act with renunciation of its fruit is not something mechanical, something done without application of mind. In fact, when we apply this test, it becomes clear which actions are worthy of doing and which are not so. Some say that the Gita enjoins us to act with renunciation of the fruit; it does not suggest which actions should be done. It does appear so, but it is not true. When it is said that one should act and renounce the fruit of actions, it becomes clear which actions should be done and which should not be done. Actions intended to harm others, actions full of falsehood, actions like stealing can never be done if their fruit is to be renounced. The sun illuminates

all things, but does darkness gets illuminated? No, it disappears altogether. That is what happens to selfish or forbidden actions. All the actions should be subjected to this test. When we intend to do something, we should see whether it is possible for us to do it without any attachment and expectation of returns. Renunciation of the fruit is the only unfailing test for actions. When this test is applied, actions with desire or selfish motives show themselves up as fit to be rejected. They must be renounced. Then pure and *sattvic* actions remain. They should be done with detachment, selflessness and humility. Renunciation of selfish actions is also an action and it should also be subjected to this universal test. Renunciation of selfish actions should not require any efforts.

Thus, we have seen three things : (i) Whatever actions we do, we should renounce their fruit, (ii) When the test of renunciation of the fruit is applied, *rajasic* and *tamasic* actions, selfish and forbidden actions stand rejected, (iii) The same test is to be applied to such renunciation too. There should not be any vanity about renunciation, any feeling that 'I have made so much sacrifice.'

5. Why should *rajasic* and *tamasic* actions be abjured? Because they are not pure; so they smear the mind of the doer with the impurities. But on deeper observation, one finds that *sattvic* actions too are flawed. In fact, every action has some or other defect in it. The *swadharma* of farming comes to mind as a pure and *sattvic* occupation. But even in such

work, which is of the nature of *yajna,* some violence is involved. Ploughing and other operations destroy a number of living beings. When we open the door in the morning, the sun's rays enter the house and kill a number of germs. What we call purification turns out to be a killing operation. Even *sattvic* work is thus flawed. What is then to be done?

6. I have already said that all the virtues have not yet been fully developed. We have been able to have just a fleeting glimpse of qualities like wisdom, devotion, service and non-violence. It is not that they had fully blossomed sometime in the past. Mankind is learning from experience and making progress. In the Middle Ages, it was thought that agriculture involves violence; so it should be avoided by the non-violent people; they should prefer trade and commerce instead. To grow grains is sinful, but to sell them is not so – is it not strange? To avoid actions in this way does no good. Restricting the sphere of actions in this way will ultimately prove suicidal. The more a man thinks of escaping from actions, the more will he get entangled in them. If you have to trade in grains, is it not necessary for someone else to grow them? If so, are you not an accomplice in the violence involved in farming? If growing cotton is a sin, it should be equally sinful to sell it. Not to produce cotton on the ground of it being an impure work is a sign of warped thinking. An attitude that goes on rejecting actions of all types on different pretexts is not a sign of compassion; on the contrary, it shows lack of true compassion. We should understand that when

the leaves are plucked, a tree does not wither away; it rather gets fresh foliage. In the contraction of the sphere of activities, there is contraction of the Self.

103. The right way to extricate oneself from activity

7. The question then arises, 'If all the activities are flawed, then why should not all of them be renounced?' This question has already been answered. Renunciation of all the actions is indeed a very attractive and fascinating idea; but how to renounce innumerable actions? Is the way of giving up *rajasic* and *tamasic* actions applicable to *sattvic* actions too? How to avoid *sattvic* actions that are flawed or impure? The curious result of saying 'इंद्राय तक्षकाय स्वाहा'[1] ('Let Indra alongwith Takshak be offered as sacrifice in the *yajna*') is that Indra, being immortal, does not die, and Takshak too escapes death and becomes stronger. *Sattvic* actions have a good deal of merit and a little flaw in them. When you try to sacrifice them because of that flaw, the merit in them does not die because of its inherent strength, but the flaws survive and grow behind the shield of the merit. The flaws which otherwise could have been removed, get strengthened because of such indiscreet sacrifice. If we drive away the cat because it kills the rats, we shall have to suffer violence by the rats. If snakes are killed because they are violent, a lot of pests will multiply and destroy the crops,

---

[1] King Janamejay performed a *yajna* named *sarpasatra*, involving sacrifice, that is, killing of all the snakes as a snake had killed his father, King Parikshit. The snake chief Takshak then took refuge with Indra, the King of the gods, who was immortal. Alongwith Takshak, Indra too was then offered in sacrifice.

resulting in the starvation of thousands of people. Renunciation must, therefore, be accompanied with wise discrimination.

8. There is a story that Machchhindranath asked Gorakhnath, his disciple, to give a boy a good wash. Gorakhnath literally washed the boy like a piece of cloth by thrashing him on a washing stone, squeezed him and put him on the clothes-line for drying! Is it the way to give a boy a wash? Clothes and boys are not washed in the same way. Similarly, there is a lot of difference between renouncing *sattvic* actions and renouncing *rajasic* and *tamasic* actions. *Sattvic* actions are to be renounced in an altogether different way.

Actions bereft of wise discrimination can result in something adverse and unexpected. Has not Tukaram said, 'त्यागें भोग माझ्या येतील अंतरा । मग मी दातारा काय करूं ।।' ('If I outwardly renounce the desires and passions, they will enter my heart. O Lord! What am I to do then?') Even if one tries to make a little sacrifice outwardly, the subtle urge for indulgence remains in the mind and grows there in strength, rendering that sacrifice meaningless. If a little bit of renunciation is going to lead us to build palatial houses, it makes no sense; it would have been better to live in a hut. It is better to continue to be dressed in the coat and the turban than to wear a loin-cloth and amass wealth and wallow in worldly pleasures. That is why the Lord has prescribed an altogether different way for renunciation of *sattvic* actions : they are to be done, but their fruit should be severed from them. While some actions themselves are to be renounced, fruit of some other is to be severed from them.

9. There is a story about a man, who thought that his house was filthy and inauspicious and therefore left and went to another village. He found filth in that village too and therefore went to a forest. There, as he sat under a mango tree, a bird's droppings fell on his head. Disgusted, he cursed the forest and went and stood in a river. There he found big fish eating up the small ones, and that heightened his disgust. Convinced that the whole of creation was abominable, and there was no way out except through death, he came out of the water and kindled a fire to end his life. A gentleman who was passing by enquired, "Brother, why do you want to end your life?" The man replied, "Because the world is an abominable place; it stinks." The gentleman said, "But imagine how it would stink when your flesh begins to burn! How awful the stench is when even a single hair burns! What would happen when your whole body gets burnt? We live nearby. How would we bear it? Where could we go?" The man was bewildered and exclaimed, "One cannot live in this world, nor can one die! What is one to do then?"

10. The moral is that if you go on condemning everything as abominable and try to escape from it, you simply cannot carry on. If you try to avoid a small flawed act, an act with a bigger flaw will become inescapable. The nature of *karma* is such that it cannot be got rid of by outward renunciation

only. If a man tries to fight the *karma* that has come to his lot in the natural course, if he tries to swim against the current, he is bound to get exhausted in the end and be swept off by the current. His interest lies in acting in tune with the current of *swadharma*. Then the coatings on the mind will peel off gradually and the mind will go on getting increasingly purified. Activities will wither away of themselves even though actions will continue to be done. *Karma* (action) will remain, but *kriya* (activity) will disappear.

11. There is a difference between *karma* (action) and *kriya* (activity). Let us take an example to explain this. Suppose there is a great commotion at a place and it is to be stopped. A policeman goes there and shouts at the top of his voice. To make the people silent, he has to do the intense action of shouting. Someone else may just stand up and raise his finger; and that will be sufficient to quieten the people. Another person may just go there and his very presence will stop the commotion. In the first case, activity is intense; in the second case, it is gentle; and in the third case, it is subtle. But action is the same – that of quietening the people.

As the mind gets purified, intensity of activity will go on diminishing. Activity will go on becoming gentler and subtler, and will altogether cease in the end. Action and activity are different things. Even grammatically, these two terms are different from each other.

This must be clearly understood. A man may express his anger either by shouting or by keeping silent. He may thus resort to different activities for the sake of one and the same action. A *jnani* does no activity, but his action is infinite. His very existence induces innumerable people to take to the right path. Even if he is just sitting still, he does infinite action. As activity goes on becoming subtler and subtler, action goes on growing. Thus, one can infer that when the mind is completely purified, activity will cease altogether and action will become infinite. Activity will progressively become gentler and subtler till its complete cessation in the end, and then infinite action will take place by itself.

12. Action cannot be got rid of by rejecting it superficially. It is possible only gradually through selfless, desireless work. There is a poem by the poet Browning wherein a man asks the Pope, 'Why do you bedeck yourself with robes etc.? Why do you have all this paraphernalia? Why do you keep a serene face? Why this pretence?' The Pope answers, 'I do all this because it is possible that as I go on play-acting in this way, faith may touch me one day, even without my realising it.' One should, therefore, go on doing desireless activity; it will finally culminate in the state of no activity.

104. An insight into *swadharma*

13. In short, *rajasic* and *tamasic* actions are to be renounced without exception and *sattvic* actions that come to us in the natural course should be done,

even if they have some flaws in them. Let them be defective. If you try to avoid their defects, other defects will overtake you. If your nose is crooked, let it be so. If you attempt to cut it to make it beautiful, it will look more frightful and ugly. *Sattvic* actions may be defective, but as they come to us in the natural course, they should be done; only their fruit should be renounced.

14. There is one more thing to say. You must not take up the action that has not come to you in the natural course, even if you feel that you could do it quite excellently. Do only what has come to you in the natural course. Do not go out of the way to take on new tasks which are not naturally yours. Avoid the work which needs a lot of deliberate efforts, even though it appears attractive. Do not be tempted by it; for, renunciation of fruit is possible only in the case of the actions that come to you in the natural course. If a man begins to run after each and every action, imagining that 'this is good and that also is good', renunciation of fruit is inconceivable. This will make a mess of one's life. One will try to do such actions for the sake of fruit only, but the fruit will elude him. Life will then always be unsteady and unsettled. The mind will get attached to that action. Even if *sattvic* action is found tempting, one should keep away from that temptation. If you try to pursue a variety of *sattvic* actions, *rajas* and *tamas* will creep into them. You must therefore restrict yourself to the *sattvic* actions which come to you as your natural *swadharma*.

15. *Swadharma* is comprised of *swadeshi*[2] dharma, *swajateeya dharma* (duties arising out of one's being a part of a particular community) and *swakaleen dharma* (duties appropriate for the time). These three together constitute *swadharma*. While deciding about one's *swadharma*, one is required to take into account what is appropriate to one's nature and tendencies and what are the duties that have fallen to him. You have something in you which makes you what you are. That is why you are different from others. Everybody has something that is distinctively his own. A goat can develop itself as a goat; if it aspires to be a cow, it is impossible. It can never give up its 'goatness'. To give up the 'goatness' it will have to give up its body; it will have to die to take a new body and acquire a new *dharma*. In the present birth, that 'goatness' alone is sacred for it. You must be knowing the story of the bull and the frog. There is a limit beyond which a frog cannot inflate its body. It will die if it tries to become as big as a bull. It is not right to imitate others. That is why it is said that taking up another's *dharma* is disastrous.

16. *Swadharma* consists of two parts; one changes while the other does not. I am not today what I was yesterday, nor shall I be tomorrow what I am today. I am changing continually. A child's *swadharma* is to seek all-round development. A young man's *swadharma* is to use his abundant energy for service to the society.

---

[2] *Swadeshi* has been defined by Mahatma Gandhi as 'that spirit in us which restricts us to the use and service of our immediate surroundings to the exclusion of the more remote.'

Swadharma of a mature adult man is to give others the benefit of his knowledge. A part of *swadharma* thus changes, but the other part remains unchanged. To use the language of the scriptures, we may say that a man has *varnadharma* (duties that follow from being in a particular *varna*) as well as *ashramdharma*[3] (duties that follow from being in a particular *ashram*); *varnadharma* does not change while *ashramdharma* changes.

Ashramdharma changes. What does this mean? When we successfully pass the stage of *brahmacharyashram*, we enter the next stage – become a *grihasth* (the householder) – , then enter *vanaprasthashram* and finally become a *sannyasi*. But *varnadharma* does not change. I can never go beyond my natural limits. Any attempt to do so will be foolish. You cannot overlook your distinctive attributes and personality. The scheme of *varnadharma* is based on this idea. The concept of *varnadharma* is quite appealing. Is *varnadharma* absolutely unchangeable? Is belonging to a *varna* akin to belonging to a species? Is it that just as a goat will always be a goat, a *Brahmin* will always be a *Brahmin*? I concede that it is not so; one should take

---

[3] *Ashram* here means a stage or period of life. Four such stages had been prescribed: *Brahmacharya* (roughly, first 25 years of life when one is supposed to remain celibate and concentrate on his studies), *Grihastha* (next 25 years of life when one is supposed to carry out the duties of a householder and discharge family responsibilities), *Vanaprastha* (next 25 years of life when one is supposed to retire from the family responsibilities, assuming the role of an advisor and devote oneself to the service of society) and *Sannyasa* (when one should completedly renounce worldly life).

a balanced view. When *varnadharma* is used as the basis for social order, exceptions are inevitable. The Gita has acknowledged this.

The key point is that one should understand these two types of *dharma* and keep away from any other *dharma*, even if it appears beautiful and alluring.

105. The full meaning of the renunciation of fruit

17. From the elaboration of the idea of the renunciation of fruit of actions the following points emerge :

i) *Rajasic* and *tamasic* action should be completely given up.
ii) The fruit of the action of renunciation should also be renounced. There must not be any pride or vanity about it.
iii) *Sattvic* action should not itself be renounced, but its fruit should be renounced.
iv) *Sattvic* action, whose fruit is to be renounced, should be done even if it has some impurities in it.
v) When *sattvic* actions are done continuously and their fruit renounced, the mind will get purified. Activity will go on becoming gentler and subtler, and will cease completely in the end.
vi) Activity will disappear; but actions for the sake of *loksamgraha* – to bring the people together and show them the path of righteousness – will continue.
vii) Only that *sattvic* action should be done which comes to us in the natural course. One should keep away from other actions, howsoever good

they may appear. One should not be tempted by them.

viii) *Swadharma* that comes to us naturally consists of two parts. One is subject to change and the other is not. *Varnadharma* does not change, while the *ashramdharma* keeps changing. The part of *swadharma* that is subject to change must change. That will ensure purity and avoid stagnation.

18. If a stream stops flowing and water stagnates, it begins to stink. Similar is the case with *ashramdharma*. A man first accepts family life. He submits to the restraints of family for the sake of his growth. There he gets different experiences. But if he remains bound there permanently, it will spell his doom. The family-life, which was his *dharma* at one stage, becomes *adharma* at a later stage, as it then binds him. If the changing part of the *dharma* is not given up in time because of attachment, the result is disastrous. There should not be attachment even to a good thing. Attachment inevitably leads to terrible consequences. Germs of tuberculosis may enter the lungs unawares, but they will nevertheless eat away the whole of our life. If, through our carelessness, the germs of attachment enter into *sattvic* action, that will then result in the rotting of *swadharma*. The *sattvic* *swadharma* will then degenerate into *rajas* and *tamas*. The part of *swadharma* that ought to change must be left behind at the appropriate time. This is true for the *dharma* about family as well as the *dharma* about nation. If attachment creeps into patriotism, it will degenerate into dangerous chauvinism. That will

halt development. Attachment will corrupt the mind and cause degeneration.

106. *Fulfilment is nothing but the culmination of sadhana*

19. In short, if you aspire for the fulfilment of your life, the principle of the renunciation of fruit of actions will free you from all the worries. It would show you the right path. This principle also tells us the bounds within which to act. When we have this guiding light with us, we shall know what to do, what to discard, what to change and when, and so on.

20. But now let us consider something different. Should the spiritual seeker have his attention riveted on the ultimate state marked by the complete cessation of activities? A *jnani* continues to act without doing any activity. Should a seeker have this aim in mind?

No. Here too, the principle of renunciation of the fruit should be applied. Our life is so wonderfully fashioned that we would get what we want even without paying any attention to it. *Moksha* (the state of oneness with the Supreme) is the highest fulfilment of life. But one must not covet even *moksha*, or the state of *akarma*. That state would be reached without one being aware of it. *Sannyasa* is not something that can happen at some particular moment. It is not something mechanical. You will not even notice how it grows in your life. Let us not therefore worry about *moksha*.

21. A *bhakta* always says to the Lord, "*Bhakti* is enough for me. I do not have desire for *moksha*, the ultimate fruit of *sadhana*." After all, *moksha* too is a kind of fruit – something that is to be enjoyed – and it too must be renounced. But when we renounce *moksha,* it will not move away from us; rather, it will be more surely ours. Only when you give up the desire for *moksha*, you will advance towards it without your being aware of it. Let *sadhana* be done with such single-minded dedication that there is no thought of *moksha* in the mind; then *moksha* itself will seek you on its own. Let the seeker be totally immersed in his *sadhana*. The Lord had already said, 'मा ते संगोऽस्त्वकर्मणि' ('You should not covet the state of *akarma*, or *moksha*'). Now He is again saying in the end, 'अहं त्वा सर्वपापेभ्यो मोक्षयिष्यामि मा शुच: ।' ('I shall release you from all sins; be not grieved.')[4] 'I am here to accord you *moksha*; forget about *moksha* and be concerned about your *sadhana*.' *Sadhana* will attain perfection when you forget *moksha*, and then *moksha* will itself be attracted to you. *Moksha-Lakshmi* garlands him who is not concerned about her and is fully absorbed in his *sadhana* without any thought of *moksha* in his mind.[5]

22. When *sadhana* reaches its zenith, the moment of fulfilment comes. If a man in a forest wants to reach home, but just keeps sitting under a tree in the forest, chanting 'home, home' all the while, the home will

---

[4] Gita, 18.66.

[5] Please refer Chap. 3.1.

remain away. If he succumbs to the temptation of rest, he will miss the ultimate rest. He should keep on walking; eventually he will find his home right in front of him. If I lose myself in dreaming about the *moksha* and relax, slacken my *sadhana*, the *moksha* will remain distant. The surest way to attain *moksha* is to fling away any aspiration for it and concentrate on *sadhana*. One must not hanker after the ultimate rest, after the state of *akarma*. Have love for your *sadhana*, and then *moksha* will be yours without fail. You cannot solve a problem by shouting for the answer; you should rather stick to the correct method and that will step by step lead you to the answer. How can you reach the end before the completion of the process? How can you have an answer without following the method fully? How can you attain the state of liberation when you are still a seeker? When one is struggling for life in a flooded river, will it do if he thinks of the pleasures awaiting him on the other bank? At that time, all the attention should be riveted on swimming, all the strength should be applied to inch towards the other bank. *Sadhana* should be carried to the end; the ocean should be crossed, and you will find *moksha* there waiting for you.

107. *The triple state of the realised one*

23. All the activities drop off in the final state of a *jnani*. But this does not mean that in the final state there would necessarily be complete absence of activity; activities may take place or they may not. This final state is extremely fascinating and sublime. The *jnani* is not concerned about what is taking place

in this state. Only that which is invariably pure, good and beneficial will take place in that state. The *jnani* stands at the zenith of *sadhana*. There he would be untouched by all the actions even while doing them. He may even bring about destruction, and yet he will not be the destroyer; and even if he does good, he will not be the benefactor.

24. The final state of *moksha* is the zenith of *sadhana*. In this state, *sadhana* becomes natural and effortless. Then there is not even the thought that 'I am doing something.' This final state of realisation (*Siddhavastha*) is not a state of morality. A child speaks truth, but it is not a moral act, as he has no idea of untruth. To speak truth while being aware of untruth is a moral act. In the final state, untruth does not exist; truth alone exists. So there is no question of morality. What is forbidden, what is worth abjuring comes nowhere in the picture. Ears do not hear what should not be heard; eyes do not see what should not be seen. Only that gets done which ought to be done; one does not have to do it consciously. One need not have to avoid consciously what is worth avoiding, but it does get avoided. It is in this culmination of *sadhana*, when it has become natural, amoral – or you may call it supra-moral – that morality reaches its supreme height. We may call this a state of *sattvic sadhana* wherein *sattva* has been transcended.

25. How is one to describe such a state? Just as one gets indications of the coming eclipse, there are indications in this state that *moksha* is to follow the

death of the body. Experiences of the state of *moksha* begin even while the physical body is still in existence. Words fail, language falters while describing this state. Whatever violence a man in this state commits, he does nothing. How to judge his actions? Whatever is done at his hands will be nothing but *sattvic* action. Even when he no longer performs any activity, he shows right path to all in the world. This grand vision makes one speechless.

26. This final state is three-dimensional. One of them is the state in which we find sage Vamadeva. His declaration is well-known : 'All that is there in this universe, that am I.' A *jnani* becomes completely egoless. He loses any sense of identification with the body. His activities cease. Then he attains a particular state of consciousness. In this state he is no more confined to a single body. This state is not a state of activity. It is a state marked with intense and pervasive emotions and feelings. All of us can have experience of this state on a small scale. A mother takes upon herself the virtues as well as vices of her child. The child's sorrow makes her sad and his happiness makes her happy. But this state, this experience of identity in the case of a mother is limited to her child. She takes upon herself the child's faults. A *jnani* takes upon him the faults of the whole world. He becomes sinner by the sins of the world and the virtues of the world make him virtuous. And yet he is absolutely untouched by the merits and the sins of the world.

27. In the (Vedic) Rudra Sukta, the sage says, 'यवाश्च मे तिलाश्च मे गोधूमाश्च मे' ('Give me barley, give me sesame, give me wheat.') He is continually demanding something or the other. How big is his stomach? But then he, who is demanding all this, was not one contained in a single physical body measuring three cubits and a half; his Self had become one with the whole universe. I call this 'Vedic *vishwatmabhava*' (The Vedic attitude of identification with the whole universe) as we find this attitude and spirit at its height in the Vedas.

28. Narsi Mehta, the Gujarati saint, says, while singing the Lord's praise, 'बापजी पाप में कवण कीधां हशे, नाम लेतां तारूं निद्रा आवे'. ('O Lord! What sin have I committed, that I should feel sleepy while chanting your Name?') Was Narsi Mehta feeling sleepy? No; in fact, those who had assembled to listen to him were sleepy. But Narsi Mehta had identified himself with them; he was in a particular state of consciousness. This is the state of the *jnani*. The *jnani*, in this state, may be seen doing all conceivable virtuous and sinful acts, and he would himself concede it. Does not the Vedic sage say, "I have done a lot of things that should not have been done, I am doing such things, and will continue doing them." When such a state of consciousness is attained, the Self begins to soar high in the sky like a bird. It transcends the limitations of earthly existence.

29. Just like this state of consciousness, the *jnani* has also a state of activity. What sort of activities will the *jnani* do naturally? Whatever he will do will be nothing but *sattvic*. Although he is still bound by the limitations of the human body, his whole body, all his organs have become *sattvic*; so all his activities are bound to be *sattvic*. If you look at it from the point of view of practical affairs, his behaviour will reflect the ultimate perfection of the *sattvic* nature; if you look at it from the point of view of *vishwatmabhava*, he appears to be doing all the sinful and the virtuous deeds in the universe, and still he is untouched by them. It is so because he has peeled off and flung away the body stuck to the Self. It is only when one flings away this worthless body that one attains the state of identification with the whole universe.

30. Besides the state of consciousness and the state of activity, the *jnani* has a third state too. That is the state of *jnana*, the state of knowledge. In this state, he can neither bear with sin nor virtue and flings aside everything quickly. He is ready to set fire to the whole universe. He is not prepared to undertake any action. Its very touch repels him. In the final stage of *sadhana* or in the state of *moksha,* these three states are conceivable for the *jnani.*

31. How is one to imbibe this state of no activity, this last state? The way is to train ourselves not to take upon our shoulders the burden of being the doer of the actions we do. We should keep reflecting, 'I just happen to be instrumental. I am not really the doer

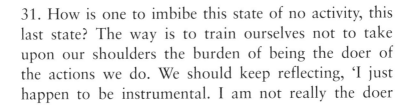

of actions.' We should first assume this stand with humility. This, of course, will not immediately result in the complete eradication of the sense of being the doer. It can happen only gradually. Let us first feel that 'I am nothing, I am just a puppet in His hands. He is moving me.' The next step is to feel that 'the activities do not touch the Self; they are of this body. But I am not this transient and mortal body; I am full of divine consciousness.' And, meditating over this feeling, you should remain completely untouched by the fetters of the body. When this happens, the state of *jnani* will be attained wherein connection with the body is, as it were, completely severed. This state will be three-dimensional as we have already referred. In the state of activity, wholly pure and perfect activities will be done at the hands of the *jnani*. In the state of consciousness, he will have the feeling that he is the doer of all the sinful and virtuous deeds in the universe; yet he will remain untouched by them. In the third state of *jnana*, he will not let any action touch him and will burn down all the actions. A *jnani* can be described in terms of all these three dimensions of the final state.

108. 'Thou alone – – Thou alone'

32. Having said all this, the Lord then asks Arjuna, "Have you listened to all this carefully? Now ponder over it fully and then do what you think right." The Lord thus magnanimously gave complete freedom to Arjuna. This is a unique feature of the Gita. But then compassion welled up in Him and He took back that freedom. He told Arjuna, "Give up your will, your

sadhana; give up everything and come to Me; take refuge in Me." What this means is that you should not have any indepedent self-will; you should do what He wills you to do. Let His will prevail. With full freedom, you should feel that you need have no freedom. Reduce yourself to zero. Let there be the Lord, and the Lord alone, in the universe. The goat, while alive, bleats 'में - - - में - - -', that is, 'I - - - I - - -.' But when it is dead and its guts are made into strings for carding cotton, the strings, as saint Dadu says, give the sound 'तुही - - - तुही - - -'. ('Thou alone - - - Thou alone - - -'). Now there is nothing but 'Thou alone - - - Thou alone - - -'.

(19.6.32)

Glossary

Aahara: Food

Abhang: A kind of devotional poems

Abhaya: Fearlessness

Abhishek: See footnote on p. 157

Abhyasa: Constant practice

Adharma: Unrighteousness

Advaita: See footnote on p. 248

Aghorpanthi: A tantric cult

Ajiva: Refer p. 130

Akarma: Refer Chap. 4.15,16 and Chap. 5

Akshar: Imperishable

Anadi: One that is without beginning

Artha: Refer p. 142

Artharthi: Refer p. 142

Ashram: See footnotes on p. 93 and p. 384

Asuric: Demoniacal

Atman: Self

Bhajan: A kind of devotional song

Bhakta: Devotee

Bhakti: Devotion

Bhaktishastra: Science of *bhakti* (devotion)

Bhavana: Sentiments and genuine feelings (Vinoba has defined it as the reason which is fully convinced and settled)

Brahmachari: See footnote on p. 56

Brahmacharya: See footnote on p. 56

Brahman: See footnote on p. 26
Brahmanirvana: Union with Brahman; the spiritual liberation
Brahmavidya: The science of realizing the Brahman
Brahmin: See footnote on p. 9

Charkha: Spinning Wheel
Chaturvarnya: See footnote on p. 291

Dakshina: See footnote on p. 47
Dakshinayan: Six months of the southern course of the sun
Dana: Charity, sharing
Daman: Subduing/Repressing
Daya: Pity, compassion
Dharma: See footnote on p. 7
Dhwams: Destruction

Falatyaga: Renunciation of the fruit of actions

Garba: A form of dance popular in Gujarat
Ghee: See footnote on p. 119
Guna: See footnote on p. 31
Gunateeta: One who has transcended the three Gunas
Guru: Master, teacher

Japa: See footnote on p. 53

Jiva: The individual self

Jivanmukta: One liberated from the cycle of births and deaths

Jnana: (Spiritual) Knowledge

Jnananishta: One who is committed to the (Supreme) knowledge

Jnani: See footnote on p. 56

Karma: Action (Referred to in the Gita as action done selflessly and without attachment in the pursuit of *swadharma*)

Karmayoga: The way of selfless and desireless action with a sense of surrender to the Supreme

Karmayogi: Practitioner of *Karmayoga*

Kshatriya: See footnote on p. 9

Khadi: See footnote on p. 52

Kriya: Activity

Loksamgraha: See footnote on p. 95; also see p. 341

Mantra: Sacred verse; spirit

Maya: See footnote on p. 129

Mimamsa: See footnote on p. 89

Mimansaka: Adepts in Mimamsa

Moksha: See footnote on p. 36

Naad: Sound

Nama: Name

Nara: Man

Narayan: God; a Name of Lord Vishnu

Nirguna: Without attributes. See footnote on p. 96

Nishkaam: Desireless

Nishtha: Ordinarily means faith or settled conviction; In Chap. 5, used in the sense of the ultimate state

Paradharma: The dharma which is not one's own

Parva: A part, section of the text

Pooja: See footnote on p. 57

Prakriti: See footnotes on p. 31 and p. 128

Prasad: Grace; See footnote on p. 57

Purusha: See footnotes on p. 128 and p. 309

Purushottam: The Supreme Person (God) See footnote on p. 309

Raga: Modes of Indian classical music

Rajas: See footnote on p. 28

Rajasic: Full of *rajas*

Rajayoga: Refer pp. 173-192

Sadhaka: The spiritual seeker

Sadhana: See footnote on p. 96

Saguna: With attributes. See footnote on p. 96

Sakaam: One with desires

Saakaar: With form. See footnote on p. 96

Samadhi: See footnotes on p. 6 and p. 165

Samsara: See footnote on p. 75

Samskara: See footnote on p. 147

Sangh: Association

Sankhya: See footnote on p. 20 (Vinoba used the term for the basic principles of life. See Chap. 2.2)

Sannyasa: See footnote on p. 12

Sannyasi: One who has renounced the world

Sat-Chit-Ananda: See footnote on p. 29

Sattva: See footnote on p. 31

Sattvic: Pure, noble, sublime

Satyagraha: See footnote on p. 40

Shastra: Science

Shudra: See footnote on p. 9

Siddha: One who has achieved spiritual liberation

Sthitaprajna: See footnote on p. 39

Surya-namaskar: See footnote on p. 49

Swadeshi: See footnote on p. 383

Swadharma: See footnote on p. 12

Swara: Musical note

Swayamvara: See footnote on p. 45

Tamas: See footnote on p. 31

Tamasic: Full of *tamas*

Tantra: Technique; also a cult

Tapa: Penance

Upanishad: See footnote on p. 7
Upavas: Fast; Etymologically, 'to dwell close to God'
Uttarayan: Six months of the northern course of the sun

Vairagya: Non-attachment
Vaishya: See footnote on p. 9
Vanara: See footnote on p. 68
Varna: See footnotes on p. 9 and p. 384
Veena: A stringed musical instrument
Vibhuti: Divine Manifestation
Vijnana: A type of knowledge
Vikarma: See p. 72
Vishad: Despondency
Vishwaroop: See footnote on p. 84
Viyog: Separation
Vrata: Vow
Vyaghra: Tiger

Yajna: Sacrifice; the Vedic ritual involving sacrifice
Yoga: See footnote on p. 19. The art of practising the principles of life
Yogi: Practitioner of the Yoga